ASPECTS OF EDUCATIONAL
TECHNOLOGY

Aspects
of Educational Technology
Volume XV11

Staff Development
and Career Updating

*Edited for the Association for Educational
and Training Technology by*
Ken Shaw

General Editor
A J Trott *Bulmershe College*

Kogan Page, London/Nichols Publishing
Company, New York

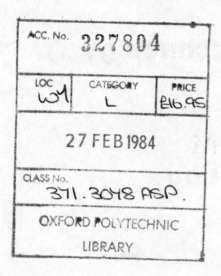
First published in Great Britain in 1984
by Kogan Page Limited
120 Pentonvile Road, London N1 9JN

British Library Cataloguing in Publication Data
　　Staff development and career updating.—(Aspects
　　of educational technology; v.17)
　　1. Great Britain — Occupations
　　I. Title II. Series
　　331.7'02'0941　　HF5382.5.G7

　　ISBN 0-85038-761-2 (UK)
　　ISBN 0-89397-175-8 (USA)
　　ISSN 0141-5956; 16

Printed in Great Britain by Billings & Sons Limited, Worcester

Published in the USA by Nichols Publishing Company
PO Box 96, New York, NY 10024

Contents

Section 7: Theory and Applications of Educational Technology

Author Index

Educational Technology International Conference 1983

Every so often one calendar year is devoted to some particular theme. We have had in recent times the International Year of the Child, and latterly Information Technology Year. The idea is a splendid one, but unfortunately there is an element of catharsis about it, in that once it is over people assume that some national or international need has been fully met.

The whole point about information technology, however, is that the needs have barely been defined, and that is why ETIC 1983 is both important and timely.

Some of the most recent developments such as the microcomputer, Prestel, direct broadcasting by satellite, cable TV and various others can offer to education the possibility of substantial advances. When I sit down in the university library and use the Lockheed Dialog system to retrieve information about educational research, I often browse through the other files. I discover that there are now millions of pieces of research in files such as Chemistry Abstracts, or Biology Previews, and that one only needs a keyboard and screen, a source of electrical power, and a telephone link, to be connected to the largest multi-media libraries in the world, whether these be in Britain or in Palo Alto.

One of the major advances in recent technology is that the micro, Prestel and cable TV offer interactive facilities of a kind and on a scale never before available. The potential of such technology is way beyond the rudimentary hand-cranked behaviourist teaching machines of the 1960s. It is most important, therefore, at this present time that teachers are trained to use new technology intelligently, that suitable software is made available, that the place of this technology in teaching and learning, both at home and in school is fully explored, and that some of the errors associated with earlier educational technology are avoided.

I am sure that AETT members will make an important contribution to the debate and to future practice as a result of their experience here at the School of Education in Exeter University.

Professor E C Wragg

Editorial

The early 1980s are full of signs that change, never slow since the end of the last century, is accelerating. The two great linked factors are alterations in the pattern of employment, especially for young workers and the impact of new technology, including information technology. We are seeing something beyond the substitution of new techniques and processes for old, beyond the steady and progressive up-dating in people's skills and knowledge for which education and training have always had a major responsibility. We are seeing a de-stabilization of the curriculum at the top end of secondary schools; in further education there are signs of yet another surge of change beyond the reorganization involved in setting up TEC and BEC courses, followed by the New Training Initiative; and there are new elements and new partners in the education and training of the 16 to 19 age group. There is urgent and widespread criticism of the heavily-weighted rote-learning type of arrangements by which the overwhelming bulk of preparation for life and work takes place before adult life and work has really begun, and a more serious acknowledgement that other training agents from commerce, industry, the youth service, and the armed forces, in addition to qualified teachers, have a role to play in the preparation of the next generation of young people.

Listening to some of the sessions and editing the papers of ETIC 83 has left me with better grounded and more deeply confirmed beliefs with which to face this both alarming and exciting future. First, a valuable, and to me unexpected, reaffirmation of the importance of creative imagination, not merely analysis, logic and systematic development, in the application of technology to learning and teaching. One of Professor Jalling's commandments about course development was 'always include the unexpected'. Excessive pre-programming of the course is more common in training than in education: often the purposes, too readily described in the narrow vocabulary of objectives, require it. Spontaneity is sacrificed in the interest of clarity and sequence in the explanation (which is usually top of the list in students' demands). This style readily leads to 'product' skills — fixed in the possession of the learner, easily tested and ready for use. What if 'process' skills are at a premium in the future? Skills which are flexible so that they can serve several purposes, skills which are applicable in unexpected situations, capable of being redeployed and updated to suit new work areas, skills which don't become obsolescent? To promote these skills calls for more advanced teaching and study methods, which include the unlocking of creativity, imagination, improvization and positive attitudes to innovation, in addition to the normal fostering of skill and imparting of information. Doing the unexpected, and more importantly leading course developers and learners to accept elements which because of their unexpectedness, raise anxiety and demand imaginative solutions, is one of the few known ways of drawing out adaptiveness, the ability to respond quickly to unexpected demands, and confidence in unfamiliar situations.

Complementary to this was the emphasis on support for the learner, help with more advanced learning skills, the creation of 'learner-friendly' not just efficient packages. If training of the next generation is to be spread over a longer period, if more people drop-in and drop-out of education and training as they change jobs or reach new life stages, we can find out more about how to support learners who may not always have direct access to institutions, tutors and counsellors. This conference has shown that a good deal of steady work in what surely must be a growth area has been going on. Process skills are harder to develop than product skills; the learners need more support.

The conference scene is becoming more volatile. Participants are tending to delay finalizing their commitment to attend; promised papers take longer to materialize; rescheduling at the last moment becomes more frenetic.Cost of sustenance and travel get higher, and the logistics of conference running get harder all the time. The strain on the host institution, now that clerical and technical staff have been cut to the bone, is ever more noticeable. There has always been a lot of work behind the scenes; this is now complicated by increased anxiety about organizational aspects when resources are limited. In the event, a wide range of participants — over a hundred — attended, with excellent overseas representation. The social aspects of the conference, which this year included a wine party in Exeter museum, were well appreciated. The time is approaching when the Association may have to think long and hard about the format of future conferences.

K E Shaw
School of Education
University of Exeter

Keynote Address

Hans Jalling
National Board of Universities and Colleges, Sweden

STAFF DEVELOPMENT FOR SURVIVAL!

Most staff developers have fought an uphill battle the last few years. It is unfortunate that organizations which suddenly find that they have to cut their expenditure almost always panic. It is indeed understandable, particularly in the case of the systems of higher learning that have seen an unparallelled growth since the Second World War, but expenditure in fact becomes much higher than is necessary.

In our academic world, innumerable committees have hunted for 'unnecessary' costs. Based on the assumption that academia does not change, they have been on the look-out for items that are not traditionally 'academic', and have, more often than not, ended up with organizations that can do more of what they traditionally have done — which by definition is wrong, as the crisis has its roots in Society's demand for *new* ventures, not more of the proven unnecessary ones.

Faculty/staff training/development has been the victim in many cases. I do not have to remind you of the fate of the CTUT in the UK which — in spite of a very favourable review — was found redundant. Strangely enough, its 'sister committe' (for the training of university administrators) was allowed continued existence under the auspices of the Committee of Vice Chancellors and Principals (CVCP). I believe that one of the questions we should ask ourselves is *why* this is so? How come that the development of administrative staff is found necessary in an economic shrinking world? After all, research and teaching is done by the academics, is it not?

As I see it, there are two reasonable explanations. First, many staff development organizations have tried to 'copy' academic behaviour in the same way that they have maintained that they are 'research' institutions. Unfortunately, the 'research' carried out has very often been below academic standards, and consequently one must agree, from a pure academic point of view, that in this sense they do not belong to the academic community.

Second, many staff developers have insisted that they have nothing in common with the management of the universities. Although they do a good job, are 'experts' in their field, etc, they do not share views held by the management. It is, as we all know, a cherished belief amongst staff developers that any collaboration with the Vice-Chancellor's Office would destroy their credibility with their academic colleagues.

Seen from the point of view of the management — and I should at once like to make it quite clear that I would side with the management, as it is their job to get the organization out of the crisis — such organizations would have to go. They are sub-academic and are therefore not trustworthy.

Yet, it is a costly and unfortunate mistake, and I believe that many Vice-Chancellors and Presidents have axed their staff developers with deep regret. If there is anything an organization that has to meet new challenges needs, it is a working staff development unit.

The worsening economic prospects tend to make staff development more important than ever, and I would maintain that this is something all leaders of organizations realize today, including university management. It has been proved that successful service organizations have two things in common: first, they have committed leaders, and second, they have made the goals and policies of the organization clear, and indeed accepted, by all members; that is, the leaders have used staff development to 'market' their policies in the organization.

It is true that this implies a profound change in the behaviour of the public sector. It has been accustomed to govern by rules and regulations rather than by sharing common beliefs, but I believe that the *examples* set by the commercial world very strongly point also to a need for a change of *policies* for the public sector, including the system of higher learning. Let me use two examples that seem to have made an impact in my country (Sweden).

Ericson Telephone Company has been marketing mechanical telephone switchboards for a long time. Some years ago they decided, however, to go digital, and it is easy to realize that this necessitates some very profound changes in company structure and company policies. You will be interested to note that the management did not issue new sets of rules and regulations, but instead increased their budget for staff training in the main company from 4 million krona a year to 80 million krona a year — a sum that corresponds to £600 per employee per annum in Sweden. The results: increasing profits.

Like most airlines, the Scandinavian Airlines System has been losing money for a long time. A new President was appointed; a President that believes in making goals and policies absolutely clear to everybody in the organization, in the belief that everybody would then come to the same conclusions as the management in individual cases. Instead of trimming his organization, which, incidentally, everybody was expecting, he made intensive use of staff development to implant his basic idea: no passenger should leave an SAS aircraft dissatisfied. In one year he managed to change 45 million krona in the red to a profit of 450 million krona! In spite of an enormous bill for staff development!

Having watched this happening, the Swedish Government decided to adopt the same policy. It is quite clear that the public sector in Sweden will have to be diminished, become more efficient, and, above all perhaps, more oriented to the results of its activities than the procedures. Hence, the Government decided to invest a considerable amount of money in better leadership within the Civil Service, and to make an extensive use of staff development to try to market their ideas of an effective Civil Service within the members of the Civil Service. It may be worth noticing that our change of government last autumn has not affected this new policy — the present (social-democrat) Government seems to be as convinced of the necessity of staff development to improve administrative leadership as the previous (non-socialist) Government.

Last year the Prime Minister sent an invitation to a compulsory two-week course to all Director Generals and their Deputies within the Civil Service — a group of some 300 persons which was divided into 10 sub-groups. The message was the need for a more efficient Civil Service and the method prescribed: each and every Director-General was responsible for a massive use of staff development within their respective organizations. As a direct consequence of this, my Department has spent some £200,000 of tax-payers' money on compulsory training for all Vice-Chancellors of the Universities and Colleges, all Registrars and their senior administrative staff this academic year. In spite of cuts within all public sectors, the Government provided some fresh £150,000 for this purpose.

Consequently, I believe that the tide is turning and that staff developers can look at the future with great confidence. At the same time, I can hear you say that this development might be true for one of those small Polar countries, but it will never happen in the UK. I think that you are utterly wrong.

In fact, I am convinced that the same thing *will* happen in the UK, and that the pertinent question is not *if* staff development will be used but *who* will be asked to run the show. As my Department has managed to survive some of the critical years at the end of the 1970s and the beginning of the 1980s, and, indeed, managed both to increase the quality of our work and the respect of the academic community for our work, I have ventured to compress our experience into '10 Commandments for Staff Developers in the 80s'.

Let me first give you some information on our background. My Department is part of the National Board of Universities and Colleges, which is the Government agency supervising research and higher education in Sweden. The Department is responsible for staff training and development of all university and college staff in our country, which comprise some 30,000 people. I should like to emphasize that our brief does not only include academic staff but everyone — secretaries and technicians as well as porters. At the Board we have a staff of some 10 people and further staff at every university and college. We provide about 40 centrally directed activities every year, supplemented with a much larger number of local training and development programmes.

Our work started in 1970 when I was asked to build an organization for 'teaching university teachers how to teach'. Fortunately, we very soon realized that staff development — particularly at the universities — comprises much more than classroom behaviour, and already in 1972 we included administrative training in our programme. Our current activities can be divided into three areas:

1. research and research contact
2. teaching
3. administrative training

The emphasis of our programme is shifting, but in the last few years the administrative training programme has been the dominant one.

I should like to stress that we are a department within the National Board. We are *not* a group of 'expert consultants' who wander off to all sorts of countries running seminars and workshops. In fact, I believe that our relative success in the field of staff development is due to the fact that we have never regarded ourselves as experts, or, indeed, have allowed individuals of the Department to take on consultancies, domestic or overseas. As will become obvious from my '10 Commandments', we actually avoid performing ourselves — we ask 'real' people with 'real' expertise to do that. The strength of my Department has nothing to do with the expertise of the 10 or so people within the National Board — our strength is our access to leading experts within and outside the universities who can really contribute to the development of qualified staff.

When we started our work some 15 years ago, we spent most of our resources on the rank and file of the universities, well knowing that senior people would regard us at best as harmless, but normally with suspicion. One of the significant changes over the past 10 years is our move to leadership training.

It is a slow process, but it can be made. Last year the Chancellor of the Universities and all our Vice-Chancellors (VCs) went to Ontario in Canda as part of our programme; Ontario having very many similarities to our own country. This might seem silly to you — VCs are known as frequent travellers — and what could possible be achieved by such an exercise?

This was not a tourist trip, however. My Department had spent three years establishing contacts with the appropriate Canadian organizations to make an intensive study programme possible. Each VC had some particular issues to study, and as a final part of the programme the VCs reported to the Chancellor of the Universities on their particular topics. The success of the programme was obvious, and I believe that this was a useful preparation for the more ambitious programme of compulsory administrative training which my Department has run this academic year. Although no VC liked the word 'compulsory' in the invitation, all attended, and some have even expressed their great satisfaction with this opportunity. More details of this particular programme can be found in *A National Staff Development Organization at Work*.

In successful organizations goals are fixed and methods are free. Within the public sector, including the universities, the opposite is very often true: methods are fixed while the goals are unclear. There is no doubt in my mind, however, that we will see a change in the 1980s in this respect, and, as a consequence (as has indeed been demonstrated by the Swedish Government) the need for staff development will increase to achieve such a situation.

For the staff developer this will mean a change of emphasis from training to attitude development. The simple courses on various techniques will become obsolete and will have to be replaced by much more sophisticated activities concentrating on priority goals and attitude change.

It also means that an important task for the staff developer will be to tell people that 'they do not know what they do not know' (including professors who are Nobel Prize laureates). This can only be achieved by a respected and trusted staff development department — by management as well as by staff. This leads me on to my 'Commandments'.

1. Regard Yourself as Part of the Management

As I maintain that all staff must be committed to the same cause as the leadership, it is obvious to me that the very frequent tendency amongst staff developers not to regard themselves as part of the management is fundamentally wrong. In my experience it is a myth that co-operation with the management equals loss of credibility.

2. Build Up Competence in Many Fields

Problems vary from time to time. 'Small group teaching techniques' is not a major problem of today's universities. The staff developer will constantly have to change his or her competence if she or he wants to be regarded as an asset by his or her institution. If you want institutional support, it seems to me that you would at least have to concentrate on problems that the institution finds relevant.

3. Get the Best People to Do the Job

This is a corollary to the second commandment. It is literally impossible for a person, or a small group of persons, to have competence in the great variety of issues that staff developers will have to cover at the universities.

Do not attempt to do the job yourself — get the real experts to do it for you.

4. Make Provisions for Competent Course Administration

Staff development activities should be intense; it is not a pleasant holiday for tired academics. This makes the job of the course director very demanding.

We want our course directors to concentrate on the intellectual contents of the activity. Consequently, we do not want them to be distracted by questions such as whether there should be red or white wine for dinner, if the bus for tomorrow's excursion has been confirmed, or who has a telephone message.

In our experience the cost-efficiency ratio very much increases when a competent course secretary is made available. We have made this a rule without exception.

5. Take Good Care of Your Course Staff

We do not 'hire staff'. We ask prominent experts to join us because they share our commitment. As commitment cannot be turned on and off at will, it necessitates an organization that can make provisions for the development of staff developers. This may, in fact, mean the setting up of a special staff development programme just to train one or more potential staff members.

At present, our most difficult problem is to cater for all former course directors whose expertise we do not need at the moment. Their commitment to our cause is a source of enormous strength — but a source that must be properly looked after.

6. Do the Unexpected

Academics can read and write. If they want to get facts about something they are eminently capable of doing this.

Our task is to draw the attention of our colleagues to aspects which they may have overlooked — in other words, to teach them 'what they do not know that they do not know'.

7. Take Risks

In innovative centres it is common to say 'She or he who has never had a flop has not tried hard enough'. I believe that the same goes for staff developers.

8. Remember that Attitude Change Takes Time

Taking risks does not mean the acceptance of impossible tasks. As most of our future activities will involve some kind of attitude change, we must insist that our principals allow adequate time for staff development — or decline the offer.

9. Have the Soul of a Head-Waiter

A staff developer is a manager of creative groups. She or he is there to co-ordinate various specialists' efforts, remove obstacles and take the blame when something goes wrong. She or he is not there, however, to win the applause when something goes right.

Thus as I see it, the ideal staff developer should have the soul of a head-waiter.

10. Enjoy Life — You Have a Good Job

Unless you are committed to staff development, your organization is not very likely to be a successful service organization.

Instead of bewailing times long past, pity ourselves and complain about the wrongs of an evil world, we must look at the many fantastic sides of our job. Are we not a privileged group who — as part of our everyday life — meet and talk to some of the most interesting people in our respective countries?

I have the best job in the university system of my country!

A NATIONAL STAFF DEVELOPMENT ORGANIZATION AT WORK

Perhaps I should start reminding you that I have a national responsibility for staff development. This may seem very grand but it also has some very obvious limitations. Someone said the other day: 'I do not believe in seminars, workshops, courses etc; I do things differently'. At the university level this is true in Sweden where all types of individual counselling or long-term organizational change efforts are being launched by our staff developers. Although these activities fall within my responsibility, at least partly, I have chosen to describe the national level rather than the university level, principally because this is something you do not have in the UK. Your colleagues in university administration receive funds from the CVCP. They also attract some rather good persons to run their programme; as you may know, the present Training Officer has just been appointed Registrar at London School of Economics which has been described to me as a plum job in university administration.

I shall thus be pleading the case of the need, possibly even the necessity, of a national interest in staff development in universities — with all the drawbacks that may come from this concept. It is, for instance, quite clear that a national organization has serious limitations in its choice of methods. I can never approach a whole department as someone has to be left to entertain the students and to cope with the letters from the VCs office. I cannot work with an input of a small number of hours spread over a long time, such as two hours per week for an academic year.

In Sweden, and also probably in this country, many academics tended to look at national and local organizations as an 'either/or'. I believe that we have now passed this stage and that most people would agree that the two types of organizations supplement each other. I think it is fair to say that the previous competition between the national programme and the local programmes is dying out and that we have found different 'niches' to pursue our various activities. At the national level we do not only put on activities that stem from the wishes of the Chancellor of the Swedish Universities but also, on the suggestion of individual universities, activities that are needed but cannot easily be arranged at local level.

Although we have to resort to conferences, symposia, seminars, workshops — to put different names to groups of people meeting and working together for a limited period of time — there are some advantages of a national level. The most obvious one is probably a much wider selection of good people to do the actual job. (Third Commandment, see p 16.)

While most university staff developers will draw their experts in different fields from the university (although this may not be formally required, I believe that good psychology and a wish to survive at that particular university makes this necessary), I have a nation's academics at my disposal. I am not only talking about star performers who may be invited for a lecture or to a three-hour seminar, but about persons who take the responsibility for a particular series of seminars or courses, or, to use my terminology, our Course Directors.

Incidentally, I should like to point out that the situation of our Course Directors to a certain extent corresponds to the secondment of academics to Centres of Educational Technology in this country. It is true that they do not physically move their offices to the National Board, but there is little doubt that the period of work for a Course Director — which is never less than a year and may well extend to several years — means an affiliation to my Department.

Let me illustrate this with the case of the Dean of the Law School who is running a series of seminars with Harvard University on computers in higher education. We decide on our programme for the coming academic year at the end of March, so he was appointed at the beginning of April 1982. From this day we have tried to expose him to various experiences which we think would be useful for someone who has to conduct a series of seminars to very critical colleagues. We have arranged a series of meetings with a well-known American expert in the field; we have appointed the Head of the School of Electronics at the same university, who is good at programming and also uses computers in his teaching as Deputy Course Director; we have provided relevant literature based on several data banks, and we have sent this Dean on two study tours on both coasts of the US. My colleague at the National Board who is in charge of this operation has — on average — spent a day every third week at Lund discussing the seminars, and we have had a couple of slightly more formal meetings in my office.

Discounting the time for reading the relevant literature, it is my guess that we have provided actual events relating to the seminar for this Course Director amounting to between two and three months full-time this academic year — a net period of time which, I believe, would come very close to a secondment in the UK.

I should also like to stress that the problem the Dean is working at is a real problem. It is not related to any particular department — such work would be carried out at the university level — but it is a significant problem for the entire university system. It goes without saying that a possible re-introduction of computers in higher education in Sweden would necessitate capital investment of a magnitude that would demand fresh public money. The raising of such funds may not be of interest to the individual lecturer, yet it is a job that has to be done — and which may, in the long run, be even more important than the reshuffling of a department's curriculum. I can see no reason why academics should not take an interest in this, and I would maintain that our national staff development programme, on many occasions, has helped to focus interest among academics on issues of great importance to the system as a whole.

Having discussed the way we treat our Course Directors (fifth Commandment — see p 17) before with British colleagues, I expect that many of you would say that if you had this kind of money you would have solved the problems of British universities 10 years ago. You may be interested to know that so far we have actually spent £3,500 almost entirely on foreign travel. This is, of course, a ridiculously low sum if you take into account that I expect to expose around 75 leading Swedish academics to a series of 10 days seminars on this topic — some £50 per head in preparation costs.

Recently, a British colleague and I talked over coffee about the way non-educational organizations, like, for example, industry or the armed forces, put the findings of educational technology into use — or abuse, if you prefer that point of view. However, there is very little doubt in my mind that they are far superior to us educators in this field. Anybody who has been to an international trade fair cannot help being impressed with their use of the techniques we are trying to sell to our colleagues. I should like to suggest that one vital difference between them and us is that they prepare themselves for whatever task they have, while we start out thinking that no preparation is needed. They have a goal that they want to achieve and which is specified — not in meaningless terms such as 'to promote' but in terms that allow for quality as well as quantity. They also observe my eighth Commandment (see p 17). They know that attitude change does take time, and, consequently, develop a long-term strategy in a way we very rarely do.

Returning to my case with the Dean of the Law Faculty, it is, of course, fair to point out that I have not paid for his or the Assistant Course Director's time. The reason for this is that both are in a position to choose between alternative activities, to do research, increase their load of undergraduate and graduate teaching, sit on the building and catering committees of their university, or to give a hand with staff development.

When we started our operation some 15 years ago we had to hire everybody. That very often meant people from outside the universities who professed that they had special skills that were badly needed by us. Those consultants were often very expensive, and therefore one of my first strategic targets was to build an organization of at least equal, but preferably superior, competence within the universities — an organization in which we would not hire people but invite people who shared our commitment to a progressive university system. Some five years ago we stopped hiring people.

We offer our Course Directors a learning experience, arranging events for them which they hardly can do for themselves. With pleasure, we see an increasing

number of really top academics on our staff; admittedly the nearest we have come
to a Nobel Prize Laureate is a researcher with two nominations but no prize, but for
a staff development outfit this is not bad.

Again I can hear you saying that this does not apply to the UK. In this case you
are wrong, however. Since Leo Evans and I first discussed the possibilities of a joint
venture many years ago, our ties with Britain have increased. It is indeed surprising
that so many academics and top administrators in the UK are willing to put
themselves at our disposal, putting in a lot of work, as an alternative to their other
activities, without any compensation for loss of time. I only hope that we are able,
or will be able in the future, to offer them some learning situations which are or
will be of value to their work.

I believe that both adequate preparations and international contacts are more
easily arranged at a national level than at university level, and I would therefore add
them as cases in point for a national organization. In my plea for national
organizations, there are two more points I should like to make.

First, the more autonomous the universities, the more important it is that
academics and staff meet at a national level to discuss mutual problems — not
connected with their individual disciplines (there are other fora for that) but related
to structural difficulties. In the old days, when our various disciplines and
sub-disciplines were not as specialized as they are today, academics used to meet
to decide on university policy in general. Today, we seem to regard anything
outside research in our own disciplines as ephemeral, and consequently, complain
about the idiocy of other people not understanding our problems while we do not
give a second of our valuable time trying to understand theirs. I understand that
the way the University Grants Committee (UGC) performed its task two years ago
of trimming your university system is often quoted as an example of not doing the
right thing. Yet, if it is going to come to a real confrontation between the AETT
and the UGC, I am afraid I am going to put my money on the UGC— and not
because of relative power but because of relative competence.

What I am trying to say is that I believe that the 'super-industrial society' will
see some very profound changes in its systems of higher learning, and that I believe
that the preparations for such changes are a worthy cause for staff developers.
I think, however, that a national organization is better equipped to do this job
than organizations based at individual universities.

My final point in this pleading for national organizations is that we can set an
example. It is easy to prove that the now compulsory induction course in teaching
methods for new academics at all our universities is a result of the work of my
Department. But you can be more subtle than that. Suppose that the UGC, or the
CVCP, or indeed the Department of Education and Science, had a staff
development organization that suddenly concentrated its effort in one direction, do
you not think that this would be noticed, and that the signals would be received
and understood, by universities in the UK? Some years ago in Sweden we were
worried about the status of our research technicians — their training was becoming
obsolete and the universities seemed to do very little to keep them abreast with
research and development. So we created a nationwide in-service training for
research technicians. The message was clearly understood, and, although we do a
few courses of a more specialized kind, we do not have to supply this kind of
training nowadays — the universities have taken over.

My five points — in this case, suggestions rather than commandments — for a
national organization are that:

1. we have easier access to the best people;
2. we can spend more — and badly needed — time and money on preparations;
3. we have a wider access to international organizations, and, through them, to
   individuals of interest to us;

4. autonomous universities need varied fora for a discussion on structural changes — the CVCP fulfills only a part of this need;
5. a national organization can set an example, or, 'we sometimes fly our kite'.

I should also like to clarify one point in our system — we have no control over the participants in our activities; they are selected by the individual universities. There has been one exception — the Course for Vice-Chancellors and other senior administrative officers — but this is the only exception to the rule.

At the start we had very much the same situation as many of you seem to have — we ran courses for a group of addicts who really did not need our training, while those who needed it stayed away. As my first Commandment (see p 16) bids me to remember that I am part of management and therefore not paid to organize a choir of believers, a second strategic decision was to move away from sending out invitations and instead gradually to rely on the VCs offices to pick out people for our activities. We are not quite there yet, but this academic year I have an agreement with 10 out of 11 VCs that they 'suggest' — as they like to put it — to various individuals that the VCs would like them to represent the university in most of our activities. The result has been noticeable — not only do we meet more powerful academic people but the faces of old friends from previous conferences become increasingly scarce.

After this apology for our existence I should like to continue to do what I had planned to do, that is, try to describe what we actually do. First, however, I should like to dwell a little on our different conceptions of time required. You think, and many of our academics think, that our activities are too long — for example, one of our most successful management courses is a 10-day course.

If you look at industry's way to tackle problems of staff development it seems quite clear to me that this time argument is not well founded. It also seems to me that there are two possible ways of avoiding this trap. By:

(a) having your academics meet the demands of the extra-mural world (where they very soon would find that the world at large which actually does finance their work is not terribly impressed by the time standard of the academic world); and
(b) cheating (which might mean, for example, that you place your activities in a place where airline regulations necessitates a stay of not less than 13 days).

I have always found it very interesting that academics who cannot be away from their departments more than a day or two, because they fear that the departments might disintegrate, can nevertheless add a two-week study visit in a country overseas to a 13-day staff development activity. Somehow the time argument becomes less credible.

I hope that my Department is doing a little bit of both. It is, however, a serious conflict of interest, and I believe that every staff developer should spend some time debating this issue with him/herself. Are we going to accept impossible briefs for the sheer joy of having otherwise unreachable academics join our events, or should we follow the rulings of our professional competence and refuse to take on assignments which are clearly unrealistic?

On the whole, I think that my Department has lived up to the eighth Commandment (see p 17): that attitude change takes time. If you study current literature on management and organizational theory you will find that this is the most important issue today. I shall not try to argue why this is so — although I think that each of us would come up with some pretty good arguments for such a line — but simply note that this is the message of all successful organizations of today.

I have to admit, though, that it is a bit doubtful whether we lived up to our own rules in the case of the compulsory course for the Vice-Chancellors. I may be able

to give some valid explanations as to why we behaved as we did, but I have no other
excuse than that I believe that our behaviour is in line with our long-term strategy
(which might be looked at as a slightly bent set of Commandments!).

Let me now turn to the compulsory course for Vice-Chancellors, Registrars and
senior university administrators — the event you are so sure could not happen in the
UK. Let me also say that I believe that you are wrong: such an event will take place
in Britain within the next three to four years. It may not be labelled 'staff
development', and you may have nothing to do with the event — this it seems to
me, depends on whether you accept my first Commandment (see p 16) of regarding
yourselves as part of the management — nevertheless, I am prepared to put some
money on the event happening, although it may be organized by the CVCP, the
UGC or the DES. If you have the soul of a head-waiter — ninth Commandment (see
p 17) — the organizational frame is not important. The contents are, however.

So we have the following situation: an adamant Chancellor of the Universities —
who had not been asked by the Prime Minister whether or not he would like to
attend the Director Generals' course — has called the following people to attend a
nine-day compulsory staff development event.

- ☐ Vice-Chancellors   (11)
- ☐ Pro-Vice-Chancellors   (11)
- ☐ University College Presidents   (13)
- ☐ Registrars   (24)
- ☐ Senior Officers of the National Board   (17)
- ☐ Senior Academic Administrators   (98)
  - — Heads of Undergraduate Ed
  - — Heads of Planning Depts
  - — Heads of Budget Depts
  - — Heads of Personnel Depts
  - — Heads of Information Depts

Total: 160 people

The following restrictions were issued by the Government — in fact, by the Ministry
of Finance:

- ☐ the course should comprise 3 x 3 days
- ☐ the three parts should cover
  - — university and society
  - — leadership, and
  - — more effective operation, eg by better planning
- ☐ the National Board Officers should have at least Parts 2 and 3 separate from
  the universities
- ☐ university administration's Civil Service role must be discussed
- ☐ there must be a one-day follow-up in 1984

As you can see, there were no budget restrictions. This does not mean that I was
given *carte blanche* — on the contrary, I have had to fight for every krona spent on
the course — but I find it very rewarding that the Ministry of Finance was more
interested in results than in budgets. I believe it is Peter Drucker who has coined the
phrase that 'public organizations tend to do the wrong thing'. In this case, I think
that the right thing was done.

If you sum up the situation, we found ourselves dealing with:

- ☐ 160 or so participants who would be
  - — unwilling
  - — pressed for time, and
  - — often outranking potential course staff
- ☐ time
  - — inadequate for needed attitude change

Within my Department we added another restriction. It was quite clear that we would use the enormous prestige of the Chancellor — previously a very successful and much respected Vice-Chancellor of the University of Lund — as much as possible. Thus, while we would have wanted to divide the participants into some six groups with 25 to 30 people (which would have amounted to 30 days for the Chancellor in a period of five months which clearly was not possible), we had to divide into three groups for university and society and into four groups for the two following events.

I very clearly found myself squeezed between Commandments 1 and 8 (see pp 16-17) — regard yourself as part of management versus attitude change takes time. In the end, the first Commandment took precedence, and we decided to go ahead. I admit that this was not a very happy position but we decided to play down leadership as there was very little we could do in the allotted time, and concentrate our efforts on universities and society and better planning procedures.

Incidentally, the 'we' I have used refers to my Department but not to our permanent staff. When faced with the rather full order to run this thing for Vice-Chancellors etc, we followed our normal procedure of organizing a planning group comprising real people: two Presidents, one Registrar, one Head of Undergraduate Education and one Deputy Registrar. I do not have to tell you that they did not charge us for the considerable time they spent on this, but you may be interested to know that one of the meetings took place in my office between 5 pm and midnight on 22 December 1982 which may be taken as proof that even some of the academic leadership are committed to the cause of staff development in our country.

Again, I hear you say that this is all very well but unfortunately it does not apply to the UK. Again, I think that you are wrong. I know at least two Vice-Chancellors and a couple of Registrars in the UK who would be very happy to allot some of their time and energy to staff development — provided that you give them the chance and that you choose topics they would find pertinent to the problems of British universities today.

What did we finally do? We thought it a good idea to divide the three occasions into:

- [ ] one 'nice'
- [ ] one 'nasty'
- [ ] one 'semi-nice'

The 'nice' session would comprise lectures by eminent experts in various topics. The 'nasty' session would involve a lot of group-work with a fair amount of decision-making, all reported to the Chancellor. The 'semi-nice' session would be a gradual retreat from the group-work situations to more safe lectures on the elements of good leadership.

The final programme looked like this:

Day 1	Day 2	Day 3
Trends in Swedish society — political — economic — immigration — information	Situations of our competitors — UK — Federal Republic	Concept of risk-taking mangement — Dept Minister of Higher Education — Chancellor — one Vice-Chancellor
	Group work*	
	Civil Service role	

* Listing problems that have to be solved by 1987 to maintain universities of international standing

First three days

As we divided all sessions into eight groups, and we had three sessions for each, we had results from 24 groups. The results were processed and systematized, and in a televised speech the Chancellor gave instructions for group work in the second — 'nasty' — session. Fortunately, all groups had listed evaluation procedures as an important issue, so this could be an important part of the second of the three days.

Day 1	Day 2	Day 3
Group work: A strategy plan for universities	Group work (continued)	Each university makes its own strategic plan to be handed in to the Chancellor
	'Humanistic lectures'	
Strategic plans in an industrial setting	Industry *evaluates* strategic plans (as presented in group work)	

Second three days

We had some really worried people by now. Most Vice-Chancellors expressed their hope that the Chancellor would accept that the strategic plans had not been approved by the University Councils, and therefore could not be taken as evidence of the future policies of the universities; and this quite apart from their dissatisfaction with the session which must be regarded as unsatisfactory (in clear contrast to the nice and well structured first three days.

The third part of the course — the 'semi-nice' part — had the following structure:

Day 1	Day 2	Day 3
Industry's view on university administration	— selling your ideas in your own organization	Discussion with the Chancellor
Reorganization plans for universities (Dept of Higher Education)	— information systems — equality between men and women — I am a successful Civil Servant	I am a successful leader of a large corporation
	Innovative organizations	

Third three days

Have we been successful? I will tell you in five years time!

Whatever its results, the staff development activity I have just described certainly needs — and I should like to say calls for — a national organization. As my industrialist friends would say: for whose benefit do we have staff development? For universities, for teachers, for students, or for ourselves?

Section 1:
Staff Development in
Open Learning

1.1 Staff Development for Tutors in Open Learning

Roger Lewis
National Extension College

Abstract: The Council for Educational Technology (CET) has, since 1976, been very active in developing open learning schemes. As part of this work it defined three areas in which development was needed: learning materials, management structures and tutoring strategies. This paper considers the work CET has carried out in the third of these areas, in helping tutors in open learning systems to acquire strategies that facilitate student learning. The paper outlines the circumstances of students or trainers working in open learning schemes and discusses the ways in which these affect the role of the tutor. What qualities and capacities does the tutor need? How best might they be acquired? The first CET package is described — its content, method of presentation, the way in which it was piloted, and the results of the piloting. The genesis of 'How to tutor in an open learning scheme' is then described; this publication was followed by a series of regional workshops held during 1982. The aim of the workshops was to promote the 'How to Tutor' package together with other staff training initiatives for tutors in open learning. Finally, the paper considers likely future developments: what challenges will tutors, supervisors and others face as new open learning schemes come into being, such as those sponsored by the Manpower Services Commission's Open Tech Unit? How might CET and others help tutors to meet these challenges?

INTRODUCTION

In the late 1970s the CET Open Learning Systems Project identified three areas in which development was needed before open learning could really take off: firstly, more suitable learning materials available more easily, secondly more flexible management and resourcing arrangements, and thirdly, tutoring. This paper focuses on the third of these, on strategies tutors can acquire to support students and facilitate their learning. Unfortunately, we have no simple word that conveys this; 'teaching' and even 'tutoring' do not adequately describe the role of a tutor working in open learning, ie in a context which does not centre around the physical presence of a teacher in a particular building with a group of people called 'students'. This paper will consider the following: the context of the student working in an open learning system, the role of the tutor, CET's initial development work in this area, the genesis of 'How to tutor in an open learning scheme', the regional workshops based on the 'How to tutor' package, and the future. Many of the references will be to local or distance contexts (eg Flexistudy, Doncaster Quarrying) rather than to tutors and students in learning workshops (eg Bradford Maths workshop). This is simply because most well known examples are in the first two categories; the general points apply equally well to workshop-based schemes.

THE STUDENT IN AN OPEN LEARNING SYSTEM

The rest of this paper follows from the situation of the open learner. She/he is not in frequent, regular face-to-face contact either with a teacher or, equally importantly, with peers. The content of his or her learning is transmitted not by a teacher but by a more or less specially designed package, developed to help individuals study on their own. Sometimes the open learner can feel isolated and, especially if an adult with many commitments, can all too easily get behind with study, lose touch and drop out. Open learners thus need to have or acquire such qualities as maturity, staying power and autonomy. They also need to be able to set short- and long-term goals and to monitor progress towards these.

I'm still in England. Seriously though I am sorry for the delay in getting this first E008 assignment to you.

These last few weeks have been hectic and I am only just returning to something like sanity. I have not been able to stick to the times set by myself as regards studying. This has not been for want of trying I should add; it has been due to umpteen unforeseen 'happenings'.

The first of these was connected with my return to normal working. On my return to normal work I found that there was a certain amount of overtime available and because I desperately needed to amass some savings I reluctantly had to accept and work over. This overtime work was in the form of working one in three weekends and although I did not usually study during the weekend I found I could not manage without doing some studying on my return from working over. This meant that I fell behind in certain jobs usually reserved for weekend attention.

Then fate took over and suddenly we were inundated with visits from friends and relatives whom we had not seen for months. This put paid to any studying after work and I was forced to study when and where I could.

I started on E008 and I even managed to start on the essay part of the assignment. It was then that something happened which was alien to me; no matter how hard I tried I could not come to write beyond two paragraphs. I was stuck and no matter what I did I could not write. I was too ashamed to phone you and I went through a phase where I was completely depressed. I picked up the phone several times and tried to phone you but I couldn't. I apologise for this because I know you would have helped but at the time I was truly ashamed of myself and I felt as if I had let you down.

Anyway things got better and I started again and this time there was no difficulty in writing; only in how to say it. I have tried hard with this enclosed essay and deep down I am still not happy with it.

Then fate stopped work again, this time in the shape of a flooded kitchen. I returned home from work one night to find the kitchen under two inches of water. A tap had been left on and there had been pots in the sink and the sink had overflowed. This meant I could not study that night and the night after due to clearing up the mess. Luckily I am insured for such occasions and a new carpet is in the pipeline.

Student working towards an O level in English (This is from a genuine letter though admittedly the student is rather more articulate than is often the case.)

THE ROLE OF THE TUTOR

How should the tutor respond? As I have said, it is impossible to carry out what is still the most usual role for the tutor — information giver. Contact is too sporadic for that and the learning materials are designed to fulfil this role. This is true of most forms of open learning, eg the tutor in a workshop context moves from one student to another, is not responsible for the structure of each student's learning. One vital quality the tutor needs is the ability to work with this learning package, supplementing it and modifying it as necessary but never undermining it in the eyes of the learners since that is all they have access to for most of their study time.

The tutor has to bear in mind that his other main job is to support the student, usually by distance means such as letter, marked assignment or telephone. The learner should feel cared for — in contact even if at a distance. The tutor's role is to provide reassurance but also to help the student to acquire and strengthen a sense of autonomy with its concomitants, such as the ability to assess progress realistically, to work to self-imposed deadlines and to diagnose and resolve problems. It follows that the counselling dimension is paramount — such activities as clarifying motivation, deciding whether a particular course will meet an individual's requirements (pre-entry counselling), dealing with any problems that arise — these are vital and are not necessarily part of the way in which many academics define their role.

> *Thank you for your reply, I have been waiting for it as if it was a cheque from Littlewoods. Every morning I have eagerly awaited the postman, I even started to open the door so I could get the mail that bit sooner...*
>
> *Next you ask me if my wife supports me, yes she does. She has told me to get on with my studying while she baths the kids and she makes sure I am not disturbed. I do not know if she understands why I want to study but she has gone out of her way to help me to do so.*
>
> *Sorry I have missed a question of yours out, you asked if I wanted you to draw my attention to my numerous spelling mistakes, yes please, you can see my need for 'O' level language now. Thank you for asking, like I said before you should have been my teacher, I don't think this would have been necessary then. Please do not think I am greasing round you, it just makes a change for someone to take the time to show an interest without their being forced to.*

Student response to the tutor (from the student quoted previously)

THE OPEN LEARNING SYSTEMS PROJECT'S EARLY WORK ON TUTORING

In 1978 CET established two working groups. One looked at student learning and asked such questions as: How do students learn? What problems do students face at different stages of their courses? The other considered tutoring — what skills and capacities do tutors need? How might they acquire these? Would training best be carried out by using packages, or face-to-face? As part of existing pre- or in-service provision or separately? These groups were of course looking at the two facets of one problem, so they were merged. The next stage was to plan a package of materials based on the needs of students studying by open learning. This would be aimed at tutors, helping them to define and practise the intervention skills they needed in order to support learners.

What were the principles on which this package was based? It was decided to remove the 'expert' trainer and to rely on tutors' responsibility for generating their own learning. The package was built around raw material of a case study type designed to elicit the tutor's own existing theory and practice. It covered the problems of students in 'mid-course' and included questions for the tutors to discuss and decisions for them to take. Tutors were then presented with the personal views and reactions of others rather than with 'expert' analyses. These they could compare with their own responses. The materials were flexible as to mode (group or individual), order of study, and time, and an important role was to be played by materials that the tutors themselves would generate while working on the pack, eg diary notes, cases studies of their own students, marked scripts.

The package was made available in two forms, for group and for individual use, and both were piloted. Barnet tutors worked on the peer learning group form; tutors from Shrewsbury worked on the individualized form of the same material, exchanging their responses with colleagues through the post.

An evaluation found that the original principles were borne out (Gibbs, 1981). Tutors liked being responsible for their own learning and used the material flexibly, as planned. They valued the support of their peers saying that working with colleagues sharpened their sense of commitment, removed any element of threat and offered plenty of opportunity to compare practice. It was planned to extend the approach into other areas and to cover other topics.

THE GENESIS OF 'HOW TO TUTOR IN AN OPEN LEARNING SCHEME'

Unfortunately the ambitious project could not be completed. This was partly the result of financial constraints but it was also a matter of priorities. Open learning schemes had been multiplying: Flexistudy alone expanded from five colleges in 1978 to 60 colleges in 1980. As the numbers of tutors involved in these schemes increased so too did the need for training materials. Certain areas were identified as in need of urgent attention. These included the role of the co-ordinator of a scheme, marking student work, using the telephone, running face-to-face sessions, counselling, advising the student on study strategies, providing opportunities for practical work and keeping adequate records. As far as possible, the earlier principles were observed: the materials consisted of a series of questions, linked by a skeletal framework. The questions were asked in a variety of contexts during piloting and answers were collected. These answers formed the basis of what was later published as tutor responses. Thus the principle of excluding any prescriptive advice was maintained; instead, tutors could compare their own responses with the views and comments of a variety of other practitioners.

What is your own view on corrections?

'I correct very fully — spelling, grammar, sentence structure as well as errors of fact or interpretation. I do this without making a great "song and dance" about it but if the student is to achieve a good O or A level grade they must be capable of reasonably error-free work.'

'Hum. As will be seen by anyone reading these notes I am absolutely useless at English — spelling, etc.

I mark only that work that I am qualified to mark, which at the moment is: basic electronic workshop projects.

If I can read and understand the students' electronic argument then that is all I am concerned with.

Poor spelling is not something to be marked in engineering/scientific subjects unless the meaning if the word can be misconstrued.

In my experience, most engineers with problems in this area, already know about it, but still find being marked on or having comments on this aspect of their work (a) very discouraging (b) very annoying.

Damn it, when will some people learn that other people cannot spell no matter how hard they try. (If you do not know a word is incorrect, you will not look it up in a dictionary.) Also, if you suspect every word you write, you will hardly proceed to write at all, this is exactly what happens to some students who have been subjected to spelling correction fanatics marking technical scripts.'

Extract from section on assignment comments and marking

After the piloting the materials were quickly rewritten and then published in two formats. The self-study version was an A5 booklet, with a fold-out flap to enable the tutor to cover up the responses while considering his or her own answers to a particular question. The group version, for tutors working together in peer learning groups, was A4 in size and contained sheets of paper in two colours. The sheets could easily be detached from the folder in which the package was presented. White sheets were used for the questions and the framework; buff sheets contained the responses. The buff sheets could be fed into the group discussion as desired. The aim was for maximum flexibility: sections and questions could be studied in any order, with or without the use of the responses; tutors could work for as long or as short a time as they wished. The sheets could also be used for workshops, as a basis for role-play or by tutors in correspondence with one another. In both versions the intention was for tutors to reflect about their own scheme and to decide what, if any, changes they wanted to make to their own practice. One centre, for example, discussed marking and brought into the discussion scripts produced by their own students. They then sent out a questionnaire to find out what students felt about the way in which their work was marked. The tutors discussed how they would change their approach to marking in the light of the student response.

Work with the group version has shown the importance of a co-ordinator in managing the use of the package, particularly now when the climate is not especially favourable to staff development. A respected tutor with some 'clout' is needed to ensure that the staff development activity is co-ordinated and that practical facilities (eg a room, refreshments) and moral support are forthcoming. The good co-ordinator (facilitator or animateur) will also help a group to co-ordinate its discussion and to structure its meetings. To use the group version to the full, co-ordinators need a very good knowledge of the package. They can then modify and adapt it, as is necessary with any materials to be used in an open learning context.

THE REGIONAL WORKSHOPS

During 1982 CET ran five regional workshops to promote not only the 'How to tutor' packages but also staff development in open learning more generally. The workshops were planned for 'college co-ordinators of open learning schemes and for open learning tutors'. The objectives were:

- ☐ To introduce 'How to tutor in an open learning scheme' to participants.
- ☐ To provide an opportunity for participants, working in groups, to use extracts from 'How to tutor' in order to explore tutoring in open learning.
- ☐ To provide an opportunity for open learning tutors and co-ordinators to meet to share experience.
- ☐ To give participants the opportunity to listen to the tutoring experiences of an established open learning scheme.
- ☐ To provide an opportunity for participants to consider the priorities for student learning in their schemes, and what is necessary for these priorities to be met.

The fourth objective was met by inviting a co-ordinator from a well established open learning scheme to summarize the main experiences of that scheme. Short plenaries alternated with intensive small group sessions working on extracts from the 'How to tutor' package. Groups were varied so that each participant encountered the maximum possible range of experiences.

The five workshops attracted over 200 participants from around 140 different institutions. A wide range of institutions was represented including further education colleges, training boards, a grammar school, regional management centres, polytechnics, SCOTEC, the Open University, the Cement and Concrete Association, Lucas CAV and British Leyland. Thus the workshops attracted a very diverse audience. The most important topics seem to have been working with learning materials, keeping records, pre-entry counselling and how to move students towards greater autonomy. Was open learning expected to produce better results and a higher standard of tutoring than conventional classes? Appraisal of tutors, even self-appraisal, would seem to be an unusual experience in further education. This was a revelation to the participants from industry, for whom regular appraisal is an accepted part of the working environment. One or two colleges were moving to such systems, some also asked all candidates from any new job in college what was their experience of, and attitude to, open learning. The 'How to tutor' packages were well received; it was also suggested that CET might consider complementing the print-based package with other media such as audio-tape, video-tape or tape-slide.

POSSIBLE FUTURES

There is currently an increasing interest in open learning at all levels and in all subjects. Flexistudy continues to grow in the general, non-vocational area and it is expected that this scheme will carry an increasing proportion of technical and business material. Adult education, schools and industrial training are also using open learning methods. The Open Tech is underway and is likely to generate not only further interest in open learning but also more tangible results: new materials, new systems of delivery and support, new ways of marketing courses, new kinds of qualification. Some colleges are trying to introduce a general policy for open learning across departments and to initiate not just one system (eg Flexistudy) but several (eg workshops as well).

What are the implications for tutoring? Raising quality remains important. Colleges and other institutions will have to develop their own training models within their own institutions but they will need some help in activities such as identifying and developing suitable co-ordinators — and in resourcing the activity. The Open Tech is likely to announce a staff development support project; new kinds of people will be coming into the orbit of tutor training — supervisors in industry, volunteers — as well as lecturers initially trained but new to open learning. It is likely that all this activity will produce both an enhanced use of existing training materials and also new ways of enhancing the skills of those people, whatever their job title, required to support open learners.

REFERENCE

Gibbs, G (1981) Training tutors at a distance: an alternative strategy. *Teaching At A Distance*, 20. Open University, winter.

1.2 Information Technology and Open Learning: The Interactivity Analogue

N Paine
Scottish Council for Educational Technology

Abstract: The paper will try and pick out the generally accepted features of interactive print material and trace the development of these features. These will then be applied to learning material emerging from the new technologies such as interactive video, CBT, Viewdata, etc to show how these features can be built into different media. The paper will show that there is a danger that new technologies can simply recreate old mistakes and end up producing bad learning material, unless the lessons gleaned from print-based experience are applied to other media.

INTRODUCTION

'Educational Technology is successful in so far as it increases the range of procedures open to the individual learner in a specific task. [Media] ... are effective not merely because they are affecting more senses but because they increase the strategies open to the learner of grouping, organising, categorising, image-fixing and associating.'
I G Morris (ETIC 76)

This paper is concerned with discussing the possibility of extending the progress made in defining successful qualities of interactive learning material in print into other media; in other words building analogues of print interactivity on the one hand, and getting around the limitations of print interactivity on the other.

According to Ian Morris' ETIC 76 lecture in Dundee, media other than print offer a greater range of learning strategies for the materials producers which in turn make a wider variety of learning opportunities available to the student. The principles of instructional design which work for print should form the starting point for design in other media. What I am anxious to look at is the way we can formulate some conditions for that base which are not specific to one particular medium.

There appears to be an increasing tendency, which I call technolunacy, to consider as many different media as possible to be essential to a particular learning package for no better reason than that they exist. Some packages I have looked at bear witness to this. One had Viewdata modems built into a costing to fulfil a function which could be handled by print at a fraction of the cost. The purpose of this paper is not to lay down prescriptive rules but to debate the points which emerge and suggest some general guidelines which may or may not be taken up. At this stage, in a sense, to generate some debate on this issue is more relevant than attempting to resolve it.

HOW MUCH OF AN ANALOGUE CAN PRINT OFFER?

Print material has certain physical limitations and production constraints which are obvious:

☐ It needs to be examined more or less linearly.
☐ Multi-coloured materials are expensive to produce.
☐ 'Hiding' what comes next can be unnecessarily complex.
☐ It tends to be dominated by words rather than images.
☐ Production is slow and expensive.
☐ Material is difficult to alter once printed.

But it also has certain advantages:

☐ It is portable.
☐ It needs no special equipment to be made use of.
☐ It can act as a permanent record or reference bank.
☐ It is a familiar medium.
☐ Distribution is relatively simple.
☐ It can be weighed up very quickly.

Indeed a course like the CNAA postgraduate diploma in educational technology by distance learning provided by Dundee College of Education, has, over the years, *reduced* its multi-media content at its students' behest. This, in spite of the fact that a proportion of the course is designed to encourage experimentation in designing learning materials with other than a print-base. This, I believe, is a general tendency. Students like print — mainly for the first three reasons I have listed above.

To develop the analogue concept, we must build upon the strength of print-based material linking this to the peculiar strengths of the medium chosen for a learning task.

There are obvious advantages for a student dealing with a print-based learning package which are taken for granted: a student can weigh-up the size of the package, flick quickly through its pages to get an idea of content and style. It can quickly be marked or personalized. We can reassure ourselves about its content and feel familiar with it before sitting down to work.

Many computer-based training packages or Viewdata packages, however, invite the student onto an unknown journey: he or she has no idea of direction, length or expected commitment, and only a vague idea of content. This must create resistance in the student or at least unease. Many packages have no more than a title frame before the sequence begins.

A Prestel Information Provider offers users a 'guided tour' to the data-base. In 30 or so frames, taking from two to five minutes to work through, a user can look at the main features of the data-base: its areas of coverage and method of operation. At any point on the guided tour, the user can key 1 and return to the main index, ie the beginning of the data-base. This simple, but effective, technique could be extended to training packages which cannot normally be viewed selectively and quickly. By looking at some of the testing, and a summary of the content, a student could decide quickly on the appropriateness of the course in the same way that someone can browse through a book.

Many print-based packages offer selective revision facilities, where the student can select one key section to revise his or her knowledge. Some offer a pre-test which, if successfully completed, obviates the necessity for the student to work through a particular part of a unit. Both of these techniques could be used in non-print media. Many CBT programs I have worked through simply do not allow a student to stop at any point and return to it at will. A break in the middle of a 'lesson' necessitates down-loading the lesson again and working through it to the point previously reached. And similarly repetitive drill and practice testing has to be relentlessly pursued to the final example before the machine will deliver more goods. The great print facility of 'skipping' needs some kind of analogue, as does the increasing use of checklist revision sequences.

The great advantage of Viewdata, CBT, video-cassette and video-disc is their ability to move beyond a linear page-turning function into more or less random access. Much material, however, simply translates the linear restrictions of the programmed text into a different medium. In a sense running a feature film on video-disc is the same kind of software-imposed limitation on the hardware. Fifty-four thousand random access frames are simply viewed in sequence and the interactivity of the medium is mostly lost. On one level it would be possible to conceive of a learning programme that was almost entirely student driven. The routing system through the materials could be chosen according to the students' interests and abilities. This would present significant problems for the materials designer and would need an interface that could analyse the students' learning needs in terms of the available data-base. Other developments are more modest in scope:

- ☐ The student could select how many examples he or she required of a particular sequence.
- ☐ A contents list would allow the student to opt in and out of a particular sequence, perhaps through a 'help' key.
- ☐ Testing could be related to progress through the material.
- ☐ The student could present him or herself for testing.

A typical checklist for print-based materials might include:

	Identification of the course/unit/title/author
	List pre-entry requirements
	Time required to complete unit
PRE-STUDY	Contents list
	Any prerequisites for use
	Any instructions for use
	List aims, objectives
	Overview
	Define different kinds of interactions within unit
STUDY	Student-assessed questions
	Further activities
	Post-tests — tutor-assessed questions
POST-STUDY	Summaries and review sections
	Any additional reading

This list is printed in a linear way and usually follows this sequence in a unit:

UNIT TITLE → Prerequisites → contents → aims and objectives → UNIT interspersed with SAQs → summaries and conclusions → further activities → TAQ → additional reading.

Professor Noel Entwistle and others have shown that students develop learning styles that reflect partly on what a student wants or needs to know and partly on an intrinsic pattern of knowledge acquisition — the distinction between holist and serialist learners, for example. That sequence in a printed unit could be breached at any point: a student might leap to the summary then back to a medium position SAQ and its answer, before starting off on one particular section. Menu driven packages could offer that facility as simply as print, but few cater for the variety of learning needs of the student.

My particular interest lies in open learning systems designed to offer flexible learning opportunities to adults. The notion of flexibility ought to be extended right through the course on offer as well as in its delivery. Experience with adult distance learning students in Dundee has shown the wide variety of ways they tackle standard units and, by extension, the course as a whole. If a student achieves suitable learning outcomes, does the route to these outcomes matter a great deal?

I can list at least 12 kinds of student-assessed questions ranging from the close Yes/No answer to more open short essay questions:

☐ Multiple choice
☐ Matching
☐ Sequencing
☐ Filling in blanks
☐ True/false
☐ Completion . . .
☐ One-word answers
☐ Short essay type
☐ Case study.

There are, I am sure, many others not mentioned here. Often different media actually enhance the kind of testing opportunities available and make the experience more attractive and interesting.

Barclays Bank use Viewdata as a training medium more extensively than anyone else in the UK. They have over 100 hours of material on a private data-base serving banks in Greater London. One sequence tests the students elementary knowledge of cash-drawer layout by drawing a cash-drawer, filling it with money and then asking the student a series of questions about the location of money withdrawals and deposits. Each correct answer modifies the cash-drawer graphic. It is effective and simple.

Much CBT and interactive video assessment routes the student back to the relevant part of the 'text' if their assessment choice is incorrect. This should be optional and based on the significance of the assessment for the achievement of learning objectives. Much print assessment is designed purely to increase interactivity: the response is not crucial or all responses are in a sense correct. These fast assessments are as necessary in print as elsewhere. Even gimmicks such as latent-image printing for a doctor's diary proved highly successful in 'hooking' the student to the learning experience. Electronic and audio-visual materials offer far more possibilities for testing in a wide variety of ways including simulating case study work, building testing and graphic design into one package, etc. The key point is that what makes print material interactive and successfully interactive should not be ignored when working in other media. There is a higher tolerance amongst adults when working with non-print material. I have watched basic education students happily play a simple game of hangman on a PET which they would feel insulted by if it were presented in print. But that power of the new should not be exploited in order to develop worse material than the print equivalent and the insights already gained with print need not be lost when shifting to other media.

Roger Lewis (1981) defines the characteristics of self-study materials as:

☐ Make clear to the learner what he needs to know or be able to do.
☐ Provide objectives.
☐ Give the learner the chance to see how well he is mastering the objectives by providing questions and answers in the text.
☐ Give any necessary study advice.
☐ Unpack difficult concepts and relate them to experience.
☐ Break the subject up into manageable chunks for study.
☐ Converse with the student in a lively and interesting style.

You could add:

☐ Signpost the material carefully and continually.
☐ Offer some form of escape or 'help' sequence (to a tutor or further explanation) if the student gets into difficulties.
☐ Review the material at regular intervals.

☐ Offer checklist sequences for revision.
☐ Systematic evaluation of the materials.

W T Beveridge (1982) has developed this simple list into a straightforward annotated checklist for those writing computer packages under headings such as educational objectives, package structure and design, interaction, learner control, etc.

Beveridge's paper and Lewis' book link together very well. One could be seen as an annotation of the other in a particular specialized context. What Beveridge considers 'the components of a good package' fit the educational technology principles discussed above. It would appear to be unnecessary to draw up specific checklists for each medium, rather keep the principles in mind when material is being developed. The analogues of print interactivity should be built around these clear indicators:

☐ Some kind of list of objectives.
☐ An indication of the nature of the package and its learning outcomes.
☐ Self-assessment in a variety of forms.
☐ User-friendly.
☐ Well structured and signposted data-base.
☐ Review/revision sequences.
☐ An attempt to monitor the student's experience in evaluation.

Each will have a variety of analogues, for example 'user-friendly' for a computer program will mean, friendly error codes (not just ERROR 107 but PRINTER NOT CONNECTED [Beveridge, p 8]), acceptance of 'YES', 'yes', 'Yes', 'Y' as correct indicators, etc. In Viewdata it will mean a routing system that does not lose the student, and access to the menu at regular intervals. For interactive video it will mean, simple control systems; as short a time lag as possible for cueing, reviewing, etc.

If we have accepted that we cannot control the use made of print materials, then we must make other media as flexible and accessible. Rather than add blanket value judgements such as the one adumbrated by De Cecco and Crawford (1974) from a small piece of research into visual representation:

'Rampant colour, the existential realism of European motion pictures and other excesses, whatever their artists appeal, are not sound bases for the development of visual materials for instruction.'

The sound bases come from the ed tech model which should hold good for any medium, where non-print materials increase the available strategies for learner and and package writer rather than restrict those opportunities.

Paul Copeland's (1982) media quadrant presented at a recent ETIC looks at five or six different media and places them on the following quadrants:

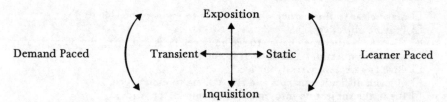

Only interactive video, in his analysis, falls squarely in all four quadrants. My point would be to develop a medium, for what it can achieve educationally rather than expect it to fulfil every category. Print, after all, only fills the righthand half of the diagram. The choice of medium is often based, not on ideal qualities but on more pragmatic features such as cost, available resources, time and expertise. Any medium can be made to work if the points I have listed are taken into account. Any can fail in spite of their theoretical potential.

CONCLUSIONS

1.0 There are examples of good practice which can be generalized from print self-learning materials. Each one of these can be given an appropriate analogue when working in a medium other than print.
These points include:
☐ Listing aims and objectives.
☐ Giving a small description of the pack including the approximate time taken to complete it.
☐ Full and varied SAQs.
☐ User friendliness — 'help' sequences.
☐ Frequent signposting.
☐ Review sequences.
☐ Student evaluation of package.
1.1 The points do not need minute development for every conceivable medium, but need to be borne in mind when materials are prepared.
2.0 Regardless of the theoretical potential of a particular medium, its suitability will depend more on development materials according to the points above than on intrinsic capabilities of the hardware.
3.0 Even information-based technology can be harnessed for suitable educational aims, provided the limitations are recognized.
3.1 Media other than print should offer the possibility for a wider range of self-assessment than print which would stretch the interactivity of the medium to its limits.
3.2 The medium is not necessarily the message.
4.0 The 'hidden qualities of print (such as abilities to skip, skim, weigh-up, etc) also need analogues in other media.

REFERENCES

Beveridge, W T (1982) *Educational Computer Package Evaluation and Design.* SMDP.
de Cecco, J P and Crawford, W R (1974) *The Psychology of Learning and Instruction* (second edition), p 399.
Copeland, P (1982) The educational significance of electronic media. In *Aspects of Educational Technology,* **XV**, pp 231-237.
Lewis, R (1981) *How to Write Self-study Materials,* p 14. CET.

1.3 The CET Open Learning Systems Programme: A Contribution to Career Updating

John Coffey
CET Open Learning Systems Consultant

Abstract: The current Council for Educational Technology (CET) open learning systems programme ended on 31 March 1983. CET is now embarking on a new OLS programme with very different concerns from hitherto. It seems an appropriate time therefore to review the work to date, to assess its impact, and attempt to identify the most important factors which aided its success as an innovatory programme.

This paper comprises a brief report on the programme as a whole and its achievements since 1976. The aims and objectives for each of the three phases are given. The main aspects of the work are outlined but no attempt is made to describe any part of the programme in detail. Good timing, a clearly identified target group, the early identification of a transferable model, and carefully considered programme objectives are identified as crucial to the effective promotion of open learning systems by project staff. Examples of methods used to overcome inertia in the system preventing innovation are outlined. Though the programme has not been subject to formal evaluation, a subjective assessment of its major achievements is given. The main problems facing further spread of open learning systems in public sector institutions are listed. A very brief outline of the next stage in CET's OLS work is given.

INTRODUCTION

In the Russell Report, 'Adult Education: A Plan for Development', published in 1973, there was a reference to the potential of open learning systems in the education of adults. This was perhaps not surprising since the Open University had been established recently and had already shown that distance teaching using multi-media materials and some face-to-face tuition could be very successful. It might therefore have been expected that an institution similar to the Open University would be proposed for courses below degree level. However, the Russell Report resisted this temptation and proposed the following:

> 'It is not likely and not reasonably desirable that a permanent institution or a range of institutions like the Open University should be created for adult education below degree level. What is desirable is not a super organisation, but an organisational framework.' (DES, 1973)

CET too, had begun to take an interest in open learning and a brief article by Geoffrey Hubbard, 'Analogues of the Open University', took up the Russell challenge and set out some parameters for an open learning system (Hubbard, 1975):

1. It identified mature students seeking academic, vocational or professional training and qualifications as the main target group for open learning.
2. The aim for an Open University analogue would be to make available to students anywhere in the country courses leading to a wide range of academic, professional and vocational qualifications at times and in ways that conformed with the students' requirements.
3. Open learning systems would grow from within existing institutions, in particular those in the further education system, and there would be a need

for some central initiatives and support to enable them to reach their full potential.

Phase I

These ideas were presented at a conference on open learning convened by CET in April 1976. The conference urged CET to undertake an investigation into the levels and range of current open learning provision for mature students. The subsequent but brief investigation unearthed a surprising number of innovative open learning activities in colleges. It also provided sufficient background information to identify criteria by which open learning systems could be described and to map the broad outlines of a national open learning provision (Davies, 1977). Concurrent with this investigation was another project in which CET was involved. CET joined with the Post Office (now British Telecom) and the Technician Education Council in the development of learning materials for an external students programme in telecommunications. This project gave a detailed insight into the problems concerned with establishing open learning systems inside further education establishments and the role of educational technologists in learning materials development teams outside the OU (Coffey, 1978).

From these beginnings it was possible to plan a second and a much more ambitious phase of the programme to promote the widespread development of open learning systems.

Phase II

The aims for the second phase of the programme were to:

- ☐ Increase awareness in further, adult and continuing education of the contribution open learning systems could make to education and training.
- ☐ Produce guidelines, evaluated case studies, or studies of new open learning experiments, on which open learning developers could base their plans.
- ☐ Propose action necessary for the continued development of OLS.

Phase II of the OLS programme ran for 19 months from September 1978. A list of projects which comprise the programme and their relationship to the aims and objectives is given in Figure 1.

The programme was remarkably successful. The very few open learning experiments under way at the beginning of Phase II were little known and isolated from each other. By the end of the programme, some 50 further education colleges had begun to develop open learning arrangements of some sort and many other colleges had expressed positive interest. Perhaps most important of all, was the increasing acceptance by senior policy makers in local authorities, validating bodies, teachers' unions, and others that open learning was a subject worth considering. A climate of interest was created in which it was possible for ideas such as James Prior's interest in an 'Open Tech' to take root.

A most effective part of the programme was the series of conferences for principals and other senior staff from colleges of further and adult education, members of HM Inspectorate, and local education authority advisory staff. These conferences were held in every region of the UK. Not only was there an effective dissemination of information about open learning and feedback to CET of a very positive and supportive response to CET's work, but requests for help arising from the conferences were followed up with practical support. This was given through sponsoring of consultancy visits, organization of various types of training workshops, and through the National Extension College Open Learning Unit (jointly funded by NEC and CET).

Probably the most important outcome of Phase II was our own deeper

ACTIVITIES

- OLS Consultant Reports - Lectures - Visits
- Comparative Case Studies
- Student Problem Investigation
- Open College Evaluation
- Tutor/Counselling Investigation
- Cost Analysis Study
- Course Design Projects
- Workshops
- NEC Open Learning Development Unit
- Distance Learning for Technicians
- Regional Conferences
- Seminars
- Publications
- Advisory Panel

OBJECTIVES

- To encourage the establishment in principle of OLS experiments in a few colleges as yet uninvolved, and advise during the early stages of development.
- To monitor and report the progress of these experiments.
- To support activities which will encourage debate of OLS issues.
- To list contacts established during Phase II for inclusion in the CET information service/
- To describe possible solutions to the six problem areas identified in Phase I, i.e., concerning student study problems, information networks, tutoring and counselling, course design, costing and administration.
- To assess the validity and transferability of these solutions.
- To produce OLS guidelines on study skills, tutoring, counselling, costing and administration.
- To distinguish between problems which can be solved using existing resources and those which require new arrangements.
- To report the outcomes of debate.
- To propose action for the dissemination of case study and other material produced in Phase II.
- To propose action necessary for the continued development of OLS using the results of Phase II activities as evidence.

AIMS

- to increase awareness in FE, adult and continuing education of the contribution OLS can make to education and training.
- to produce guidelines, evaluated case studies or studies of new OLS experiments/demonstrations, on which OLS developers can base their plans.
- to propose action necessary for the continued development of OLS.

Figure 1. Council for Educational Technology Open Learning Systems — Phase II: relationship of aims, objectives and activities

understanding of the complex network of relationships which would exist between interested agencies if the 'organizational framework', hinted at by Russell, were to be achieved. The Russell phrase implied that existing institutions such as colleges, libraries, advice centres, broadcasting organizations, publishers, correspondence colleges, and so on have the basic skills required to operate open learning systems provided that the appropriate links could be established. It became clear from our own regional conferences and other aspects of our work that despite the undoubted existence of this considerable body of untapped expertise, and the entrepreneurial spirit in further and adult education colleges, and elsewhere, some central co-ordination would be required. An early attempt to show the relationships between different parts of an open learning system is shown in Figure 2 (Coffey, 1978).

Information exchange, pump priming of learning material development, training support, and mechanisms to identify the needs of students and industry would be required. Many of the financial arrangements on which education and training was (and continues to be) based were inappropriate for open learning.

Phase III

In order to help find solutions to these and other related problems, CET agreed to support a third phase of the open learning systems programme for three years from April 1980. The programme was given two main aims, one concerned with 'policy makers', and the other with 'operational' questions. The aims were:

1. *Policy making.* To continue to supply policy makers with information about the potential and need for OLS, to keep them up-to-date with developments, and to alert them to problems concerning policy; to consult with other organizations about the need for nationally co-ordinated support for OLS, and to submit appropriate action recommendations to government.
2. *Operational.* To encourage support and evaluate developmental work in OLS administration and management, learning materials design, and staff training, in order to create a foundation on which open learning opportunities can become an established part of further education provision, and to leave good working examples in the field.

The projects supported during Phase III and their relationship to the aims of the programme are shown in Figure 3.

The start of Phase III unfortunately coincided with a substantial cut in CET's government grant. The net result was a cut in the OLS programme budget of 35 per cent. Nonetheless, it was possible to concentrate effort on production of a consultative document (CET, 1980) to assess the degree of support there might be for some form of national co-ordination and promotion of open learning systems based on existing institutions. This consultative document was issued in December 1980 to more than 200 representative bodies with interests in education and training. With few exceptions, those consulted strongly supported the CET recommendation that government should nominate and support an existing agency or agencies, or form a new one to take responsibility for the development and continuation of open learning systems. Further, the council was urged to emphasize that open learning systems should as far as possible, be fully integrated into existing education and training provision.

At the same time, the Manpower Services Commission (MSC) had been asked by the minister for employment, James Prior, to put together proposals for an 'Open Tech'. It has been possible to work closely with MSC and provide advice and consultancy throughout the development of their programme. As Richard Freeman has pointed out in his article 'Reflections on an "Open Tech" ', the 'Open Tech' was a long time in coming and went through several important metamorphoses

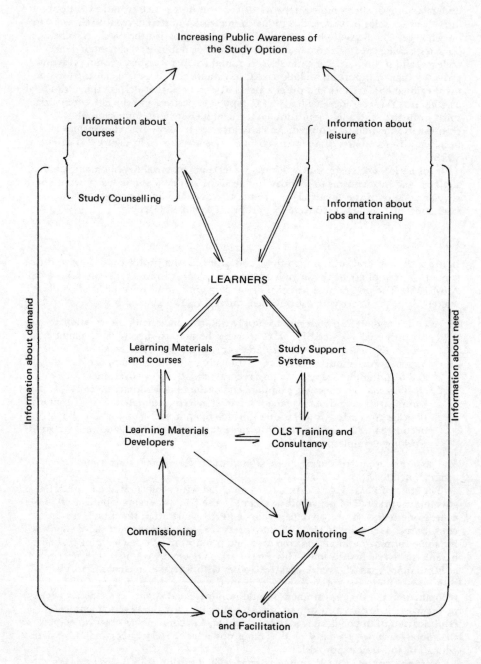

Figure 2

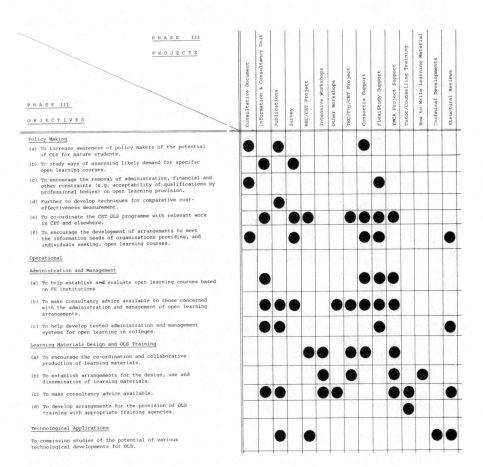

Figure 3

during its development (Freeman, 1982). In the early stages, a central institution, similar in many ways to the Open University, was envisaged. However, the CET programme had demonstrated that other collaborative models based on existing institutions were more likely to meet the requirements of an 'Open Tech' and it is not really surprising that MSC adopted a model which embodied many of the principles set out in the CET consultative document (MSC, 1982). The fact that 'Open Tech' was able to begin its work in a climate which had already been prepared to receive it is perhaps the most important legacy of the CET programme.

Other bodies too have worked with the programme. The Further Education Curriculum Development and Review Unit, the Technician Education Council, Business Education Council, the Scottish Council for Educational Technology, and some local authorities are among those which now put the promotion and development of open learning as important priorities for their work.

Training of staff in open learning schemes in the tutoring and counselling skills, so important to the support of independent learners, has also been a high priority in this phase of work. Training materials have been prepared (Lewis, 1981) and promulgated in a series of regional staff development workshops. Roger Lewis describes this aspect of the activity in another paper at this conference. This programme has also supported a study of the problems students have in working within open learning schemes, an aspect of the work Anita Morris describes in another paper at this conference.

Throughout Phase III, CET continued to support individual colleges and training establishments which set up open learning schemes. Advice and consultancy on administrative questions was provided through an information unit at Coombe Lodge. A variety of workshops were set up to train staff for specific roles within new developments. A newsletter was established to provide a forum in which open learning systems developers could promulgate their own work and ideas. A register of information about open learning schemes in England, Wales and Northern Ireland was put together (Monaco and Latcham, 1982). (SCET has produced a guide to open learning schemes in Scotland.)

At the end of Phase III, some 200 institutions, which before 1976 had taken little interest in open learning, had set up one or more open learning schemes. While many of these schemes can trace their origin directly to the influence of the CET programme, it is now more and more the case that institutions receive their advice and guidance from one or more of the other national bodies including a professional association, The Open Learning Federation, which have begun to support the interests of those working in open learning.

THE INNOVATION STRATEGY

The open learning systems programme, at modest cost (£310,000 since 1976), has been very successful in stimulating innovation in further and adult education and in training. How was this done?

The Starting Points

It is easy to be wise after the event, but one of the main factors was good timing. At the time the programme started, the success of the Open University was becoming widely recognized, and thought was being given to how similar techniques might be used elsewhere. Demographic trends indicated that there would be spare capacity in further education colleges unless new clientele from the adult population could be found. Awareness of the implications of widespread use of new technologies on training and employment was beginning to stir. HMI had set up a study group on development of distance learning. It was reasonable to suppose that at a future stage government would have to fund some development to provide for the education and training needs of mature students, and that open learning systems might be among the methods proposed. Given all these factors, it would have been difficult to fail. Nonetheless, there were pitfalls to be avoided. Dissipating limited resources on a programme which attempted to satisfy all needs at once was one such. CET however, decided to focus its efforts on one group only, namely, mature motivated adults seeking recognized qualifications below degree level. If schemes could be begun under that fairly precise umbrella, then they could later become the starting points for broader schemes.

Good management early on ensured that the objectives for the programme were clear throughout. Not only was there the work by Geoffrey Hubbard, referred to above, but the assistant director responsible for the open learning programme, Leslie Gilbert, insisted at the beginning of Phase II that project staff develop a paper analysing the OLS concept and its implications. This analysis (Coffey, 1977) and subsequent work done by Doug Spencer (Spencer, 1980) kept the aims of the programme firmly in view throughout.

The early identification of Flexistudy as an OLS model which colleges would see as transferable to their own situations (Rowlands, 1977), and the support of that model by an innovatory correspondence college, NEC, helped would-be-innovators to experiment (Sachs, 1980). This enabled many individuals to acquire experience of OLS and encouraged them to identify closely with national initiatives.

Avoiding 'Catch 22'

Despite the fortunate timing, a clearly identified target group, clear objectives and a model, the programme, like so many other innovatory projects before it, was faced in many educational and training institutions, with the familiar buck-passing arguments in favour of doing nothing. Almost any individual, whether he or she be teacher, administrator, adviser, or union official, would claim to appreciate the value of open learning but assert that some other group or individual would prevent it happening. The strategy adopted in the programme to combat this inertia was therefore to proceed on a broad front providing, as far as practicable, appropriately focused help and advice to all groups concerned. It is not possible here to go into detail of all the activities undertaken but some examples illustrate the point. (Some of these have already been mentioned above.)

Regional Conferences

LEA advisers and college principals were invited to attend regional conferences to promote the idea of open learning. At these conferences participants were given a genuine opportunity to help shape the thinking which eventually resulted in the production of the CET consultative document (CET, 1980).

Consultancy

Colleges and LEAs which wished to embark on open learning experiments were given access to consultants with special expertise. Consultants were selected from the staff of existing schemes and, therefore, not only understood the concerns and anxieties of their clients from firsthand experience, but also were perceived by their clients as credible. CET staff retained a degree of detachment throughout. The 'honest broker' role was very helpful in discussions with groups at all levels in the system.

NATFHE

The teachers' union principally concerned, NATFHE (National Association of Teachers in Further and Higher Education), were understandably hesitant about accepting OLS. Rumour had it that politicians saw open learning as a neat way to reduce the size of FE! The programme therefore accepted the validity of the concern and set up a joint CET/NATFHE study group to ensure that each group knew what was going on. The programme supported a special conference on open learning systems for union representatives which was very well attended. The result of this activity was qualified support throughout, a positive response to the CET consultative document and to MSC proposals for an 'Open Tech', and the publication of a union statement favourable to open learning (NATFHE, 1981).

Learning Material

Shortage of suitable learning material over a wide range of subjects has been a major problem throughout. Among the many activities undertaken by the programme were:

- ☐ Studies of the role of educational technologists in writing teams (Coffey, 1978; Morris, 1981).
- ☐ Encouraging correspondence colleges to collaborate with colleges in development of OLS.
- ☐ Providing training workshops to groups of staff in individual colleges and consortia.
- ☐ Developing new technologies for learning material generation such as collaborative intensive writing workshops.
- ☐ Publication of guidelines on 'How to write distance learning material' (CET, 1980).

Tutoring

The problems of tutoring were also examined and novel techniques developed, though cuts in funding prevented completion of the task (Gibbs, 1981).

Resources

The OLS information and consultancy unit at Coombe Lodge provided access to papers on staff resource questions (Birch and Latcham, 1981).

There were many other activities undertaken in the programme but the guiding principle has always been first to identify the problem and then find appropriate solutions. This approach has been particularly appropriate in technician education where the needs of different industries have placed specific constraints on course providers. This has already been discussed in detail in the report on a project on open learning for technicians sponsored by MSC and TEC and managed by the CET OLS programme (Guildford Educational Services, 1982). The problem-solving approach has also been taken up by the MSC in the Open Tech Programme (MSC, 1982).

DISCUSSION

As is so often the case in development projects of this kind, no formal evaluation of the programme was undertaken other than project reviews within CET. Therefore, the detailed assessment of effectiveness of the programme as a whole has to be subjective though there are evaluation reports on some of the specific activities within it. Some very public results do however confirm that the programme has been successful in achieving its main aims. Nonetheless, there has been a widespread adoption of OLS as a means of provision and much of this innovative activity can be traced directly to the work of the programme. The government too has decided to fund a major development programme for technicians through the MSC and, while the initial impetus for the innovation may have begun elsewhere, the approaches eventually adopted for its implementation are traceable to the programme. Open learning and distance learning are now becoming important considerations in the DES Pickup programme through its links with the Open University and the Further Education and Curriculum Review Unit (FEU). These developments too are traceable to the programme. OLS models other than Flexistudy are now receiving much more attention. Perhaps the most significant of these is the workshop mode developed at Bradford College of HE which uses many of the principles of operation used in programmed learning centres.

CET is therefore pleased with its work, particularly so since the positive responses have come both from policy makers as well as from practitioners within the system. This breadth of response augurs well for the eventual institutionalization and integration of the innovations within the education and training systems. It would, however, be wrong to try to give the impression that the work is finished and that there is no further need for development.

The initiatives by government, LEAs, colleges, and training institutions at present meet the needs of a tiny proportion of those who might wish to study through open learning systems. This is very worrying since the youth training initiative of the MSC is swamping innovative potential of FE colleges and, for a time at least, is likely to push the development of OLS well down the priority list.

Despite the positive and welcome support for 'Open Tech' and Pickup by government, there is still no recognition by government that OLS and new information technologies make it absurd to deprive anyone of study or training opportunity simply on the grounds that the potential student lives in the wrong place or cannot study at a particular time. There has been no positive governmental encouragement to LEAs to support development of OLS. The existing accounting procedures used in education and training continue to be inappropriate to open learning. In fact, these procedures often inhibit developments. The dependence of OLS on independent learning material requires an element of risk capital before students can be enrolled and pay fees — at present the most obvious means to repay the costs of developing such material. Most public institutions are governed by annual budgeting arrangements and find it hard, or even impossible to recycle funds in order to support development work.

In my view, and that of many others, a need for co-ordination of open learning developments remains, despite the undoubted central roles that 'Open Tech', and bodies such as the Open Learning Federation will exercise. The argument put in the CET consultative document for co-ordination remains unanswered. At a more practical level, there are a number of promising methods and ideas tried in the programme which need further development. It is to be hoped that opportunities for this will occur in the 'Open Tech' programme, FEU projects, and the work of the Open Learning Federation. In particular, approaches to development of learning materials through intensive writing workshops and use of study guides, methods of training OLS tutors devised by Graham Gibbs (Gibbs, 1981), and approaches to pre-entry counselling all need considerable further work.

THE FUTURE FOR CET'S INVOLVMENT IN OPEN LEARNING

CET is not a body which takes responsibility for course provision. It is a development agency and it reduces its active involvement in specific developments once there are others able and willing to carry CET initiatives forward. This stage has been reached in the case of OLS and this phase of the programme therefore ended on 31 March 1983.

A new and very different programme began in April 1983. The concept permeating this programme is student negotiated learning. This concept links work on learning exchanges, student self-help groups, study circles and open learning in small companies, as well as giving an opportunity to explore the extraordinary potential for application of information technologies in open learning. Some support for OLS in colleges will continue to be provided, but at a much lower level. A series of booklets on different aspects of OLS development, preparation of learning material, and OLS tutoring will be published; the newsletter, *OLS News*, will continue to be published; workshops on tutoring in OLS and on preparation of learning material will be held from time to time; but the development effort will be concentrated on new work.

REFERENCES

Barnet College of Further Education (1978) *Flexistudy — A Manual for Local Colleges*. National Extension College.

Birch, D W and Latcham, J (1981) *Accounting for Academic Staff Resources for the Tutorial Support of Open Learning*. Coombe Lodge.

Coffey, J (1977) Open learning opportunities for mature students. In Davies, C T *Open Learning Systems for Mature Students*. CET.

Coffey, J (1978) Developing an open learning system. In *Further Education: A Report*. CET.

Coffey, J (1980) Open learning systems — an overview. CET (unpublished committee paper).

Council for Educational Technology (1980) *Open Learning Systems in Further Education and Training — A Discussion of the Issues and Recommendations to Government*. CET.

Davies, C T (1977) *Open Learning Systems for Mature Students*. CET.

Department of Education and Science (1973) *Adult Education: A Plan for Development —* Report by a Committee of Inquiry appointed by the Secretary of State for Education and Science under the Chairmanship of Sir Lionel Russell, CBE. HMSO.

Freeman, R (1982) Reflections on an Open Tech. *Teaching at a Distance*, 21.

Gibbs, G (1981) Training tutors at a distance: an alternative strategy. *Teaching at a Distance*, 20.

Hubbard, G (1975) Analogues of the Open University. *British Journal of Educational Technology*, **6**, 3.

Lewis, R (1981) *How to Tutor in an Open Learning Scheme*. CET.

Lewis, R and Jones, G (eds) (1980) *How to Write a Distance Learning Course: A Self Study Pack for Authors*. CET.

Mackie, A (1980) The co-operative and intensive writing of distance learning materials by authors pre-trained at a distance. CET (unpublished report).

Manpower Services Commission (1982) *Open Tech Task Group Report*. MSC.

Monaco, J and Latcham, J (1982) *Open Learning — A Register of Participating Institutions*. Coombe Lodge.

Morris, A (1981) Directed private study and correspondence course routes to Business Education Council awards: development project. CET (unpublished report).

National Association for Teachers in Further and Higher Education (1981) Open learning — a policy statement. NATFHE.

Rowlands, G A (1977) Barnet College of Further Education: A case study. In Davies, T C *Open Learning Systems for Mature Students*. CET.

Sachs, H (1980) Flexistudy — an open learning system for further and adult education. *British Journal of Educational Technology*, **11**, 2.

Spencer, D (1980) *Thinking About Open Learning Systems*. CET.

Twining, J (ed) (1982) *Open Learning for Technicians*. Stanley Thornes (Publishers) Ltd.

1.4 Focus on Students in Open Learning Systems

Anita Morris
Council for Educational Technology, London

Abstract: As part of the Council for Educational Technology's Open Learning System's programme, an investigation was carried out to find out why students come to open learning courses, and what they want and expect to get out of them. The concept of 'orientation', used by the Open University's Learning Methods Study Group, proved to be a useful way of categorizing student aims and expections. Students had mainly vocational, mainly personal or mainly academic purposes for taking courses. As a result they had different types of concerns and wanted different things from their courses. The concept of orientation provides a useful framework for thinking about these concerns and needs, and ways of coming to terms with them.

INTRODUCTION

Background to the Investigation

The idea of an investigation of why students come to open learning courses and what they expect to get out of their courses evolved out of two concerns: the apparently high drop-out rate from open learning systems; and the need to try to make sure that students' expectations and aims were not being inadvertently thwarted by the content, structure and support systems of their courses. Recent work on student orientations, carried out by the Open University's Learning Methods Study Group, seemed to offer a useful framework for thinking about what students might want and expect to get out of a course.

The Concept of Orientation

The Learning Methods Study Group use the term 'orientation' to describe the collection of aims, aspirations, attitudes and purposes that an individual student has with respect to a course, and the institution providing that course.

> 'Orientation, unlike the concept of motivation, does not assume any psychological trait or state belonging to the student. It is the quality of the relationship between student and course, rather than a quality inherent in the student. The analysis of orientation does not set out to type students, rather it sets out to identify and describe types of orientation and show the implications these different types of orientation have for the approach a student takes to learning.' (Taylor, Morgan and Gibbs, 1980)

A study of student orientations was first carried out at Surrey University (Beaty, 1978) and four main types of orientations were found:

- ☐ *Vocational*, where the student's aims and expectations towards the courses are connected with job concerns.
- ☐ *Academic*, where the student is either wanting to follow through a particular subject interest, or wanting to carry on studying for its own sake.
- ☐ *Personal*, where personal development or proof of capability are dominant

interests.

☐ *Social*, where students' main purposes are connected with enjoying and benefiting from university life.

The first three of the above types of orientation each subsumed two kinds of sub-groups: intrinsic and extrinsic interests. Intrinsic interests are ones connected with studying the course for its own sake, whilst extrinsic ones are those where the student is using the course as a means to an end. Beaty's work also showed that the orientations to studying held by students had an effect on the focus of their studying efforts and the way they studied. Taylor (*née* Beaty), Morgan and Gibbs drew up the following table to show the connections between orientations and the kinds of things students would be concerned with while they were on their courses.

Orientation	Interest	Aim	Concerns
Vocational	Intrinsic	Training	Relevance of course to career
	Extrinsic	Qualification	Recognition of worth of qualification
Academic	Intrinsic	Follow intellectual interest	Room to choose work, stimulating lectures
	Extrinsic	Educational advance	Grades, academic progress
Personal	Intrinsic	Self-improvement	Challenge, interesting material
	Extrinsic	Proof of capability	Feedback, passing course
Social	Extrinsic	Have a good time	Facilities for sport and social activities

Table 1. *Orientations and student concerns*

The Open University Learning Methods Study Group have also examined orientations among Open University students studying the Social Science Foundation Course. Not unnaturally, they found no examples of social orientations, the students in their sample having predominantly personal, vocational and academic collections of purposes. However, as they point out, individual students' orientations were often a complex mix of two or more main orientation types. The four main types represent idealized extremes which provide a framework for understanding and explaining what students want and expect from a course and why they approach their studies in certain ways.

The Aims of the Investigation

After careful consideration, and at the suggestion of an *ad hoc* advisory group, it was decided to: investigate orientations among a wide age range of students in technical, business and 'general' (ie O and A level or general interest) open learning courses offered by OL systems with a relatively high proportion of tutor/student face-to-face contact. This meant that the investigation would, in effect, take the form of a pilot exploration whose main aim would be to see whether the concept of 'orientation' was valid for students in non-degree OLS, and if so, what kinds of orientations were prevalent. Time constraints would prevent any attempt to see how and if orientations changed during a course, and would also preclude investigating any link between orientation and drop-out.

Methodology

The aims of the investigation dictated the nature of the methodology adopted to carry out the exploration. The most sensible way to find out if the concept of orientation was appropriate for OLS students was to interview them. The interviews were, of necessity, focused around the topic of why students came to be on the course, and what they expected to get out of it. The use of interviews, coupled with the fact that the investigation covered students in three different types of OL courses, meant that sample sizes were small. However, that is not inappropriate in a pilot of this nature. All of the interviews were recorded and subsequently transcribed in full. By the end of the investigation 52 transcripts were available. These were then analysed to identify emerging patterns of orientations.

THE RESULTS OF THE INVESTIGATION

Types of Orientation

Although the majority of students described a complex mix of aims and purposes for joining a course, it was relatively easy to sort them into three categories: mainly vocational, mainly personal and mainly academic orientations. Within these categories, the intrinsic/extrinsic distinction was clearly identifiable.

1. Vocational Orientations

This was the most common main type of orientation — not surprising given the vocational nature of the technical and business courses and the fact that together their students made up approximately two-thirds of the sample. A total of 40 students showed a mainly vocational orientation.

Vocational Extrinsic: Many students were very definitely using their course as a means to an end, and that end for vocationally oriented students, was a qualification. The following quotes show this very clearly:

> 'I did a degree in accountancy and management at UCC, finishing in June '81. Few offers of employment from various people, one of which was West Midlands Gas. I took their job on the basis that it offered the quickest and easiest route to the professional qualification with the block release and that sort of thing, as compared with the others. You've got to get professional qualifications, at it were, to get on — because a degree on its own is a bit "Oh good, you've got a degree . . . Oh, but you haven't got a professional qualification".'

> 'Well . . . to get more qualifications really, which will be helpful in finding a job . . . and earning more money . . .'

> 'Basically . . . I want to get on. At the present time I'm stuck in a job . . . a quite rewarding job . . . but I'm not getting anywhere. Um . . . and I attended college — I finished in 1975 — and I ended with an HNC equivalent you see, the City & Guilds Tech . . . absolutely of no use to me at all. So I decided that I'd go back to college and get electronics qualifications to go with it — probably stand me in good stead.'

Vocational Intrinsic: However, a number of vocationally oriented students were taking the course in order to help them gain a better understanding of aspects of their job, or to help them do their job better.

> 'Well, what I do at work . . . um . . . I deal a lot with sort of *boxes*. I know what they do, and I add a bit more together. But I really want to get down to the root levels of what's going on. So, to know how to do that. And also how to get the small bits together in the first place . . . how it works and how to test them . . . bits and pieces now and again . . . checking them . . . building bits and pieces which hook into computers, *that's* interesting.'

'Just a better insight into work that I *do*. I'm not studying just for the sake of studying. I want a better insight into the equipment I'm looking after, 'cos at the moment — although I can look after it, I've been to various manufacturers' specialized courses — you learn nothing about the *basics* and the principles in that. You just learn to make various checks at various points and that you should or shouldn't get certain things happening. And you learn how to take the appropriate action if something is going wrong, but they haven't got the time to teach you any basics.'

'You know, I thought that it would help a lot in the nursing training and at the same time, English language . . . It's surprising how often you have to write reports and one thing and another. And in my job at the moment, as well as warden, I have to write quite a few letters, and I thought that it would help in that way.'

2. *Personal Orientations*

This type of orientation was the next most prevalent but it was a long way behind vocational. This is the reverse of the order which the OU group found in their sample. A total of nine students revealed a mainly personal orientation to their course. Once again a distinction could be made between 'intrinsic', where students were wanting to widen their horizons, to develop personal skills or to become more capable because they feel inadequate; and 'extrinsic' where students seem to be more concerned with testing their own capabilities — to show themselves how much they can do, or prove their capabilities to others because they feel they have been undervalued in the past.

Personal Intrinsic: Several students wanted to widen their horizons, wake themselves up, 'improve' themselves in some way:

'I hoped it would stimulate me . . . I feel this would be a challenge.'

'I really ought to be doing something, y'know — the children are getting bigger — and make preparations for going back to work. Because everybody else will have caught up on their German so much in between time, so I thought . . . and also I needed something to keep the grey matter going as well, so that was one of the main things as well. My husband's away a lot and I need something to get my mind going in the evening when the children are in bed.'

'. . . improve myself . . . I've been able to write letters, but I've always thought — they probably weren't good English — they were . . . well . . . to the point. And I thought I wanted to learn to "read" and "write".'

Personal Extrinsic: Other students with a personal orientation were trying to prove to themselves that they were actually able to get down to studying:

'I blew my chance at school . . . I've always loved English literature — I wasn't planning for it to lead anywhere: just for my own satisfaction I think, basically. To prove that my brain hadn't quite stagnated as I thought it had done . . . It was just for my own satisfaction, I think.'

'Really, my major, shall we say, issue in doing it — not necessarily to get the qualification at the end of it — but just to prove to myself that I could knuckle down to do the work.'

'I thought it would give me a bit of self-confidence; especially if I passed and after all this time — it's 30 years since I've done any studying; to be able to make myself sit and study and take the exam and pass it — I thought I'd have achieved something . . . I just expected to learn whether I could stick at something because I'm rather prone to taking something up enthusiastically, then dropping it . . . that was my main reason.'

3. Academic Orientations

Only two of the students interviewed had a mainly academic orientation. The OU group make a distinction between those students who want to carry on studying, to keep on with their education (extrinsic) and those who want to follow up a subject that particularly interests them (intrinsic). Both of the mainly academically oriented students seemed to fit into the extrinsic category:

> 'Well, basically because I've just finished (the) Radio Amateurs exam — got my radio amateurs licence and I wanted to . . . eh . . . continue doing a bit more study and I saw the advert in the paper and . . . eh . . . it seemed an ideal opportunity.'

> 'Yes . . . umm . . . a couple of years ago . . . umm . . . I decided that I'd like to have a go at some academic studying. Previously to that the last studying I'd done was 10 years ago when I was at technical college. Eh . . . and I've done no studying since then . . .'

This does not mean that the students interviewed were not interested in the subject they were studying. Academic intrinsic orientations were mentioned:

> 'I *like* accounting.'
> 'I've always loved English literature.'

but they always emerged as secondary considerations rather than main aims:

> S. '. . . because I wanted to get a qualification . . . So, it's important that I get A level English — very important I think.'
> I. 'Why did you choose that one?'
> S. 'Because I thought it was one that I could pass, because I enjoy reading. I like English and I thought I stood a better chance of getting that.'

Orientations and Student Concerns

In Table 1, Taylor, Morgan and Gibbs suggest that different orientations are linked to different sorts of concerns associated with a course. Some of these concerns did not emerge at all during the interviews. Others did, but were not necessarily connected with the same orientational types. In fact, from the present interviews, it looks as though students with an extrinsic interest are, whatever their orientation type, more ready to 'learn the course'. They seem more concerned with grades and use external standards to judge how well they are doing. They also take exams more seriously. Students with an intrinsic interest seem less interested in 'learning the course'. They appear to appreciate the strong supportive framework that their courses offer them, and seem to regret that there is not always enough time or opportunity to follow up topics that are of particular interest to them. Table 2 summarizes the connections between orientations, interests, aims and possible concerns of the students interviewed.

IMPLICATIONS

As these findings show, the concept of orientation is applicable to students in non-degree level open learning systems. It has great potential as a framework for describing and thinking about what students want and expect from open learning and what we, in our turn, can and should be offering them. Some more work is obviously needed to determine the prevalence of various types of orientations in different systems. And to establish clearer links between orientations and various student concerns. This information could then be used to analyse existing courses to see how well they were meeting student needs; or to help in the design of new types of courses and systems.

Meanwhile the framework could be used as it stands to encourage tutor-student discussion about what students want to get out of their courses and ways of

Orientation	Interest	Aim	Possible Concerns
Vocational	Extrinsic	To become 'qualified' in general terms, for an unspecified job, or career	Grades; progress through course; tutors' opinions; passing the exam; probably happy with course package as it stands
	Intrinsic	To be trained in order to do a specific job, either as pre-entry training or on-the-job training. To understand, or do existing job better	Relevance of course content to job. May want room to follow up relevant topics
Personal	Extrinsic	To test capability to own satisfaction, or to prove capability — perhaps because of missed educational opportunities	Feedback; grades; progress through course; tutor approval; passing the course. Probably happy with course as it stands
	Intrinsic	To widen horizons; to overcome a sense of inadequacy; to develop personal skills	Interesting, challenging material; tutor-student discussion about content; time to 'do' course in depth, freedom to follow up interesting topics
Academic	Extrinsic	To return to study; to continue studying; to take next step on educational ladder	Grades; academic progress; progress through course. Probably happy with course package as it stands
	Intrinsic	To follow up an interest in a subject, perhaps as a hobby	Interesting, challenging material; freedom to follow up particular interests; time to thoroughly explore certain issues.

Table 2

achieving this, within the constraints of the situation. This would be a way of making open learning more 'open' than it is at present. It might even, by narrowing the gap between what the student wants and what the college can provide, help to decrease drop-out.

REFERENCES

Beaty, E (1978) The student study contract. Paper presented at 4th international conference on HE, University of Lancaster.
Taylor, E, Gibbs, G and Morgan, A R (1980) *The Orientations of Students Studying the Social Science Foundation Course.* Study Methods Group, report 7. IET, Open University.

Section 2:
Improving Learning in
Institutional Settings

2.1 Images of Culture and Technology

Cynthia Stoane and A M Stewart
Dundee College of Technology

Abstract: Using technological expertise and the principles of educational technology, a package has been designed which aims to present opportunities to explore themes of communication, stylization and symbolism and the effects these have on society.

INTRODUCTION

'Cultural Images' is the outcome of co-operation between a college department, a film company and the Egyptian Ministry of Tourism. Through the use of the four films and other materials in the package, children in the upper primary school may achieve a greater understanding and deeper appreciation of influences upon society and of those things in society which are of value.

Although the many aspects of Egyptian history and culture are worthy of study in themselves, the broad aim of the package is to provide a view of one culture in order to help pupils to look at their own culture and society. In a highly technological society like ours children have come to expect high speed and power, automation and technological expertise. Like adults, they are easily influenced by the images, social pressures and symbols which are part of our high-powered society. Images of pop idols flash across our screens, advertisements pressurize us to own more and more gadgetry, and signs and symbols direct us through high-speed lives. Is there any place left for cultural images in our society? Must beauty, art and craftsmanship be forfeited for progress and new technologies? Technological expertise and the principles of educational technology have been used in the design of this learning resource for primary education, to present opportunities to explore such themes and look for a balance.

Basic Resource Material

Four films, produced by an Egyptian media psychologist were seen, by chance, by an educationalist. The films had been produced for tourism but it was felt that they were more than touristic documents and could, in fact, become the basis of an educational package. Underlying the films were messages about communication, stylization and symbolism and how these can develop, influence and motivate society. Whether the film producer's ability to communicate with his audience could be used to advantage in the attitudinal training of children became the challenge.

Previous work has demonstrated that translation of aims into worthwhile behavioural objectives (Rowntree, 1973) can influence the application of knowledge gained and resultant change in attitude (Henerson, 1978; Simonson, 1977; Zimbardo, 1970). Research in primary education had shown that it is possible to apply the principles of educational technology and the use of technological expertise to the affective zone and bring about attitudinal change (Stoane, 1980; Stenhouse, 1967).

'Cultural Images' was designed as an educational resource package at the Centre for Educational Development at Dundee College of Technology. A team worked with an educational technologist/trained school teacher as project designer. The team consisted of a writer and a designer, an artist and a photographer, with full technical back-up support to produce materials 'in-house'. The aim of this paper is to:

☐ Demonstrate how resource material was turned into a major educational package.
☐ Suggest that the approach can affect the attitudes of children and teachers.

METHOD

Approaches to Study

In studying Egypt there are a number of possible approaches, depending upon whether interest is in Egyptian writing, building, the Pharaohs, animal life or farming. A broad general study of ancient Egypt might give a review of a large number of topics; ancient Egypt could be contrasted with modern Egypt. A detailed study of paintings does not necessarily remain within the discipline of art, but leads into education, writing, cults, religion and everyday life.

The films of the 'Cultural Images' package cover a very wide range of topics. They have not been produced as a series and it is not necessary to use them as such, although there is considerable overlap within the four areas.

The study material was first divided into 12 topic areas. This then divided the subject matter into curricular areas (Figure 1). The films and resource materials based upon them lead across the curriculum (Figure 2) and can be used to suit the individual interests and abilities of pupils. The Route Map or concept map became

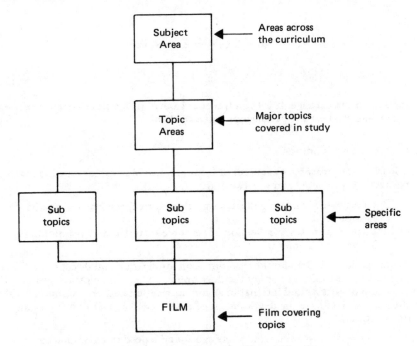

Figure 1. *The curriculum map links the films and subject areas*

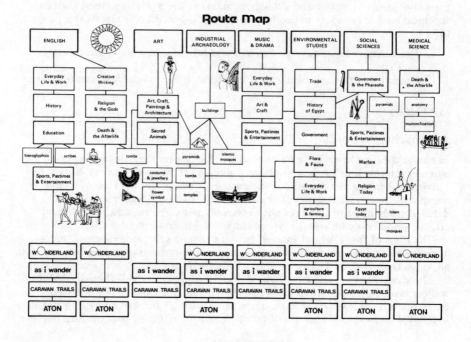

Figure 2. *Curriculum (Route) Map*

the key to the package. It is the advance organizer which ties together the topics and demonstrates the relationships between them.

Content and Themes

The films are presented as sources of inspiration. In developing an educational package the projected aim was twofold:

☐ To provide stimulating ideas, suggestions for expression and creativity in the classroom.
☐ To provide notes, a collection of resource materials and inspiration for further development.

'Wonderland' is a film about expression, communication and direction in life. It presents opportunities to study the development of communication systems, the evolution of writing and international communication barriers. Resources within the package facilitate the development of such topics as the following example demonstrates.

The Egyptians five thousand years ago found a need to communicate and express themselves in more ways than verbally. A highly imaginative system of communication symbols evolved from the earliest picture writing to the highly symbolic hieroglyphs. It is possible that the Egyptian hieroglyphic writing inspired the Phoenician alphabet, the prototype of the modern Latin alphabet. Yet the development of writing is a comparatively recent innovation in the history of human communication. If, as has been suggested (Williams, 1981), communication were to be squeezed into the 24 hours of a single day, we would spend all of the a.m. and most of the p.m. hours with very little change. In fact, most of the technologies which are inundating us today have been invented in the few moments before midnight. We have only been using writing for about one-sixth of the period for which we can trace our evolution. Relatively speaking then, it is a new invention.

The evolution of symbolism into the twentieth century can be traced, making the topic not only interesting but also relevant for children of a modern society (Figure 3). As the world grows increasingly smaller, it becomes more important to find a means of easy international communication. The following question has been raised: Has humanity come fill circle — from prehistoric symbols, through sophisticated language and now back to symbols to help us to live together in today's Tower of Babel?

In the film you saw wall paintings from the tombs at Beni Hassan showing SPORTS and ANIMALS of ancient Egypt and ARTISTS at work in ancient Egypt.

LOOK at the following symbols used in modern society to illustrate the same topics.

These symbols were used in the 1972 Olympics.
What SPORTS do they represent?

These ANIMAL symbols are used as signs of the Zodiac.
Name them and match them to their GRAPHIC symbols below.

Figure 3. *An example from pupil's worksheets which looks at the topic of modern symbolism*

Structure and Content

The four films with related multi-media material make up the package, which is separated into four independent units. The content of each of the four units is divided into six areas.

1. Four video tapes have been made from the original films which together provide realistic and cultural experiences for pupils. Each film comes with notes for teachers. For the experienced teacher the resources can be adapted and developed in a way that best suits the class. But for the less experienced teacher there are guidelines and plans to follow.

2. Pupils' workbooks are based directly on the video-tapes. Ernest Rothkopf (1968) and others have found that a 'programmed approach' using questions can enhance pupils' understanding and retention. By presenting the student with a few key questions or advance organizers beforehand (Ausubel and Robinson, 1969) asking him to look out for answers (and more questions of his own) and giving opportunity for discussion afterwards, maximum effectiveness can be gained from films, television programmes and even excursions (Rowntree, 1982). As knowledge of results is the lifeblood of learning (Rowntree, 1982) immediate feedback is provided. The workbooks are designed to:
   ☐ stimulate pupils
   ☐ encourage attentive listening and viewing
   ☐ develop awareness of critical thought.
3. Extension projects based on the content of the films develop many of the topics with craft-based activities, problem-solving exercises, games, drama and music. Individual work and group interaction are possible.
4. Additional resources include overhead transparencies to stimulate discussion; slides made from the films to provide still shots of aspects which merit closer observation or study; and an audio-tape which presents a collection of music from modern Egypt. Appropriate activity should involve a good deal of feeling and thinking (Rowntree, 1982). If this is to be so, the media must essentially enable the pupil to shape and use the ideas being developed — contributing to them, applying them, modifying, and combining them.
5. An Information Bank is a key feature of the package, providing a resource and reference section. It is presented in book form and is divided into the 12 topic sections of the package. Many of the activities in the workbooks and extension projects require further research by pupils and the necessary information is provided in the bank. Thus the pupil can be an active producer and user rather than a passive recipient of knowledge (Sanders, 1966).
6. Finally the Teachers' Guidebook and Route Map provide notes and guidelines about how to use the package and the advance organizer — the 'mental scaffolding' on which learning can be constructed (Ausubel and Robinson, 1969).

DISCUSSION

The four films in the 'Cultural Images' package present thought-provoking images of ancient and modern Egypt; the cults, beliefs and artistic achievements of Pharaonic times and the art, craftsmanship and religion of the Islamic world in Egypt today. Although the package has been designed for upper primary school children, it is seen as suitable for social studies, liberal studies, art appreciation and other classes at early secondary level. Each package is completely self-contained, will serve a class of any number of children and materials can be used repeatedly. The aim of the designers of the package has been to present the project in a simple and straightforward manner. The materials are contained in four portfolios so that everything can be easily identified, and easily replaced. In addition to the four films and the ancillary materials based on them, other audio-visual materials have been included for use in follow-up activities.

The background to the project is Egypt and Egyptian society, a civilization which was highly developed and sophisticated 5,000 years ago and out of which were taken the first steps from civilization's infancy. Important influences of that far-off society have been carried forward, over centuries to the present day, to affect our own society. Egyptian medicine is at the roots of Western medicine. The Egyptian calendar is the basis of the modern Western calendar. Even Egyptian hieroglyphs possibly inspired the Latin alphabet. Egyptian achievements are very creditable. The four films in the 'Cultural Images' package reflect their achievements, their religion, their love of art and beauty. The use of film enables comparison and contrast to be made between ancient and modern Egypt. The films travel delightfully, enchantingly from one to the other, tracing influences. Children will enjoy spotting patterns of ancient folklore, portraits from Pharaonic times and well known symbols in the craftsmanship of the twentieth-century Egyptian.

Apart from its main aims, the package offers a number of other possibilities which can be explored:

☐ Group work and group interaction.
☐ Leadership and direction.
☐ Development of individual interests.
☐ Oral presentation and creative writing.

There is scope for the individual teacher to decide which topics are of particular relevance to his/her class, which topics to ignore in the interests of simplicity and which to develop through extension projects beyond the core of the package. The package is designed in such a way that depth of study, detail and complexity can be varied to suit the needs, abilities and backgrounds of different children.

CONCLUSION

If teachers and pupils are stimulated to think, discuss and express themselves creatively then this package will have achieved its overall objective.

The implications of a package of this nature are twofold.

1. Through the use of a structured package containing film and a range of material designed to support the film and provide active response, children in the upper primary school may achieve a greater understanding and deeper appreciation of influences upon society and of those things in society which are of value.
2. Through the use of guidelines and structured notes, teachers are shown how the films and related teaching/learning materials can be used to achieve optimum effectiveness in the classroom.

REFERENCES

Ausubel, D P and Robinson, F G (1969) *School Learning*. Holt, Rinehart & Winston, New York.
Elton, L (1977) Educational technology — today and tomorrow. In Hills, P J and Gilbert, J (eds) *Aspects of Educational Technology* **XI**. Kogan Page, London.
Henerson, M E, Morris, L L and Fitzgibbon, (1978) *How to Measure Attitudes*. Sage Publications Ltd, Beverley Hills, California.
Rothkopf, E Z (1968) Two scientific approaches to the management of instruction. In Gagné, R M and Gephart, W R (eds) (1968) *Learning Research and School and Subjects*. Peacock, Itasca, Illinois.
Rowntree, D (1973) Which objectives are most worthwhile? In Leedham, J F and Budgett, R (eds) *Aspects of Educational Technology* **VII**. Pitman, London.
Rowntree, D (1974) *Educational Technology in Curriculum Development*. Harper and Row, London.
Rowntree, D (1982) *Educational Technology in Curriculum Development*. Second edition. Harper and Row, London.
Sanders, N M (1966) *Classroom Questions: What Kinds?* Harper and Row, New York.
Simonson, M R (1977) Attitude change and achievement: dissonance theory in education, *Journal of Educational Research*, **70**, 3, pp 163-169.
Stenhouse, L (1967) *Culture and Education*. Nelson, London.

Stoane, C (1980) Educational technology in the affective zone: is it possible? In Winterburn, R
    and Evans, L (eds) *Aspects of Educational Technology* **XIV**. Kogan Page, London.
Williams, F (1982) *The Communication Revolution.* Sage Publications, Beverley Hills,
    California.
Zimbardo, P and Ebbeson (1970) *Influencing Attitudes and Changing Behaviour.* Addison-
    Wesley, Reading, Massachusetts.

ACKNOWLEDGEMENT

The author and designers of 'Cultural Images' gratefully acknowledge the work of Wassef,
without whose work in film production the package could not have been possible. 'Cultural
Images' is published by the Scottish Council for Educational Technology.

2.2 Defences Against Earthquakes: A Non-Traditional Course

M Ferraris, V Midoro and M Ott
Istituto per le Tecnologie Didattiche,
National Council of Research, Genoa, Italy

Abstract: In Italy, the mass media convey the idea that earthquakes are 'natural disasters' and that the only possible defence is predicting them. To change this widespread misconception, a non-traditional course for high school students has been produced. This course is composed of audio-visual parts (tape/filmstrips, tape-slides), a self-instructional package, tests for assessing learning and a teacher's manual. The whole course requires about 15 hours of study, including individual study. The course was tested on about 500 students in different areas of Italy.

In this paper we will describe the production and validation process of this course, the results and future developments. In particular we will discuss the methodology used for developing the instructional system.

INTRODUCTION

In Italy the main attitude towards earthquakes is that they are unavoidable catastrophes against which the only possible defence is forecast of time-location and place. From a scientific point of view this attitude is incorrect and dangerous for a seismically active country such as Italy, because it inhibits implementation of necessary precautionary measures. One of the main reasons for such an attitude is a widespread lack of information (in school, public administration mass media) about the mechanism of this phenomenon and the possibility of its control. In order to modify this situation the Geodynamic Target Project Committee (PFG) of the National Council of Research has elaborated a plan for mass education aimed at informing the public about the problems related to earthquake defence. The first step of this plan has been the development of a course for high school students (14-18 years) entitled 'What earthquakes are and how we can defend ourselves against them'. It was designed to be used by a large audience (50,000 students a year) and in various types of scholastic settings.

To produce such a course, it is necessary to use developing methodologies which, at any stage of the system production, can assure the following:

1. The quality of the product (fulfilment of the established needs, instructional effectiveness, technical and scientific correctness); if the audience is large, gaps and faults would affect a great number of students and recovery would be very difficult.
2. The real possibility of managing the product (suitability to different contexts, flexibility according to different needs).

The approach we used to satisfy all these requirements was based on a global methodology to develop an instructional system that includes:

☐ Planning of the different phases of an instructional system's life and their dynamic connections.
☐ Introduction of verification after each step of the production.
☐ Documentation of the activities carried out in each phase of the process.

This approach reflects the results of research in the field of software engineering. A strong analogy exists between software systems and instructional systems; it concerns their nature, the main problems and methodologies for their solution. On the basis of this analogy, we think it possible and useful to transfer general approaches and specific methodologies developed in the software engineering field to the field of production of instructional systems.

Our first step was the definition of a 'life cycle' of the instructional system following the analogy of the life cycle of a software system; the second step was the selection of specific methodologies for each phase of the cycle, using both indications and proposals coming from the instructional field and some technical solutions typical of the software field. The development and validation of the course on earthquakes can be considered a good testing ground for our methodological approach; in the following, we describe its main steps and underline both results and issues.

DESCRIPTION OF THE PRODUCTION PROCESS

In conformity with the general trend in systems engineering, we have defined the production phases of an instructional system. Figure 1 shows the proposed life cycle. According to our approach, the outputs of each phase document the production activities carried out and set the requirements for the following phase. As Figure 1 shows, verification is closely related to the production process; it takes place in each production phase and is aimed at:

☐ Testing of the inside results.
☐ Investigation of whether or not these results fulfil all the requirements set during the previous phase.

This interactive process should avoid deviations from the desired behaviour and should make the elimination of errors and weaknesses easier.

In the following we describe the life cycle development of the course on earthquakes.

Requirements definition

The main aims of this stage are:

1. To make explicit *why* the instructional system must be developed.
2. To define, roughly, *what* are the general features of the system, ie aims and content domain.
3. To specify *how* to develop this course, considering the conditions of our situation.

Let us examine the original situation, as it pertains to our course. As already said, the main reasons for an instructional programme on this topic were:

☐ To supply correct and homogeneous information about earthquakes according to current scientific knowledge.
☐ To modify incorrect attitudes towards earthquakes, by showing how adequate social organization can prevent their catastrophical effects.

On this basis, a production staff including educational technologists, seismologists, etc defined the goals and the contents of a course able to meet these requirements. The analysis of the situation in schools (curricula, textbooks, teaching, etc) showed that, concerning earthquakes:

1. Some curricula do not include the subject.
2. There are no textbooks dealing with the subject matter in a systematic way.

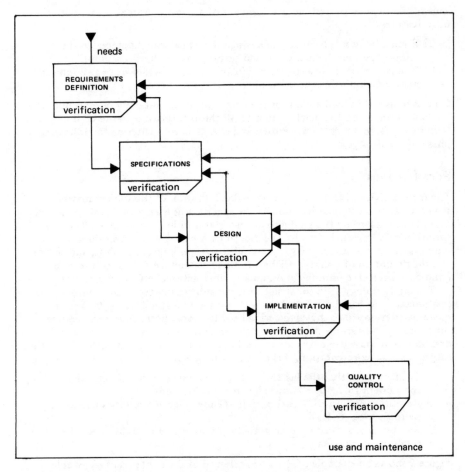

Figure 1. *Life cycle of an instructional system*

3. Generally, teachers do not have the competence required to face this subject in an autonomous way.

This situation necessitated the development of a non-traditional course with these main features:

☐ It must be usable by teachers having no particular competence in the seismology field (actually it could be used for teachers' training).
☐ It must be usable as a specialized instructional programme in any subject matter and in different kinds of schools.

On this basis we defined a plan for the course production taking into account the available human and financial resources. All this information, gathered in a 'requirements document' was verified and revised before entering the following phase of the life cycle.

Specifications

The main activity of this stage concerns the definition of the subject-matter structure, that is the identification of the specific knowledge and abilities which should be acquired by the student and the relationships among them. The specification phase includes also the identification of design constraints (learning-time forecast, students' prerequisites, economic constraints, and so on) and the definition of quality variables to be tested before the use of the course (students' interest, communication quality, instructional effectiveness, etc).

The methodology used for structuring the subject matter of the course on earthquakes was based on Petri Nets with a top-down approach. Petri Nets are a technique developed in the engineering field for constructing and representing functional specifications of a software system; recently they have been used for the description of knowledge structures. Following this approach, at each level of the subject-matter representation, it is necessary to specify:

☐ The functions that the instructional system must perform (activities leading the student to acquire knowledge in a specific domain).
☐ Resources employed in each activity (knowledge and abilities needed to perform the activity).
☐ Resources produced by each activity (knowledge and abilities acquired as a result of the activity).

Figure 2 shows an example of Petri Net referred to the contents of the whole course. A first level of refinement is shown in Figure 3. Each activity in the net may be interpreted as an explanation or as a student's performance ability. For instance, the activity 'read seismographic data' may be considered as the necessary explanation that allows the student to understand how 'seismograms can be read and used' or as the student's ability to 'read a seismogram', for example, to determine the starting point of different types of seismic waves.

Design

This stage includes three main activities: formulation of the instructional design, ie system modules, assessment tests, means and methods for presenting information, audio-visual scripts, etc; management design, ie delivery strategies, user's manual, description of the physical environment for course use; definition of the tools and procedures suitable to 'quality control'.

We can now have a look at the results of our course on earthquakes. We divided the contents of the subject-matter representation into three modules. On the basis of the stated requirements we have chosen the methods and the tools appropriate

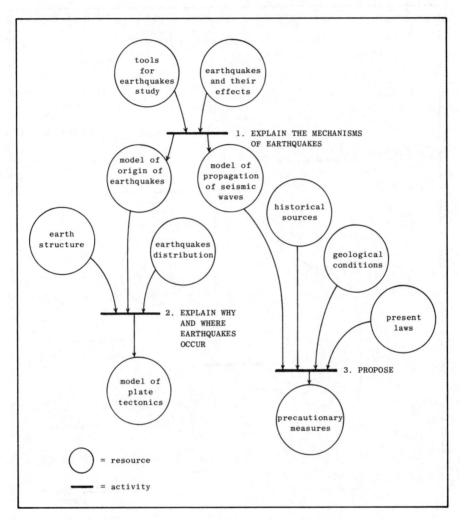

Figure 2. *An example of Petri Net referred to the whole course*

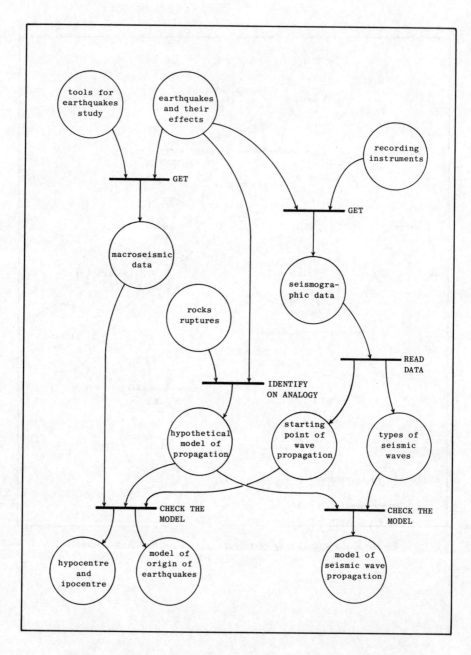

Figure 3. *A first top-down decomposition of activity 1 (Figure 2)*

to design and production of each module. Each module includes:

1. An audio-visual part for group study. It uses very simple audio-visual tools (filmstrip or slide-projector and recorder) and it tends to give information about the ground contents of the whole module.
2. A printed part for self-instruction. This consists of self-instructional textbooks, and its main purpose is to go deeper into particular subjects and to give to the students operative abilities in some of the main topics.

In such a way the instructional communication is entirely committed to audio-visual tools and textbooks; that is why we can say that:

☐ The quality of the instructional communication does not depend on teachers.
☐ It is possible to guarantee *a priori* correctness and homogeneity of information in any situation.

Each part of the course was designed to allow the active involvement of the students on the basis of closed-cycle communication models. To this purpose each audio-visual part alternates sequences of presentation and activation phases. During these phases students are asked to give answers to questions and to discuss the main proposed issues; the teacher-moderator stimulates and leads the discussion. The activation phases have two main purposes:

1. To draw the students' attention on the most important topics.
2. To give the opportunity to control whether or not a given piece of information has been correctly understood.

In an analogous way, following the Open University's model, the backbone of the textbooks is a chain of questions and exercises that takes the student, step by step, to an acquisition of the required abilities. The global structure of the course is shown in Figure 4.

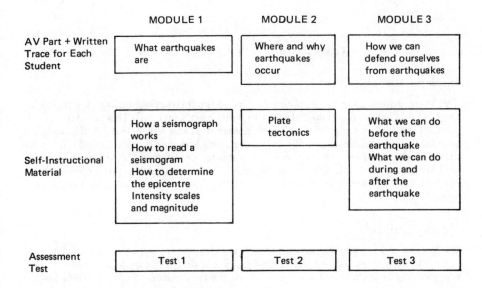

Figure 4. *Course structure*

Such a fragmented course is open to different management techniques: maximally, it can be used in its entirety; minimally, one can use only the audio-visual parts, as shown in Figure 5. The teacher himself, following the teacher's guide, can choose how to manage the course according to his particular needs.

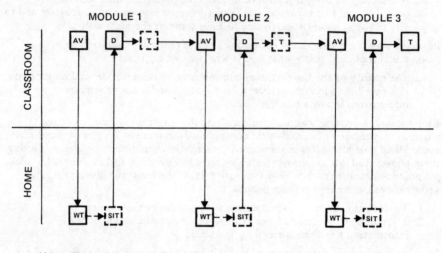

AV   audiovisual parts
WT   written trace of AV
SIT self-instructional textbooks
D   discussion
T   test
--- optional part

Figure 5. *Delivery strategy of the course*

Implementation

This stage concerns the physical production of the instructional material defined in the design phase (audio-visual, textbooks, tests, user's manual). This activity requires a lot of working time and financial resources: a well defined design avoids wasting money and time, and allows parallel, simultaneous production of different parts. This is especially true if there is no resource centre devoted to this activity, as we have in our situation. On the whole, this physical realization of the course on earthquakes took about four months, including the technical control and revision of each part.

Quality Control

Quality control is a process aimed at verifying the performance features of the system under controlled conditions and supplying diagnostic indications for revision. In our approach this stage is one of the two aspects of course validation (the other is verification, distributed in each phase of the life cycle). The course on earthquakes was tested on a sample of about 500 students in different experimental situations in order to verify:

- ☐ Communication quality (language comprehension, detection of obscure parts, etc).
- ☐ Learning (quantity and quality of information acquired for each part of the course).
- ☐ Acceptance (students' and teachers' reactions, interest, boredom, etc).
- ☐ Course management (scheduling, technical problems related to classroom use, etc).

The inquiry tools that we used to check these characteristics included formal assessment tests, questionnaires filled in, optionally, by students, and the direct informal observation of the students' behaviour during classroom sessions and individual study. Figures 6 and 7 show some of the results.

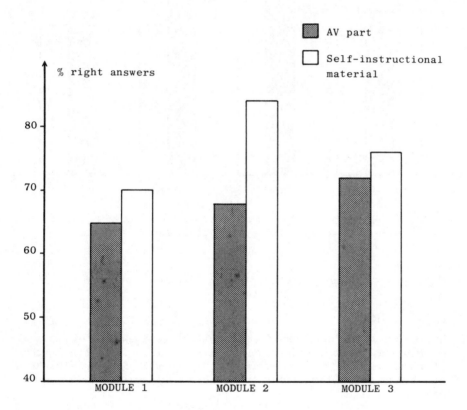

Figure 6. *Results of assessment testing*

The sample students showed a high level of interest and motivation on the topic and a general positive attitude towards the instructional strategies that we used (in particular the activation phases during the audio-visual presentation). In spite of the general positive results, the experiment revealed the necessity to revise some parts of the instructional programme. The revision stage has been facilitated by the documentation available for each phase of the life cycle and by the connection between control procedures and development stages of the course.

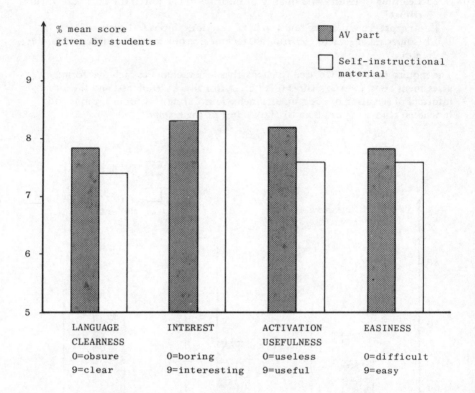

Figure 7. *Acceptance and communication quality*

CONCLUSIONS

In this paper we have briefly described the production and validation of a
non-traditional course for high school students on the defence against earthquakes.
At present, we are testing it once more with a large number of students (10,000).
At this point, our main aim is to verify the management system defined for use on a
large scale.

The overall production and testing costs amounted to about 35 million lire
(CNR researchers' work excluded) and the working time required was about 400
man-hours for each hour of the instructional programme. This working time might
seem too much when compared to a traditional lesson time, but it is reasonable
when referred to a large-scale intervention on such a special-interest topic.

Particular attention has been devoted to the methodological approach used for
the course development. This approach is based on a precise description of the
production activities related to each phase of the life cycle. It represents a powerful
guide for managing the production process and for co-ordinating the work of
people with different areas of expertise.

REFERENCES

Ferraris, M, Midoro, V and Olimpo, G (1981) Validation processes for instructional systems. In Percival, F and Ellington, H (eds) *Aspects of Educational Technology* XV. Kogan Page, London.

Ferraris, M, Midoro, V, Ott, M and Stucchi, M (1982) *Che cosa sono i terremoti e come possiamo difenderci: un prototipo di corso per una nuova didattica*. PFG/CNR n.495, Roma.

Freeman, P and Wasserman, A J (1977) *Tutorial on Software Design Techniques*. IEEE Computer Society, Long Beach, California.

Genrich, H J (1976) *The Petri Net Representation of Mathematical Knowledge*. GMD Interner Bericht ISF 76-5.

Midoro, V and Sanna, R (1977) Modello e metodo di istruzione audiovisiva tutoriale. *L'Elettronica*, 54, pp 397-402.

Thoms, D F (1978) From needs assessment to implementation: a planning and action guide. *Educational Technology*, 18, pp 5-9.

2.3 How Can Tutors Help Students to Write Essays?

James Hartley
Department of Psychology, University of Keele

Abstract: This paper is divided into three parts. In part one an account is given based on questionnaires of how university students go about the process of essay-writing in the social sciences, and how there are differences of approach between first- and second-year undergraduates. A second slightly different account which is based on interviews is then briefly given. These two accounts are then combined into a more general model of essay-writing.

In part two what students say they do is contrasted with what study manuals tell them to do. In some cases the advice from manuals largely coincides with student practice (eg making plans) but in some cases it does not (re-writing and revising).

Finally, the issue of how students can learn to improve their essay-writing skills is discussed with reference back to parts one and two above. Special attention is given to recent research on tutor's comments, and on what tutors can do to help students write more effective essays.

HOW DO STUDENTS WRITE ESSAYS?

Recent research on how students write essays has focused on students in social science courses, and has used structured questionnaires or interviews as the method of approach (Branthwaite *et al*, 1980); Hounsell, 1982). Less structured questionnaires have been used by Branthwaite *et al* in more recent (unpublished) research. Using this approach they describe the process of essay-writing as shown in Figure 1. Figure 1 is organized vertically to suggest that some activities have logical priority over others. However, this organization is not meant to imply that essay-writing involves carrying out a fixed sequence of steps. Writing essays involves some or all of the activities shown in Figure 1 and many of them are carried out several times. Furthermore, the strategies involved in each activity vary for different students. Some brief descriptions and elaborations are as follows:

1. *Choosing a topic.* Sometimes the topic is set for the student by the tutor, but often students are given some freedom of choice in this respect. Students generally chose a topic that interested them, but other strategies were apparent. For example, some students said that their choice was based upon how much information was readily available, or on how easy or difficult the topic was thought to be, or on how wide-ranging or narrowly focused they wanted their essays to be.
2. *Obtaining information and material.* The next and possibly the most difficult stage was to find useful and relevant material. Books seemed to be the main source here, with lecture material playing a less prominent, but nonetheless important role. The over-riding aim at this stage seemed to be to find *relevant* material. Students described various strategies of using books, eg choosing the simplest book available and making this the main source on which to add material; choosing short books; choosing books that were not on the reading list, etc.
3. *Making notes.* Most students said that they made notes from the books that they obtained but few commented on how they went about doing this.

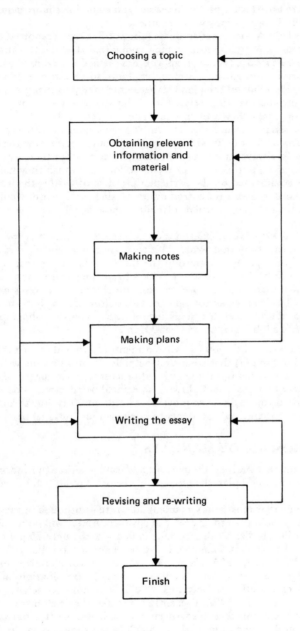

Figure 1. *The process of essay writing*

Sometimes parts of books were copied, or paraphrased, sometimes specific ideas were noted for a particular essay, and sometimes more general background observations were recorded.

4. *Making plans.* Again, most students (about two-thirds) reported drawing up a plan for an essay (with more women saying that they did this than men). As in Hounsell's study, two main approaches seemed discernible: some students simply arranged their notes and material into some sort of logical order; others predetermined the plan by the points they personally wished to raise. Only a few said that they revised their plans as they went along.

5. *Writing the essay.* Few students gave specific details about how they wrote particular essays. Some, however, mentioned strategies such as paraphrasing those parts of the books which seemed relevant; interpreting the book in their own words; always stating authorities and evidence for their assertions; trying to answer the question set — or trying to look as though they had. Several students commented on the particular problem of writing the introduction and conclusions, with the introduction causing particular difficulties. None commented on one particular difficulty, knowing who you were writing the essay for.

6. *Finishing-off the essay.* One-third of the students (again more women than men) said that they first wrote their essays in rough, and then made a fair copy. Similarly, only one-third of the students claimed to read over their essays (to check for errors and mistakes in spelling, clarity and coherence). Very few students made more than one rough draft. An even smaller number said they left their essay for a day or two before coming back to complete it. A few specifically mentioned adding references and/or bibliography at the end: 'Write a bibliography and hand it in'.

In considering these descriptions of what students *say* they do when they write essays we need to note (a) that what they actually *do* may be somewhat different, and (b) that essay-writing is not the ordered process we have suggested here. Indeed we think it likely that students following a personal perspective, as described by Hounsell, would be more likely to move backwards and forwards through the stages shown in Figure 1 than would students following an institutional perspective.

ADVICE FROM STUDY MANUALS

The first thing that most study manuals advocate — although in varying degrees — is that students should plan their essays in advance. And it will be recalled that in manuals.

The first thing that most study manuals advocate — although in varying degrees is that students should plan their essays in advance. And it will be recalled that in this and the earlier studies by Branthwaite *et al* approximately 70 per cent of their students claimed to do this. Planning, however, is not without its critics. Some authors (eg Britton *et al*, 1975) claim many writers do not plan. Norton (1983) found that 42 per cent of students planned an essay in examinations and that their answers in this essay, although better ($\overline{x} = 60\%$) were not significantly better than non-planned answers ($\overline{x} = 57\%$). I recently compared the essay marks obtained on approximately 300 planned essays written in examinations with approximately 300 essays written in the same examination which did not show any evidence of planning. The mean mark obtained for the planned essays was 59 per cent and for the non-planned it was 58 per cent. In this study, however, students who made minimal plans did significantly worse (54 per cent) than students who made medium or detailed plans (60 per cent).

The next thing that most study manuals advocate — in varying degrees — is that attention must be paid to stylistic points when writing essays and reports. Many suggest writing short unambiguous sentences with simple clear vocabulary, and they point out that it is easier to demonstrate that you have understood something if you can explain it to others in simple language. Such advice, whilst helpful, does not help the writer to deal with the problem of trying to deal with several issues all at once — the basic problem of writing (Smith, 1982). It is difficult to pay attention to content, to planning, to style, to legibility and to spelling all at the same time. At this point, therefore, some authors suggest that some of the skills of essay-writing can be separated. Thus, it is argued, one should first write quickly, getting down to the main points of what needs to be said, and then go back later to work at the niceties of style. As Wason (1982) puts it, 'First say it, and *then* try to say it well'. There is little actual evidence for the effectiveness of this approach, although a recent study by Glynn *et al* (1982) does support it.

Finally, most study manuals comment on the need for re-drafting and re-writing. The argument is that new ideas occur whilst writing so that it will be necessary to read the text through in order to incorporate these, to excise extraneous details, and perhaps to re-sequence part of what has been written. Few students appear to do more than one re-write, and to appreciate (with their time constraints) the value of this advice.

IMPROVING ESSAY-WRITING SKILLS: THE ROLE OF TUTORS

Much of the advice given to students in study manuals does not appear to reflect what students do (as depicted in Figure 1). The problem seems to be that once students have been given an essay title, they are often left to their own devices. It may be overstating the case, but it does not seem unreasonable to suggest that students could be given more help with each of the stages shown in Figure 1.

Currently the only help that most students get comes from the grades and comments they receive when the essay is returned. When assessing essays one would imagine that tutors are aiming to help students learn from their essay-writing. Comments on details of grammar, style and organization should help students improve their writing skills. Comments on subject matter should help students learn more about the topic. It is generally assumed, therefore, that constructive comments provide useful feedback to the students, and that students learn from such assessments. Is such an assumption justified?

Mackenzie (1974) observed the variety of comments made by tutors on 50 student assignments at the Open University. He found that some tutors went for 'overkill', that some had a relentless eye for grammar and that some relied excessively on ticks. He found that only about half the tutors commented on what was good in the essays, and that few attempted to explain or justify the grades they gave. Similarly Sommers (1982) found that many teachers' comments were not text-specific (and thus helpful) but could be interchanged, or 'rubber stamped' from text to text.

Clanchy and Ballard (1981) analysed all the marginal, incidental and end comments added by tutors to over 300 essays written by arts and social science students. The aim of this research was to see if any common themes could be detected, and then to provide such themes, with exemplars, to students to help them interpret future comments. Clanchy and Ballard's book *Essay Writing for Students* provides four such themes, each with copious examples of tutors' comments. These themes are:

- ☐ *A concern with relevance.* It is expected that essays will be clearly focused on the set topic and will deal fully with its central concepts.
- ☐ *A concern with the effective use of source materials.* It is expected that essays will be the result of wide and critical reading.
- ☐ *A concern with reasoned argument.* It is expected that essays will present a

reasoned argument, evaluating evidence and drawing appropriate conclusions.
☐ *A concern with matters of presentation.* It is expected that essays will be
competently presented.

An additional difficulty appears to be that few students discuss their essays with
their tutors before or after receiving their assessments. Branthwaite *et al*, for
instance, noted that only five per cent of their students discussed their essays with
tutors on an individual basis, and Hounsell reports similar findings.

Thus, in practice, a dialogue between teacher and pupil which could help
students to improve their learning and their skills of written communication is sadly
lacking. This need not necessarily be so, and there are some techniques which
teachers can use to improve the situation.

First of all one can increase the length and the quality of comments given on
essay reports. Despite the fact that there is some evidence that comments can be
unreliable (that is to say that different tutors will comment in different ways upon
the same work) (Morrow-Brown, 1978; Settle, 1981) there is some indication that
students appreciate detailed and constructive comments from their tutors
(Mackenzie, 1976; Lewis and Tomlinson, 1977).

Many teachers of English circulate advisory checklists to their students in
advance so that when they are writing their comments on essays they can say things
like, 'Good work, but a lack of attention to points 5, 7 and 21 is causing
difficulties'. Indeed, appropriate numbers can be written in the margin whenever a
fault occurs. This approach, whilst typical in English departments can be applied to
other subjects. Settle (1981) for instance, suggests how it can be done in the
teaching of mathematics. Checklists given in advance, of course, inform the student
about what is expected.

Other investigators, cited by Beard and Hartley (1984) have experimented with
different ways of improving feedback. Neil McLaughlin Cook at Ulster Polytechnic,
for example, has provided students with two essays, one good and one poor, and
asked them to write answers to the following questions:

☐ Which essay deserves the higher mark?
☐ Why is one essay better than the other?
☐ In what ways could the *better* essay be improved?

The answers are then discussed in class, and finally a set of guidelines on
essay-writing is given to each student.

It is my belief that essay-writing can be improved by using techniques such as
these, and by increasing the quality of feedback given to students at all stages of the
essay-writing process.

REFERENCES

Beard, R M and Hartley, J (1984) *Teaching and Learning in Higher Education* (4th edn). In
preparation.
Branthwaite, J A, Trueman, M and Hartley, J (1980) Writing essays: the actions and strategies
of students. In Hartley, J (ed) *The Psychology of Written Communication: Selected
Readings.* Kogan Page, London.
Britton, J, Burgess, T, Martin, N, McLeod, A and Rosen, H (1976) *The Development of Writing
Abilities.* Macmillan Educational, London.
Clanchy, J and Ballard, B (1981) *Essay Writing for Students.* Longman Cheshire, Melbourne.
Glynn, S M, Britton, B K, Muth, K D and Dogan, N (1982) Writing and revising persuasive
documents: cognitive demands. *Journal of Educational Psychology* 74, 4, pp 557-567.
Hounsell, D (1982) Learning and writing. Paper available from the author, Institute for
Research and Development in Post Compulsory Education, University of Lancaster, UK.
Lewis, R and Tomlinson, N (1977) Examples of tutor-student exchanges by correspondence.
Teaching at a Distance 9, pp 39-46.

MacKenzie, K (1974) Some thoughts on tutoring by written correspondence in the Open University. *Teaching at a Distance* 1, pp 45-51.

MacKenzie, K (1976) Student reactions to tutor comments on the tutor marked assignment. *Teaching at a Distance* 5, pp 53-58.

Morrow-Brown, C (1978) Report on E262 TMA 03 Tutor Commenting Patterns. Paper from the Student Assessment Research Group, Institute of Educational Technology, Open University.

Norton, L (1983) Unpublished data from PhD thesis in preparation, University of Keele.

Settle, G (1981) A classification of tutor's comments on a mathematics assignment. Paper from the Student Assessment Research Group, Institute of Educational Technology, Open University.

Sommers, J N (1982) Responding to student writing. *College Composition and Communication* 33, 2, pp 148-156.

Smith, F (1982) *Writing and the Writer*. Heinemann Educational, London.

Wason, P C (1982) Trust in writing. Paper available from the author, Department of Phonetics and Linguistics, University College London.

2.4 Interpreting Motion in a Static Medium

Dr M Tovar
Department of Education, Concordia University, Canada

Abstract: Can young children understand and interpret the kind of cues used to suggest motion in drawings? This paper reports a careful experimental study using four- and seven-year-old children in a large sample. It is concluded that where a related context is present children's perception of the direction of implied motion in illustrations is improved. Some light is thrown on the development in children as they grow of the capacity to gain information from such cues, but a number of further factors remain to be explored.

As educational technologists, our main concern is the application of research to practical situations. This paper focuses on young children's interpretation of implied motion cues. Specifically it deals with the influence of pictorial context in children's interpretation of direction of motion as suggested by flow lines. Although it may be argued that motion can be better conveyed by media such as film, television and computers, most educational materials designed for young children are print material. Designers frequently use illustrations to convey ideas of motion, direction and speed.

BACKGROUND

In attempting to suggest motion in still pictures designers rely on different types of cues. The most commonly used cues are postural, ie portraying figures in particular stances of non-equilibrium which viewers perceive as interruptions of continuous motion. Another type, conventional motion cues, rely on graphic devices which suggest motion by analogy or 'metaphor' (Friedman and Stevenson, 1980). Examples of such cues are blurs, vibration lines and flow lines to indicate path of motion. Other cues used to portray motion are multiple image cues, contextual cues and abstract cues.

Researchers in the development of motion cues interpretation have concluded that young children have difficulty interpreting motion in illustrations where conventional motion cues such as flow lines are used as motion indicators (Friedman and Stevenson, 1975; Brooks, 1977; Saiet, 1979). Friedman and Stevenson (1975, 1980) have suggested that conventional motion cues have little meaning to young children, because the grpahic elements (blurs, line marks) used in these cues have little correspondence to live motion. They have proposed that implied motion cues can be ordered in terms of the degree of correspondence between them and real motion. At one extreme are those cues, eg postural, which are recognized by young and naive viewers. At the other extreme are those cues, such as arrows, which are completely arbitrary. Conventional motion cues are between those extremes. The authors concluded:

> 'The available evidence leads to the view that the understanding of metaphoric information [conventional] motion cues develops later than the understanding of postural or multiple information.' (1980, p 245)

This developmental conclusion seems warranted on the basis of experimental evidence. However, the researchers draw an additional, less justified conclusion:

'Contemporary children's books make use of pictorial movement information that young children have not been able to correctly interpret in experimental presentations (Friedman and Stevenson, 1975). In order to design pictures that will be understood by their prospective readers, it is necessary to have information about the type of pictorial information which can be understood by children of different ages.' (1980, p 250)

The problem with this statement is that the stimulus materials used in Friedman and Stevenson's study are not, in fact, representative of the type of pictorial motion indicators used by designers of children's illustrations. The same consideration also applied to Saiet's study. An examination of the stimulus materials used for these studies (Figures 1 and 2) shows that in an effort to separate postural from conventional cues, the researchers presented to their subjects figures that are ambiguous, unrealistic and out of context, eg human figures 'moving' with straight limbs, which children were asked to classify as still or moving. These figures, as Campbell (1979) pointed out, provide conflicting postural and conventional cue information. While these studies do show a developmental increase in children's ability to deal with this ambiguity, their conclusions have limited practical significance because the way the conventional cues are used in their stimulus materials is not representative of the way these cues are used by illustration designers.

Figure 1. *Stimulus materials from Friedman and Stevenson (1975)*

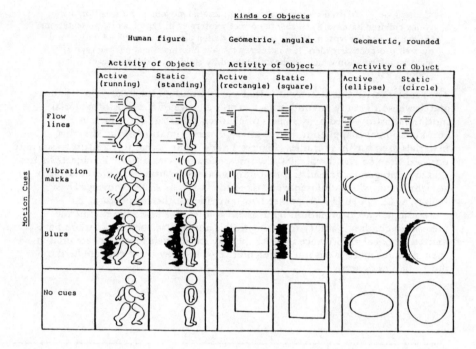

Figure 2. *Stimulus materials from Saiet (1979)*

The Campbell (1979) study is an example of how an experimenter can gain representativeness without sacrificing internal validity. She investigated the effect of postural and conventional motion cues and number of pictures (single or sequence of three pictures) on first graders' interpretation of illustrations. In order to avoid conflict between conventional and postural information, she used characters without limbs for the conventional cue condition (Figure 3).

Results showed that children performed significantly better in the sequence condition than in the single picture condition. This study did not find any significant difference between motion reported in the postural and conventional cue conditions. The stimulus materials used in this study are more representative of pictorial information found in children's illustrations than the ones of previous studies. Conventional motion cues are likely to be chosen by designers attempting to suggest motion in figures without limbs (since postural cues cannot be used).

Designers of illustrations seldom use conventional motion cues alone as movement indicators. Rather, these cues are usually combined with postural and/or contextual cues. In some cases, conventional motion cues merely reinforce the idea of motion suggested by postural and/or contextual cues, eg depicting a man running, with flow lines behind him. More importantly, conventional motion cues such as flow lines are used by designers to provide information about the quality and direction of motion. Consequently, an alternative way to assess understanding of flow lines would be to ask children to interpret the direction of motion

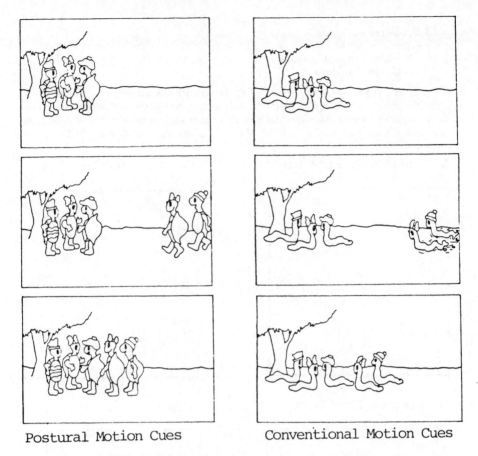

Postural Motion Cues   Conventional Motion Cues

Figure 3. *Example of stimulus materials from Campbell (1979)*

suggested by this cue.

The question of whether pictorial context may influence children's interpretation of implied direction of motion was, in fact, raised by Saiet (1979). He observed that the pictures used in his study were 'context free and in that sense were unrealistic'. He then asked: 'Would a young child be more likely to read a flow line if it helped him to interpret a picture within a specific context?' This is the primary question that the present study addresses. Does the provision of pictorial context which represents a setting in which the implied motion is plausible, facilitate young children's interpretation of direction of motion suggested by flow lines?

METHOD

A total of 96 children participated in the study (48 four-year-olds and 48 seven-year-olds). The stimulus materials consisted of black-and-white line drawings representing human or animal figures or inanimate objects (focal stimulus) whose direction of motion was to be indicated by the child. Each focal stimulus was designed to provide no cues to direction of motion other than the flow lines. Thirty-two drawings were produced from eight focal stimuli to correspond to four context flow line conditions:

☐ Both present.
☐ Context without flow lines.
☐ Flow lines without context.
☐ Focul stimulus alone.

The pictorial context was designed to be related with the action of the focal stimulus without providing any directional cues. The no-flow line conditions were incorporated to assess the effects of guessing, since no directional information was included. Figure 4 shows an example of one focal stimulus in all context/flow line combinations.

No Context/No Flow Lines   No Context/Flow Lines

Context/No Flow Lines   Context/Flow Lines

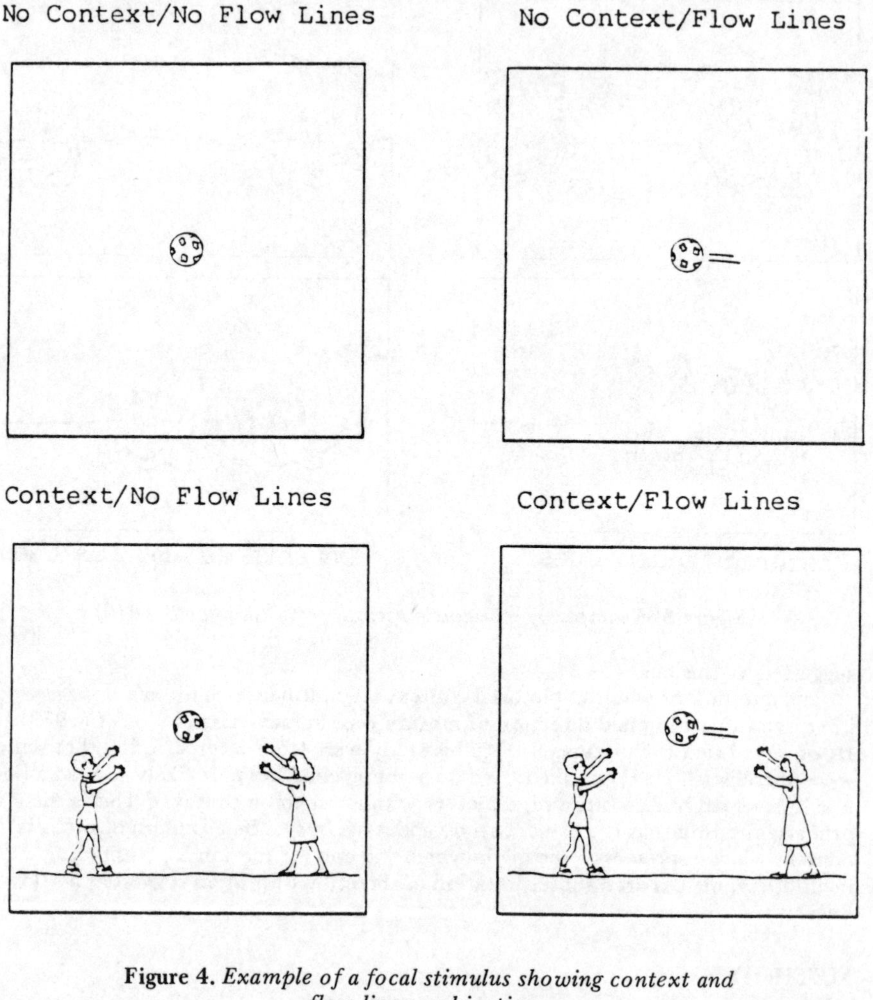

Figure 4. *Example of a focal stimulus showing context and flow line combinations*

Each child saw a demonstration picture and eight pictures corresponding to *one* context/flow line combination. The child was asked to indicate the direction of motion of the focal stimulus. If children assigned to the no-flow line conditions expressed uncertainty, they were encouraged to guess. A short interview was conducted to assess the reasons given for the reported direction of motion.

The factors of context (present, absent), flow lines (present, absent) and age (four-year-olds and seven-year-olds) were investigated in a 2 x 2 x 2 factorial design with 13 subjects per cell.

RESULTS AND DISCUSSION

Table 1 shows the mean scores obtained for each experimental condition. Older children perceived direction of motion more accurately than younger children ($p < 0.01$). Direction of motion was interpreted more accurately when flow lines were present ($p < 0.01$). The presence of a related pictorial context facilitated children's perception of direction of motion ($p < 0.05$). Age interacted with flow lines, that is, when flow lines were added to the visuals seven-year-olds showed relatively greater score gains than four-year-olds.

Age	Context		No Context	
	Flow Lines	No Flow Lines	Flow Lines	No Flow Lines
Four-year-olds	4.58	1.91	3.33	1.58
Seven-year-olds	6.58	2.33	6.66	1.08

Table 1. *Mean scores obtained for each of the experimental conditions*

This interaction supports previous developmental research which concluded that as children grow, the amount of information they derive from conventional motion cues increases. However, although the gain obtained from the presence of flow lines increased with age, four-year-olds showed a significant improvement in the accuracy of direction of motion perception in the presence of flow lines (TUKEY $p < 0.01$). This was found for both context conditions. That flow lines were noticed by four-year-olds was further supported by the fact that 46 per cent of this age group assigned to conditions with flow lines mentioned them as the reasons for their responses. Although seven-year-olds mentioned the lines more frequently than four-year-olds, the degree of association between age and mentioning the lines was not significant (λ^2 $p > 0.05$).

All of the seven-year-olds' explanations corresponded to the standard meaning of the cue. However, four of the younger children used them with consistently reversed meaning, thus reducing their total score to zero or almost zero. These children apparently were aware of the function of the cue but had not learned the accepted convention, eg, direction of intended motion is the opposite of where lines are depicted.

The question addressed in this study was whether the provision of a pictorial context which represents a setting in which the implied motion is plausible facilitates young children's interpretation of direction of motion suggested by flow lines. It was expected that context would particularly benefit the younger children's flow line interpretation. Although the data showed a trend in this direction, ie four-year-olds performed better when the flow lines were shown in context, it was not statistically significant.

In summary, the presence of flow lines facilitated children's perception of direction of motion. Although the age-by-flow-line interaction showed that seven-year-olds obtained significantly greater information gain from the presence of flow lines, four-year-olds significantly improved their performance over merely guessing in the presence of this implied motion cue. The presence of a related context improved all children's perception of direction of implied motion.

In attempting to seek possible explanation for these results it would appear that context was helpful not by merely increasing the amount of information but by presenting the action in a meaningful relationship with its surroundings. Therefore, contextual elements not related to the intended action will probably not facilitate the direction of motion interpretation since they do not add any relevant information.

Whether young children can derive meaning from cues such as flow lines is still unclear. The answer to this question is complicated by the fact that this and previous developmental studies used different procedures to assess children's understanding of this implied motion cue. Regardless of the procedures used, the findings do indicate that as children grow the amount of information they can derive from this cue increases. Investigation of developmental differences is certainly important to establish the type of information that children can process at different ages. However, if in addition to establishing developmental differences, researchers are also concerned with practical significance of their findings, they must pay attention to the way in which cues are used by illustrators.

The present study has attempted to provide a way of assessing children's understanding of flow lines more in agreement with the way this cue is actually used by designers of illustrations, ie adding information about direction of motion. In addition, the effect of a possible design variable (inclusion of related pictorial information) was also investigated.

Further research exploring the factors that help young children interpret implied motion is needed considering the important role that the depiction of motion has in illustration used for instructing young children.

REFERENCES

Brooks, P H (1977) The role of action lines in children's memory for pictures. *Journal of Experimental Child Psychology* **23**, pp 98-107.

Campbell, P F (1979) Artistic motion cues, number of pictures, and first grade children's interpretation of mathematic textbook pictures. *Journal for Research in Mathematics Education* **10**, pp 148-153.

Friedman, S L and Stevenson, M B (1975) Developmental changes in the understanding of implied motion in two-dimensional pictures. *Child Development* **46**, pp 773-778.

Friedman, S L and Stevenson, M B (1980) Perception of movement in pictures. In Hangen, M (ed), *The Perception of Pictures* **1**. Academic Press, New York.

Saiet, R A (1979) *Children's Understanding of Implied Motion Cues*. ERIC Document EDA2801. March.

2.5 Behavioural or Performance Objectives

Lt Cdr D J Freeman
Canadian Armed Forces, Ontario, Canada

Abstract: Various authors contend that the terms 'behavioural objective' and 'performance objective' are interchangeable. In certain cases, this may be so but the term 'behavioural' is used in other educational contexts. This leads to confusion and consternation over the employment and validity of objectives themselves. The author presents an analysis of the concept of an objective and discusses the merits of the terms 'behavioural' and 'performance' when used in conjunction with the term 'objective'.

Various authors have stated that there is no difference between a 'behavioural objective' and a 'performance objective' (Mager, 1962; Posner and Strike, 1975; Davies, 1976; Gagné and Briggs, 1979). My contention is that a difference does exist and the lack of understanding of this difference is one of the root causes for the misuse and misapplication of objectives in both education and training.

Before dealing with the terms 'behavioural' and 'performance', it is necessary to develop a concept of an objective, *per se*. Mager (1962) describes the qualities of a meaningful objective as one which tells us what the learner will be able to do after some form of instruction has taken place, the conditions under which this action will occur, and the predetermined criteria for an acceptable performance that we can observe.

One example which conforms to these qualities is the following objective for a basic first aider, a person of any age or station, who may be required to render first aid somewhere, sometime (Freeman, 1975). On his course of instruction, the first aider will be taught to:

Place a casualty in the 'coma' position	Given: (a) simulated unconscious casualty lying on his back on floor/ground (b) an order to put casualty in the 'coma' position (c) information that he has no injuries which would be aggravated by the 'coma' position.	1. In accordance with the manual of St John, 3rd edn, p 11, fig 1. 2. The manner of moving the casualty into position must not inflict further injuries nor cause new ones.

This example illustrates the three parts of an objective as put forward by Mager. Like a good letter with its introduction, body and conclusion, the three parts of an objective must all exist but whether these three parts are written separately as illustrated or gathered into a single paragraph, is immaterial.

A contrary case is provided by the following example:

The teacher will demonstrate the procedure for drilling two 1¼ inch holes safely in mild steel bar, one inch thick.

Although we can observe this act, this statement is not an objective because it specifies what the teacher will do, rather than what the learner will be able to do at the completion of the teaching.

There are two terms which are similar and related to the term 'objective' and which confuse many people. These terms are 'aims' and 'goals' (Davies, 1976). According to Davies, the purpose of an aim is to provide direction and orientation (for the teacher). It is an ideal which is often unobtainable; or at best, the attainment could only be guessed at, and never conclusively proven.

'To achieve a deep and abiding understanding of Canadian History'. This statement is an aim. Many professors of history, I am sure, achieve such an aim. They know this fact for themselves. We know it because they tell us. What other methods do we have for knowing it? Only by the actions of the professor himself: he reads everything in his subject area, he writes papers, gives lectures, and attends conferences. All these things and more he does, and from this we conclude that he has achieved his deep and abiding understanding of Canadian History. But has he? All the measures available to us are indirect ones. At best, such measures are circumstantial evidence, for neither science, art nor religion has yet provided us with a conclusive method of proving such an achievement.

If necessary, all the things our professor does that we can observe and measure, we could call 'performances' (more of this term later). But these performances are not aims. The aim remains an ideal, unmeasurable until humanity develops the fabled sixth sense.

The second term used by Davies is 'goal'. He suggests that a goal has three properties:

1. A general statement of values.
2. An indication of an area to concentrate on to obtain long- or short-term benefits.
3. A suggestion that some change may be necessary should circumstances so dictate.

Unlike an aim which specifies direction, the goal describes an actual destination. Hence, goals can be attained. So can objectives. Is the attainment of a BA in history a goal or an objective? Close inspection of the characteristics of and requirements for a BA would lead one to conclude that it can fit both descriptions.

Perhaps a better feeling for the differences between them is provided by this statement: my goal is to pass History 206. This fits the properties of a goal set out above. But it fails as an objective in one important area. It does not describe what observable acts the student will be able to do either in order to complete, or after he has completed, the course. Here is the crux of the matter. If the student could do, say, 42 activities in that history course, these activities could constitute 42 objectives. By completing these objectives, he would qualify for his goal, passing History 206. While similar then, goals and objectives are different.

With his idea of aims, goals and objectives, Davies has constructed a hierarchy with aims at the top and objectives at the bottom. Goals fall somewhere in between. Each is separate and distinct.

Many types of statements are called objectives but fail to meet one or more of the criteria stated earlier. Here is one example (Freeman, 1975):

Chooses appropriate criteria for decision-making	Under normal educational lecture room or seminar conditions and in written progress tests	To the satisfaction of the staff

No one should mistake this for an aim. Nor after a bit of reflection would it be called a goal. Is it then really an objective? After all, it is written in three parts! The first part does describe something that a student could do. But the second part sets down the methods a teacher will use to teach the student how to choose the decision-making criteria. The progress tests relate, perhaps, to some form of practice in this ability. But nowhere are the conditions described under which this ability will take place: given a case study? without reference to the text? The implication in the second part is what the student will do in class, instead of the conditions under which the action will occur (Mager, 1962).

At first glance the third part looks acceptable. But when and for what reasons will the staff be satisfied? If this question can be answered, then we will have described how well we want the student to choose appropriate criteria. Should he choose a minimum in accordance with certain rules? Or given a selection of 10, select the best six?

We are not told. The criteria can thus change at the whim of whoever is in charge and they can not then be called 'predetermined'. On these two counts alone the example fails to be an objective. But what is it? Basically, I feel the example is a statement of teaching intent or methodology, accidentally (?) disguised as an objective.

The phrase 'management by objectives' (MBO) is one which has caused much confusion. The term was coined by Drucker in his book *The Practice of Management* in 1954 (Howell, 1967). This phrase unfortunately coincided with the term 'objective' then coming into prominence in education circles.

MBO objectives have the properties of control, communication, common direction, planning, measurability and no duplication of effort (Howell, 1967). On the surface, they seem very like behavioural objectives. But one crucial difference is that MBO objectives are for a manager and the management and administration function (March, 1979), but do not relate to trainees in any way, not even management trainees.

Put into the three-part format, one example of an MBO objective would look like this:

Performance	*Conditions*	*Standards*
To lower the costs of producing the model 427 widget.	Nil	by 7% to 30 April; by having one operator complete operations 7, 8 and 9.

Ignoring the lack of conditions, this could pass for an educational objective in the eyes of the inexperienced. But recall the purpose. This statement has nothing to do with education or training, only management.

The definition of an MBO objective is 'the necessary aspects of the job which must be accomplished in order to fulfil the purpose'. From the definition, it becomes even clearer that these statements are similar to what Davies called aims and goals, but they are not objectives in any educational sense.

In addition to confusion between terms, there are some underlying anxieties about objectives that overshadow the thinking of many people. One anxiety is that objectives stifle creative teaching (Eisner, 1971). This is interesting for as I have shown, Mager's definition of an objective says nothing about teaching, teaching methods, teaching time, or the qualities required in a teacher. An objective only states what the learner should be able to do after the teacher has finished. And if the teacher cannot state what he wants the student to be able to do, why are they both there in the first place? Second, if the learner cannot complete the objective after the teacher is finished, then the time to correct that situation is right then, not several months later.

Another underlying anxiety illustrated by Mager (1962) is that many things taught are intangible and cannot be measured or evaluated. If this is true, how then can the teacher demonstrate that first, he is actually teaching anything at all; and second, that his students are learning something, anything? How for example does

he evaluate his students now? By a final test? If so, something must be happening.
If it isn't, then perhaps he is just wasting everyone's time. The key probably lies in
the test. This, after all, is what the teacher has determined is important and the
objectives will lie hidden in the test.

Earlier, I discussed the differences between aims, goals and objectives, and
briefly discussed two of the underlying anxieties concerning objectives. But are
these 'behavioural' or 'performance' objectives?

The term 'performance' means 'to do something'. It implies an achievement. The
following are examples of common usage:

1. Her performance in the exam was not *as good as expected*.
2. In the football game, he gave a *magnificent* performance.
3. The horse performed (ran) *well* on the muddy track.

Although value judgements are attached to each of these examples, a performance
is one that can be observed by the use of one or more of the five senses. Implicit in
the use of this word is some form of quantifiable measurement. The words
underlined in the sentences above are quantifiable measures. In other words, they
can be compared with something else and a judgement made as to whether the
performance is the same, greater or lesser.

Now the term 'behaviour' also means 'to do something'. In learning theory, it is
used to describe a response to a stimulus. Hill (1977) tells us that the terms
'behaviour', 'behaviourism', and 'behaviourist' were introduced to psychology just
prior to World War I by a man named Watson. Watson's purpose was to provide a
non-subjective way to study human behaviour, and he preferred the term
'behaviour' to those then in vogue: mentalism and consciousness. As Watson used
it, the term 'behaviour' meant the abstruse movements of the muscles (Hill, 1977).

In this sense, behaviour and performance appear identical. But their usage in
everyday English shows a distinct difference. Would it make sense, for example, to
say of a boy that his performance in cutting off his sister's pigtails was terrible?
That sentence would only be used when the lad made a poor job of the actual
cutting. The intended meaning of the sentence refers to the boy's conduct since
cutting off his sister's pigtails is not considered a nice thing to do. It is his behaviour
that we find terrible, not the actual performance of severing the pigtails.

This example illustrates a second meaning for the term 'behaviour'. In this case,
the word refers to manners and conduct. In this sense, there are many types of
behaviour: religious ('fanatical'); intellectual ('stupid'); age-related ('immature');
socially acceptable ('compassionate') and unacceptable ('deviant'), among others.

Because of the term 'behaviourist' in learning theory, there has evolved the
practice of associating any observable and measurable performances with
behaviourism (Davies, 1976). Not only is this unfortunate from the point of view of
the objectives themselves, but it is also incorrect. As Posner and Strike (1975) point
out, this 'consistent application of a behaviourist ideology to stating educational
objectives has undesirable consequences for education', not the least of which is
confusion in the minds of many people.

This double meaning to the term behaviour has led people off the narrow track
as defined by Watson. Both MacDonald-Ross and Mitchell (1972) use the term
'behave'. While they use it in the sense Watson intended, the term is misused by
others. Take, for example, Stewart's use of the phrase 'behaviour modification'
(1975). 'Performance modification' can be quite easily accepted but not 'behaviour
modification'. One could construct an acceptable argument for the latter phrase,
but to many it has sinister overtones which have no place in education. What, after
all, is a mental home but an institution devoted to behaviour modification? The
same could be said of a prison.

One could then argue convincingly that both prisons and mental homes are
'special' schools where learning occurs. But would you, as a parent, if you had a

choice, send your child to either? From this point, it is but a short step to other forms of behaviour modification: propaganda, brainwashing and indoctrination. And at least one person feels that the use of 'behavioural' objectives borders on brainwashing (Kleibard, 1971).

The term 'behaviour' relates to both internal and external actions. The term 'performance' relates only to observable and measurable actions, and has no other connotations. In the writing of objectives, it is these observable and measurable external actions we wish to note and record.

When used in conjunction with the term 'objective', therefore, the term 'behavioural' should give way to, and be replaced by, the term 'performance', and the sooner the better.

REFERENCES

Davies, I K (1976) *Objectives in Curriculum Design.* McGraw Hill, New York.

Eisner, E W (1971) Educational objectives: help or hindrance. In Kapfer, M B (ed) *Behavioural Objectives in Curriculum Development*, pp 158-67. Educational Technology Publications, Englewood Cliffs, NJ.

Freeman, D J (1975) Good objectives and bad — a case study. Unpublished manuscript. RNSETT, HMS Nelson, Portsmouth, England.

Gagné, R F and Briggs, L J (1977) *Principles of Instructional Design.* Harper, New York.

Hill, W F (1979) *Learning.* Holt, Rinehart, & Winston, New York.

Howell, R A (1967) Management by objectives is for management. *Business Horizons,* fall, pp 181-190.

Kliebard, H M (1971) Curricular objectives and evaluation: a reassessment. In Kapfer, M B (ed) *Behavioural Objectives in Curriculum Development,* pp 351-57. Educational Technology Publications, Englewood Cliffs, NJ.

Mager, R F (1962) *Preparing Instructional Objectives.* Fearon Publishers, Belmont, Ca.

MacDonald-Ross, M (1973) Behavioural objectives: a critical review. *Instructional Science,* May, 2, pp 1-52.

March, R L (1979) Management by objectives: a multi-faceted faculty evaluation model. *Educational Technology* **XIX**, 11, Nov, pp 44-49.

Mitchell, P D (1972) The sacramental nature of behavioural objectives. *Aspects of Educational Technology* **VI**, pp 48-55. Pitman, London.

Posner, G J and Strike, K A (1975) Ideology versus technology: the bias of behavioural objectives. *Educational Technology,* May, pp 28-34.

Stewart, D (1975) *Instruction as a Humanizing Science.* Slate Services, Fountain Valley, Ca.

Effective Management Through Management by Results (1969) CF Air Transport Command, Trenton, Ontario.

Managing By — And With — Objectives (1970) Studies in Personnel Policy 212, National Industrial Conference Board.

Section 3:
Military and Specialist
Career Training

3.1 The Development and Evaluation of Command and Control Simulators in the British Army

Lt Col M G S Stythe and Maj D Aitken[1]
Royal Army Education Corps

Abstract: The British Army's command and control simulators at unit level are known as battle group trainers (BGTs). The development of the present BGTs arose from the complexity of the modern battle group as a fighting unit, the command of which in war would be a formidable task. Because of limited resources maximum benefit has to be obtained from collective field training. To obtain this benefit optimum use must be made of any opportunity to develop staff command and control skills, communication skills and tactical decision-making, without the need for the costly deployment of troops in support. The BGTs were designed to subject a commanding officer and his staff to stressful situations, relating exercises to real ground and portraying battle conditions which are as realistic as possible within a realistic time frame. This paper describes the present army command and control simulators, explains how they have evolved and how their effectiveness was assessed, and suggests likely future developments.

In addition to being an essential part of staff training and development the BGTs use a variety of methodologies and resources normally associated with educational technology. Computer-assisted training, closed circuit television and slide presentations are used at various stages of the simulation to support the learning process. The three main phases of the study will be described in detail and the use of an analysis technique labelled 'scenario analysis' will be highlighted. The paper will give a summary of the analysis, review the evaluation results and suggest likely future developments.

BACKGROUND TO THE DEVELOPMENT OF BATTLE GROUP TRAINERS

The British Army's command and control simulators at major unit level are known as battle group trainers (BGTs). Two exist. One in the UK (1978) and the other with BAOR in Germany (1979). Their design was based on a number of principles:

- [ ] They should be as realistic as possible in the key areas.
- [ ] They should operate in real time.
- [ ] The complete command and control team that forms Battle Group Headquarters (BGHQ) should be exercised.
- [ ] They should be an adjunct to, and not a substitute for, exercising in the field.
- [ ] The exercises should relate to nearby ground to enable proper reconnaissance to be carried out.
- [ ] They should be used as trainers and not assessors of commanders and their staff. (Assessment would come later during field exercises.)
- [ ] They could be used to disseminate tactical doctrine but would be unsuitable to originate or validate such doctrine.
- [ ] They should be capable of bringing out tactical lessons.

1 *In addition to the two authors of this paper who are still (March 1983) serving at the Army School of Training Support, the study team also included the following two officers:*
Major R R Begland PhD US Army (now at Fort Leavenworth, USA) and
Major J F Taylor MSc RAEC (now at HQ BAOR).

Their original aim was: 'To train Battle Group (BG) commanders and their staffs, including supporting arms and air, in drills, procedures and tactics'.

Both BGTs are static. A BGHQ visits them and moves into 'mock ups' simulating its command vehicles. Its members are then exercised in real time. The exercises are set on ground nearby, over which the BG commander and his reconnaissance (R) group together with sub-unit commanders will have carried out a recce. One-sided play only is involved. Control is exercised by the nucleus of permanent staff controllers, together with temporary controllers from the visiting BG, working from a central control room containing a two-dimensional model of the ground. A microcomputer is used in the assessment of the engagements. After conducting the recce the BGHQ works from the 'mock ups' in the trainers. From the players' point of view the radio communications work as normal but are simulated by cable links. General battle noise such as artillery fire and air attack is simulated in the BGHQ by means of loudspeakers. BGs visit the BGTs for two to four days at a time and play one or two scenarios, each lasting about six hours. These are followed by a critique or debrief during which video-recordings of battle-play may be shown.

BACKGROUND TO THE EVALUATION STUDY

Financial and other restrictions on training resources increased in the late 1970s and early 1980s. Against this background the use of simulation for training commanders and their staffs at other levels became increasingly attractive and the design of higher level trainers seemed a natural extension of the BGT concept. However, the concept of the BGT system had yet to be comprehensively validated. While they seemed successful there were, of course, some criticisms. To embark upon the development of tactical training simulators at higher levels without validating the BGTs, assessing their effectiveness as trainers and taking into account the lessons learned during their development could be foolhardy and might well lead to inefficient and unsound progress. Furthermore, the BGTs themselves would require replacement of their hardware in the mid-1980s. It was therefore clearly imperative that the opportunity should be taken to evaluate the present BGT systems.

The terms of reference for the study were for the Army School of Training Support (ASTS) to carry out:

1. An evaluation of the existing BGTs taking into account their acknowledged aims and limitations.
2. An investigation into possible ways in which they could be developed to improve their effectiveness, taking into account relevant developments in commerce, industry and the armed forces of other nations.

The study is now described in outline. (Full details are in a separate ASTS report.)

METHODOLOGY

The study fell into three distinct phases:

The preliminary phase

This began in March 1981 and took the following form:

- ☐ A review of relevant literature and developments in the field.
- ☐ A series of visits to relevant military and civilian organizations.
- ☐ A study of initial comments by commanding officers of BGs which had used the BGTs.
- ☐ A study of BG operating procedures.
- ☐ A study of the BGT documentation.

At the end of this phase it was apparent that insufficiently clear or precise objectives existed for the BGTs which would enable a rigorous and objective evaluation of them to take place, although it would be possible to conduct a comprehensive subjective review. It was therefore decided that, as a first step, the evaluation study team should embark on a complete analysis of the operation activities of a BGHQ. Such an analysis would produce detailed objective criteria against which the BGTs could be evaluated thoroughly. This led to the second phase — the criterion production phase.

The criterion production phase

This started in August 1981 and took the form of three perspectives.

A training perspective

This involved the acquisition of training information from those establishments responsible for training BGHQ members. Copies of training objectives, course programmes and on-job training requirements were obtained.

A user's perspective

Here the team were concerned with the BG commander's perception of how his BGHQ operated. They were concerned initially with the activities and relationships within it, emphasis being placed on the information gathering and decision-making processes. It was possible to identify:

☐ How information reached the commander.
☐ How decisions were made: eg solely by the commander, or jointly with others, or delegated to another member of BGHQ.
☐ How decisions or other information, were passed on.

Most of this information was acquired by questionnaire. However, BG commanders were also interviewed to confirm the questionnaire data and to discuss other relevant areas, such as:

☐ Differences between individual BGHQ organizations.
☐ Critical areas of BGHQ activity.
☐ Difficult areas of BGHQ activity.
☐ Areas of BG activity that were rarely exercised elsewhere.

The operational perspective

This involved analysing the activities of a BGHQ at a more detailed level. To do this a fresh technique was adopted, called 'scenario analysis'.

This analysis involved joint activity and agreement by both BGT staffs, assisted by members of the study team, by working chronologically through a series of BG operations. As a first step in the analysis contexts were identified which were likely to cause significant activity in a BGHQ. Two examples are:

☐ Enemy threaten to capture reserve demolition.
☐ Combat team overrun.

The second step in the analysis was to agree which BGHQ members had a significant input to that context. Naturally the number of appointments identified varied according to the context, as in the case of the above. For example:

CONTEXT	
Enemy threaten to capture reserve demolition	Combat team (CT) overrun
Appointments involved	Appointments involved
BG Commander (BG Comd)	Regimental Signals Officer (RSO)
Second in Command (2ic)	Mortar Officer (Mor)
Battery Commander (BC)	Anti Tank Platoon Officer (Atk)
Watchkeeper (Wkpr)	Electrical Mechanical Engineer (EME)
Intelligence Officer (IO)	Regimental Medical Officer (RMO)
Engineer Officer (Engr)	Echelon Commander (Ech)
Total 6 appointments	Total 12 appointments

The third step was to determine and agree the activities of each identified appointment. An example of the activities of the Mortar Officer in the context of 'combat team overrun' is illustrated in the format of the analysis *pro forma* used.

CONTEXT — Combat team overrun		
Input	*Action by*	*Event description*
'A' CT reports 'B' CT's posn has been overrun.	Mor	BG reacts to one of its own sub-units being overrun.

Desired response

1. Implement DF FP.
2. Receive SITREP from MFCs and pass to BC.
3. Move Mor Base Plate if threatened by breakthrough.
4. Request ammo resupply.
5. Discuss changes to FP with BC if required.
6. Reallocate MFCs where appropriate.

As measured by

1. Accurate and timely response to FP.
2. Mors report ready in new loc.
3. MFCs ack changes to FP and new orders where appropriate.

The evaluation phase

The criterion production phase was completed immediately before Christmas 1981 and by combining and comparing the data from the various perspectives a comprehensive task list was produced of the activities a BGHQ could expect to undertake. This task list of operational activities became the basis for the questionnaires which were the *main* information gathering technique for the evaluation phase. Again, however, the questionnaire data was supported by interviews with BGHQ commanders and staffs.

Using the task list as a reference point, it was then necessary to obtain the following additional information:

☐ *Opportunities* provided by the BGTs for carrying out the operational activities.
☐ *The importance* of the activities.
☐ *Comparisons* with other forms of training where these activities are practised.
☐ The overall *context* of BGT training, in order to ascertain when attendance at BGT should occur in the training cycle.
☐ The *fidelity* of the various tasks as presented at BGT.
☐ The *reality* of the environment at BGT in which the tasks are presented. (This was termed 'physical fidelity'.)
☐ Any developments in *tactical doctrine* which might affect subsequent designs of the BGT.
☐ The *training* and *experience* of BGHQ members.
☐ The *relative costs* of the various means of this type of training.

DATA ANALYSIS

The above data were analysed in two main stages:

1. Initially each group of similar questionnaires was analysed to identify overall trends and any variance in ratings across BGHQ appointments and/or scenario contexts for the factors being rated in the appropriate questionnaire.
2. Subsequently all the data was summarized, collated and analysed following the algorithmic lines illustrated in Figure 1.

RESULTS

In a short conference paper such as this it is clearly not possible to present the results in any detail, nor would it be appropriate to do so. However, the design of the study and the analysis meant that it was possible to identify and assess for *each BGHQ appointment*, including the BG commander, the following:

☐ The detailed training opportunities provided by the BGTs.
☐ The detailed training opportunities taken while at the BGTs.
☐ A comparison of the opportunities provided and taken with other means of collective training.
☐ The fidelity level of the tasks undertaken at the BGTs.
☐ The reality of the contexts in which the tasks were set at the BGTs.
☐ The importance or criticality levels to the success of the BG's mission of each task, whether it was provided or not, or taken or not.
☐ The comparative training value of the BGTs compared with other means of collective training for each task.
☐ The relationship between the collective training provided at the BGTs and the individual training for BGHQ members previously provided at other training establishments.
☐ The training value of the various individual components of the BGT training system, eg the provision of Tac HQ, the ADP sub-system, the control room, the debriefing facility, the radio communication system and the link with real ground.

CONCLUSIONS

A number of detailed conclusions were arrived at by the study team. However, this paper will limit itself to those conclusions of a more general nature, and these can be summarized as follows:

1. The BGTs work and work well. Their concept is sound and valid and they

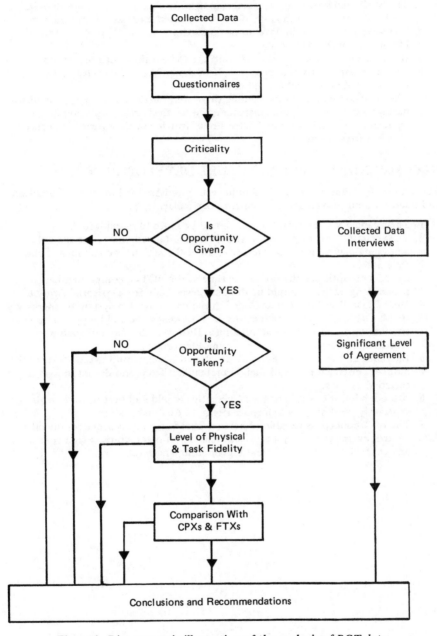

Figure 1. *Diagrammatic illustration of the analysis of BGT data*

develop both the BG commander and his staff.
2. Individual BGs bring different requirements to the BGTs. In some cases specific and specialized needs were not met.
3. The BGTs had been used as trainers in drills and procedures more than in tactics and they were capable of being exploited more as tactical trainers.
4. They were successful in developing quick thinking and flexibility of mind in both commanders and staff.
5. It was essential that they should continue to be linked with real ground.
6. Although apparently relatively simple in design they are versatile trainers and can be adapted to meet a number of needs.
7. They had some limitations. Among these were: little logistic play; unrealistic damage assessment in some instances; the relatively short duration of exercises — enough for mental stress but insufficient time for the effects of physical stress to be seen.

RECOMMENDATIONS FOR FUTURE DEVELOPMENT

Further development of the BGTs should seek to redress the limitations identified and build on their proven achievements. In particular:

1. Their capacity as tactical trainers should be more fully exploited.
2. The versatility of the simulator should be capitalized on by, for example, advancing play to learn new lessons should the action reach an identifiable stalemate.
3. In order to optimize the use of the time at the BGTs a comprehensive pre-training package should be designed, especially for Territorial Army units.
4. More flexibility should be provided in the computer sub-system by increasing the size of both read/write memory and backing store and by providing a truly multi-programmable architecture. However, the simulation should remain computer-assisted and not computer driven.
5. Exercises and scenarios should be developed which would extend further the more experienced BGs and their commanders. These should not, however, be regarded as tests.
6. Although logistic play was a weakness, this would still best be dealt with separately, probably by a purpose-designed part-task trainer.
7. The BGT concept is capable of being adapted to address other command and control exercises. The system is also capable of being up-rated as a command and control trainer for the next higher command level.

3.2 A Study of a Leadership Model in a Young Person's Environment

Major C B Beard RAEC
Army School of Training Support

Abstract: Studies of leadership models may be of value to staff developers. Using the leadership model developed by the American psychologist F E Fiedler, the writer investigated whether 247 junior leaders involved in a study during a leadership training course, could easily identify their own particular style of leadership and recognize the situations in which they could prove to be most or least effective. The model predicted that task-orientated leaders would perform more effectively in very favourable and very unfavourable situations while relationship-orientated leaders would perform more effectively in situations intermediate in favourableness.

The leadership style was categorized as relationship- or task-orientated according to the leader's answers to a 'least preferred co-worker' questionnaire. A measure of group atmosphere was obtained in a similar way and verified by instructors. Tasks were rated as of high or low structure, and position power was manipulated to give a high or low task score. Performance was rated by instructors. The median correlations between leadership style and leader performance were compared with those predicted by the model.

Although the correlations obtained were not statistically significant, when compared over the five weeks of the study 12 correlations out of 20 were in the predicted direction with five in the opposite direction. There were three zero correlations. If the two extremes of the model are ignored one can see a similar graphical shape to Fiedler's results. Thus, the study showed some, but not complete, support for the model. It is likely that further research with tighter variable controls would produce results with a higher level of significance.

The study yielded some interesting additional information including the style of leadership which some young people most preferred. Also, significant results were obtained in relation to instructor ratings, leadership tasks set, and the influence of group size on performance. Finally, the study showed that there was a significant relationship between intelligence and performance.

INTRODUCTION

A leadership study was carried out by the writer at a military Junior Leaders Unit, at the end of which a dissertation was submitted in part fulfilment of the requirements for the degree of Master of Science in the University of Aston in Birmingham (Beard, 1978).

The writer spent two years as the organizer of a 'functional leadership' course designed to make 16- and 17-year-old army junior leaders aware of the nature and practice of leadership. Part of this course involved a study of different leadership styles. There was a clearly identifiable need for research into this area to produce a better method of enabling junior leaders to recognize in themselves and in others the ingredients of success or failure in leadership. The authorities in the unit concerned were enthusiastic about the idea of a study but asked the writer to organize this so as to disrupt existing training arrangements as little as possible.

BACKGROUND

At the junior leader training unit leadership training was described as symbiotic — it flourished beside and with other training and instruction. The one-week functional leadership course was not regarded as the beginning and end of leadership development. Junior leaders could be looked upon as the Army's potential non-commissioned officers and warrant officers and in fact they go on to fill most of those posts in due course. At the unit they were organized into five separate companies on a regimental basis each with their own full-time administrators and instructors.

The one-week functional leadership course began in the classroom with an introduction to the theory of functional leadership (Adair, 1968) and this was followed by role-playing and the use of case studies. The junior leader then undertook a number of short outdoor command tasks in the course of which his effectiveness as a leader was assessed according to functional leadership criteria. A typical command task involved the leader moving a box of essential stores, with his team members, over a physical obstacle such as a river.

FIEDLER'S CONTINGENCY MODEL

Fiedler's contingency model of effective leadership (Fiedler, 1967) requires a match between a situation and one's particular style of leadership. Leaders are asked to complete a 'least preferred co-worker' (LPC) questionnaire from which a score is obtained, and then they are categorized as relationship- or task-orientated. The appropriate match between leadership style and situational control is as follows:

1. Task-motivated (low LPC) leaders perform best in situations of high control.
2. Relationship-motivated (high LPC) leaders perform best in situations of moderate control.

Situation control is made up of:

☐ Leader member relationships.
☐ Task structure.
☐ The position of power of the leader.

Figure 1 provides a summary of what Fiedler's model predicts in terms of leadership style, behaviour and performance in varying situations.

Leader Type	Situational Control		
	High Control	*Moderate Control*	*Low Control*
High LPC Relationship-motivated	*Behaviour:* Somewhat automatic, aloof and self-centred. Seemingly concerned with task *Performance:* Poor	*Behaviour:* Considerate, open and participative *Performance:* Good	*Behaviour:* Anxious, tentative, overly concerned with interpersonal relations *Performance:* Poor
Low LPC Task-motivated	*Behaviour:* Considerate and supportive *Performance:* Good	*Behaviour:* Tense, task-focused *Performance:* Poor	*Behaviour:* Directive, task-focused, serious *Performance:* Relatively good

Figure 1. *Summary of leadership style, behaviour and performance in varying situations (Fiedler, 1976)*

Figure 2 shows the eight cells of Fiedler's model in relation to the median correlation he obtained from the groups he investigated (Fiedler, 1967).

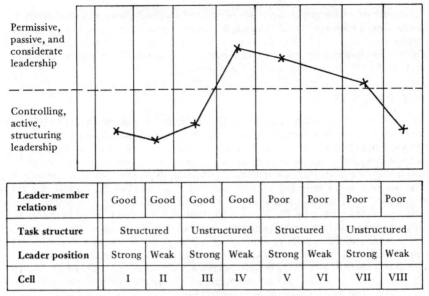

Leader-member relations	Good	Good	Good	Good	Poor	Poor	Poor	Poor
Task structure	Structured		Unstructured		Structured		Unstructured	
Leader position	Strong	Weak	Strong	Weak	Strong	Weak	Strong	Weak
Cell	I	II	III	IV	V	VI	VII	VIII

Figure 2. *How the style of effective leadership varies with the situation (Fiedler, 1976)*

Fiedler's contingency model of effective leadership seemed to offer the 247 junior leaders involved in the study the chance easily to identify their own particular style of leadership and to recognize the situations in which they would prove to be most and least effective. A general assumption was made that leadership performance can be improved by training and that the individual leader is free to influence the leadership climate. Before Fiedler's theories could be accepted into the training programme there appeared to be a need to replicate his findings at the junior leader unit in question. Evidence was needed of the validity and reliability of the model, if possible with adolescents, in a non-American military environment.

THE LITERATURE SEARCH

Before the project commenced, a literature search was made. With leadership studies appearing at a rate of more than 170 a year (McCall, 1976) this was not easy. There was no evidence that any simple definition was widely accepted. After this detailed study of the literature the writer reached the conclusion that the most useful way ahead was to look at specific leadership situations and the variables contained within them and see what combination appeared to work and what did not. There was evidence of the use of the model in a military environment at the United States Military Academy West Point (Fiedler, 1971), in a different cultural environment, with the Belgian Navy (Fiedler, 1967) and with adolescents in Japan (Tanaka, 1975). But there appeared to have been no study of the use of the model in a non-United States adolescent military environment.

THE STUDY

After a full briefing by the writer, course instructors issued junior leaders with the appropriate documentation to be used in the study.

Their leadership style was categorized as relationship- or task-orientated according to their answers to a 'least preferred co-worker' (LPC) questionnaire.

A measure of group atmosphere was obtained in a similar way and verified by instructors. Tasks were rated as of high or low structure, and position power was manipulated to give a high or low task score. Performance was rated by instructors. The median correlations between leadership style and leader performance were compared with those predicted by the model.

THE RESULTS

The data, including additional information on junior leader intelligence test scores, company membership, instructor group, leadership task and size of group, were analysed and the 247 group leaders still in the unit were assigned to the eight cells of the contingency model by dichotomizing the three situational variables of leader-member relations, task structure and position power. Leader-member relations or group atmosphere was dichotomized by dividing the leaders into those with good leader-member relations and those with moderately poor leader-member relations, as instructed by Fiedler (1976). Task structure was defined by selecting tasks according to task scores (structured and unstructured tasks). Position power was defined experimentally as a dichotomy (strong and weak power conditions); this resulted in a distribution of the groups over the eight cells of the model as shown in Figure 3. The overwhelming majority of groups fell within cells I to IV (87 per cent). Spearman rank-order correlations were calculated between leadership style (LPC) and leadership performance so that a comparison could be made with the median correlations in Fiedler's model. Use was made of the University of Aston computer and the Statistical Package for the Social Sciences (Nie, 1970).

Leader-member relations	Good	Good	Good	Good	Poor	Poor	Poor	Poor
Task structure	Structured		Unstructured		Structured		Unstructured	
Leader position power	Strong	Weak	Strong	Weak	Strong	Weak	Strong	Weak
Cell	I	II	III	IV	V	VI	VII	VIII
Situation	Favourable						Unfavourable	→
Groups	86	38	56	35	5	6	9	12

Figure 3. *Number of groups in each cell of the contingency model*

Although the correlations obtained were not statistically significant, when compared over the five weeks of the study 12 correlations out of 20 were in the predicted direction, with five in the opposite direction. There were three zero correlations. If the two extremes of the model are ignored one can see a similar graphical shape to Fiedler's results (see Figure 4). Thus, the study showed some, but not complete, support for the model. It is likely that further research with tighter variable controls would produce results with a higher level of significance.

LEADERSHIP STYLE

The only other study of leadership styles in the Army known to the writer was that by Lt Col B Barnes (Barnes, 1976). He stated that the 17-year-olds in his sample preferred democratic (relationship-orientated) styles to autocratic (task-orientated) styles. He found the opposite was the case for adult NCOs. This current study gives more support to his findings. More junior leaders (120) were classified as

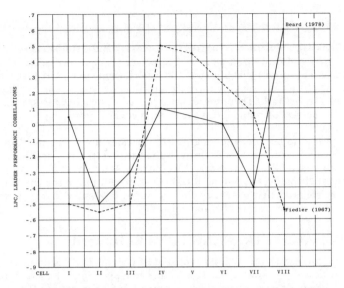

Figure 4. *A comparison between the medians of this study and Fiedler's models' median correlations*

relationship-orientated than task-orientated (106). It was interesting to see that preferred leadership style significantly depended on which company a junior leader came from. One company had junior leaders with an above average preference for relationship-orientated leadership while another had an above average preference for task-orientated leadership. It is difficult to explain this phenomenon. It may be due to the prevailing style among the full-time administrative/instructional staff in the company.

LEADERSHIP PERFORMANCE – SOME LESSONS FROM THE STUDY

Ratings

The average performance ratings made by each instructor were tested statistically and were shown to differ significantly. This meant that a junior leader's performance rating depended to a great extent on which instructor rated him. A possible way round this problem would be to standardize instructor ratings by providing both training and feedback. Closed circuit television (CCTV) was briefly used when the course was established. It was suggested to the senior education officer after the study that CCTV should be used again to provide feedback to both instructors and junior leaders.

Ranking

It was also suggested that the use of a ranking system in performance assessment could provide a group standard and might be seen to be more equitable. The problem of an inconvenient marking system should not be insurmountable. For example, in a group of 10, the top performer could be given a score taken from a table and reflecting his position. Converting scores to standard scores would allow comparisons to be made.

Tasks

The writer ranked the instructors' scores for each task and a statistical test showed that there were significant differences in the average performance ranking for different tasks. This meant that a junior leader performing one particular task had a much greater chance of doing well in that task than he would have had if he had been allotted another task. There therefore appeared to be a need to standardize tasks, and the method of running tasks to give an equal opportunity to all participants.

There appeared to be a need to create task situations simulating the daily demands of the leadership role and, through the use of extensive feedback, to allow the trainees to study their behaviour and its impact. Activities such as sports and hobbies suggest themselves as potential task areas in addition to the existing outdoor practical tasks that were used. In this way it is possible that leadership training could be made more useful and enjoyable.

DECISION-MAKING TRAINING FOR LEADERSHIP

Part of the junior leaders programme consisted of training in decision-making. As has been mentioned previously, case studies and role-playing were used with some success. The advent of computer-assisted learning (CAL) appears to offer another dimension to the instructor's resources. A system developed by Glasgow University which, in computer jargon, was 'content-free', or generally applicable, was being used successfully by Bramshill Police College. It was suggested that a similar system should be considered for junior leaders' decision-making training, and that advice should be sought from computer specialists at the Army School of Training Support.

SIZE OF GROUPS

Average performance rating scores seem in the study to have varied with the variation of average instructor group size. As the average number of junior leaders in the group went up so did the average score and *vice versa*. The shortage of instructors has produced groups of over 10 junior leaders. Some instructors were of the opinion that when this happened performance assessment became more difficult. It was therefore suggested that it was desirable to keep average group size to 10 or below to avoid a possible biasing effect here.

INTELLIGENCE SCORES

Recruits into the Army undertake pencil and paper tests which broadly measure intelligence and these scores were compared with leadership performance. The computer analysis appeared to confirm the expectation that more intelligent leaders should perform better.

CONCLUSIONS

1. There was some but not complete support for Fiedler's model. It would be unwise to generalize too much from this study without further evidence of support from research.
2. Each company seemed to have an overall leadership style preference which was peculiar to that company. This may be due to the collective style of the full-time administrative/instructional staff in the company.
3. Junior leaders had an overall marginal preference for relationship-orientated leadership styles. This confirmed previous findings.

4. The existing performance assessment system was unfair because:
   (a) Average performance ratings differed significantly with different instructors.
   (b) Average performance ratings differed significantly with different tasks.
5. Tasks used at the time of the study did not simulate the daily demands of the leadership role.
6. The size of instructor group appeared to affect the performance score an individual achieved.
7. On average the higher the apparent intelligence level of the junior leader the higher the performance score obtained.

RECOMMENDATIONS

A number of recommendations were made to the unit with the aim of improving training.

1. Fiedler's model should not be fully adopted without further evidence of its validity and reliability. Any future researcher should use tighter manipulative controls and should bear in mind recent leadership training developments with the analysis of social skills (Argyle, 1967).
2. Attempts should be made to standardize instructor ratings by providing more training and feedback, perhaps with the aid of CCTV. It was recommended that instructors should attend Army School of Training Support courses on testing techniques/validation of training.
3. Alternative assessment procedures should be explored perhaps using rankings rather than ratings.
4. It was recommended that a small working party of educational instructors and company officers should be set up to consider ways of standardizing task marking and of formulating additional tasks to simulate the daily demands of the leadership role, including such areas as sport and hobbies.
5. The possible use of CAL in decision-making training should be considered and advice should be sought.
6. It was recommended that instructor group size should be limited to no more than 10 in number, during training on leadership tasks.

REFERENCES

Adair, J (1968) *Training for Leadership*. MacDonald and Janes, London.
Argyle, M (1967) *The Psychology of Interpersonal Behaviour,* pp 122-123. Penguin, Harmondsworth.
Barnes, B (1976) Preferred and perceived styles of decision-making in an army unit. Unpublished MA thesis, Birkbeck College, University of London.
Beard, C B (1978) A study of a leadership model in a military junior leader environment. Unpublished MSc thesis, University of Aston, Birmingham.
Fiedler, F E (1967) *A Theory of Leadership Effectiveness*. McGraw Hill, New York.
Fiedler, F E (1971) Validation and extension of the contingency model of leadership effectiveness: a review of empirical findings. *Psychological Bulletin* 76, pp 128-148.
Fiedler, F E, Chemers, M M and Mahar, L (1976) *Improving Leadership Effectiveness — The Leader Match Concept*. Wiley, New York.
McCall, M W (1976) Leaders and leadership: of substance and shadow. Paper to annual meeting, British Psychological Society Occupational Psychology Section, Keele.
Nie, N K, Bent, D H and Hull, C H (1970) *Statistical Package for the Social Sciences*. McGraw Book Company, New York.
Tanaka, K (1975) An experimental study on the effects of changing task structure in the contingency model: an exercise in situational engineering. *Japanese Journal of Experimental Social Psychology* 15, 1, pp 74-85.

3.3 The Effects of Managerial Transition Training on Performance

R L Miller
HumRRO, Heidelberg, W Germany

Abstract: This research examined the effects of managerial transition on unit performance. Specifically, a structural transition guide (COMTRAIN) designed to effect a smooth and orderly change of command at company level in the US Army in Europe was evaluated. This transition guide contained a self-managed, flexible outline of topics used for conducting discussions with key personnel within the larger organization (battalion) prior to and immediately following assumption of command.

Comparisons were made between those commanders who received the COMTRAIN program and those who did not. Use of the COMTRAIN transition guide enhanced the performance of those company commanders who (a) had not served in the battalion previously, (b) had an external orientation towards success and/or (c) did not come directly from a job proximal to command. In general, the COMTRAIN approach was endorsed by both users and their supervisors.

INTRODUCTION

Transition, rotation, succession, change of command; all are words used to describe a central facet of organizational leadership: that leaders follow one another. Despite the frequent occurrence of leader successions in nearly all groups, especially in large stable organizations, relatively little research has addressed this phenomenon. An early review by Gibb (1969) reported on studies of leader emergence and succession mode. In particular, the importance of establishing leadership/followership through early, shared, significant experiences was noted. Gibb stressed that an important aspect of the organizational climate for the new leader derives from the policies of the former leader, the consequences of which shape follower's expectations, morale and interpersonal relations.

In general, studies have demonstrated that leadership succession causes turbulence and instability resulting in performance decrements in most organizations and thus constitutes a major challenge to organizations, eg, Pryor, Flint and Bass (1962), Trow (1960), Champion (1971).

As an organization, the US Army rotates leaders at a frequency substantially higher than most comparable civilian organizations. As a case in point, two-thirds of the company-sized units in the US Army in Europe (USAREUR) experience a change of command each year. Despite high leader rotation rates and the organizational challenge that they present, no USAREUR-wide formal procedure exists for effecting a smooth change of command at the company level.

Company commanders assume command with little or no transition period between assignments. To be effective in their new command, they must quickly acquire a wide range of information on the current policies, programmes, problems, priorities, and personnel in their battalion.

The early weeks in command are likely to be important determinants of long-term effectiveness. For the new commander and subordinates alike, it is a period of both raised expectations and uncertainty. In this situation, the commander's early actions are likely to establish persistent patterns in: (a) his own leadership behaviours, (b) the expectations and attitudes of his subordinates, and (c) his relationships with the battalion staff.

Thus, at the same time that the new commander's actions have a highly formative effect on patterns of leadership and followership, he is less equipped to make informed and appropriate decisions than at any later point in his command. Consequently, in the period of command transition, the need for systematic guidance and the opportunities for positive influence on leadership patterns are both high.

To meet this organizational challenge, W A Buxton developed a structured process to facilitate command transition which was designated COMTRAIN. This process guides the commander-designate through the period just before and just after assuming command of a company, battery, or troop. It is designed to assist the commander in: (a) acquiring the current and critical information needed for early effectiveness in command; and (b) establishing at the outset productive relationships with subordinates, peers, superiors, and supporting staff members. An interview guide provides the necessary structure for the COMTRAIN transition process.

COMTRAIN INTERVIEW GUIDES

Much of the information a new company commander needs to know in order for his actions to be appropriate and effective is current and specific to his own company and battalion. It is not feasible for this kind of information to be communicated through either a USAREUR-wide course or manuals. For example, effective management of the company's training requires mastery of:

- ☐ The scheduling methods used by that battalion's S-3 section.
- ☐ The community's training, duty and education cycles.
- ☐ The current training priorities for the battalion, brigade and division.
- ☐ The nature of and the constraints on training resources such as the local training area.
- ☐ Training policies and programmes currently in effect.
- ☐ The calendar of major events such as ARTEP evaluations and live firing.
- ☐ The current training status of the company and its sub-elements.

Regardless of his prior education in developing, executing, and evaluating unit training, there remains a great deal of current and unit-specific information for the new commander to assimilate.

The COMTRAIN interview guides provide the new commander with a self-managed, flexible outline for conducting discussions with individuals in the battalion who can serve as informational resources during the transition. The guides, which can be tailored and updated by the battalion before use, identify the major issues to explore with each resource-person, ie the areas of current problems, programs and priorities to discuss with each of the staff sections in battalion headquarters.

This self-managed approach, besides being appropriate for a company-grade officer, seems a practical necessity since prior staff assignments make some areas much more familiar than others. Further, arrangements for the interviews must take existing relationships, individual strengths and weaknesses, and the new commander's work schedule into account. In addition, the new commander should be able to adapt the interview approach to fit his/her own interpersonal style. Thus, the new commander is really in the best position to manage the in-briefing process.

The guide's influence on establishing productive relationships at the beginning of the command is designed to be covert rather than overt. The limited time available for the transition requires that the guide be focused directly on priority

information. However, the nature and form of the suggested interview questions are
intended to facilitate positive first impressions and productive working
relationships. In general, the guide casts the commander-in-transition in an active
listening role, seeking information that will improve the effectiveness of command,
and approaching interviewees as valued resources. Further, specific questions seek
inputs for improved co-operation and enhanced effectiveness.

The primary purpose of this research was to ascertain the impact of the
systematic transition guide (COMTRAIN) approach to command change on leader
and unit performance using a controlled experimental method. An additional
purpose was to determine the effects of other factors traditionally associated with
leader effectiveness, both singularly or in concert with COMTRAIN, on leader and
unit performance during the period immediately following command change. Five
such factors were included in the study. These were leader experience, leadership
training, leader confidence, perceived locus of control and two factors likely to
affect situational favourability: time in the battalion prior to assumption of
command, and time in/time to go of the company first sergeant.

It was hypothesized that commanders with recent leadership experience and/or
organizational knowledge would profit less from COMTRAIN since some of the
information provided would be redundant. Also, it was hypothesized that leaders
with an external orientation would profit more from the COMTRAIN approach
which emphasizes external resources, while 'internals' might be less able to utilize
effectually an approach which is inconsistent with their expectations about what is
necessary for success.

EVALUATION METHODS

Subjects were 50 company commander-designates who were randomly assigned to
either receive the COMTRAIN package or to serve as the control group.

Company and commander performance subsequent to transition was measured
using the battalion commanders evaluation form (BCEF). This form included
assessments of company administration, training readiness, maintenance and
supply, morale and discipline and commander performance. For the first month
after command transition, battalion commanders were asked to complete two
evaluations, each with a different point of comparison. In the first evaluation,
companies were rated in comparison to the other companies in the battalion along
an 11-point scale which ranged from (9) Exceedingly Above Battalion Average
through (4) Typical Company (Battalion Average) to (−1) Exceedingly Below
Battalion Average. In the second evaluation, companies and the new commander
were rated in comparison to the company's performance during the month prior to
command transition on an 11-point scale ranging from (9) Exceedingly Improved
through (4) No Change to (−1) Exceedingly Declined. On subsequent evaluations
(months 2-4) the 11-point scales were scored from (+5) Exceedingly Improved
through (0) No Change to (−5) Exceedingly Declined. These change scores were
added to the previous months' scores to create the subsequent month's score.
Additional information on the use and effectiveness of the COMTRAIN guide,
characteristics and transition activities of the COMTRAIN and control group
commanders was also collected.

RESULTS

In order to simplify the presentation of the data, two types of score aggregations
based on significant inter-item correlations were performed. First, the five separate
task ratings provided at each month were combined to create monthly composite
performance ratings. Second, the separate performance indicators across all
monthly rating periods were combined. This yielded a separate proficiency score

for administration, training, maintenance and supply, morale and discipline, and commander effectiveness irrespective of time. The performance ratings were subjected to two-way analyses of variance with use of COMTRAIN as one factor and various commander characteristics as the second. Included were time in the battalion (new: < 30 weeks; old: > 30 weeks); assignment immediately prior to command, which was coded to represent those jobs proximal (executive officer) or not proximal (student) to command; prior command experience (yes or no); completion of the Officer's Advanced Course (yes, no); completion of the company first sergeant in the battalion (new = 1-6 months in; experienced = between 6 months in and 6 months to go; short = under 6 months left); perceived locus of control (external, internal); and basis for social comparison (upward, across and downward comparison with others).

Analysis of variance indicated a main effect of previous experience on ratings of administration, F $(1, 49) = 3.86$ $p < .05$, maintenance, F $(1, 49) = 6.68$, $p < .02$ and the month 3 composite score, F $(1, 49) = 4.14$, $p < .05$. In each case, the performance ratings were higher for commanders whose assignment immediately prior had been proximal to command. Also, a main effect of Officer's Advanced Course completion was obtained on ratings of administration, F $(1, 49) = 4.62$, $p < .05$, and on the composite monthly ratings of month 2, F $(1, 49) = 4.93$, $p < .05$, and month 3, F $(1, 49) = 7.49$, $p < .01$. The means indicate that officers who had completed the advanced course scored higher on the dimensions noted above. No other main effects were obtained.

Table 1 presents the mean performance scores by COMTRAIN use and perceived locus of control for those interactions which were significant at better than the .05 level. As can be seen, officers whose orientation control was external scored higher with COMTRAIN use while those with an internal orientation scored higher without COMTRAIN. Table 2 presents the mean performance scores by COMTRAIN use and prior assignment for those interactions which were significant at better than the .05 level. Commanders whose assignment immediately prior to transition was proximal to command scored higher without COMTRAIN while COMTRAIN commanders scored higher when not coming from a job proximal to command.

PERFORMANCE EFFECTS OF COMTRAIN

The results indicate no simple effects of COMTRAIN in enhancing performance subsequent to command transition. Also, previous leadership and knowledge of the organization were not found to impact on performance. Two main effects were obtained. Both completion of the Officer's Advanced Course and proximity to command during the commander's immediate prior assignment enhanced performance ratings.

More interestingly, a significant interaction of COMTRAIN and perceived control was found on several ratings. The means indicate that commanders who believe that success is principally a product of external forces seem to profit from the use of COMTRAIN. Conversely, commanders who believe that success is primarily a product of intrinsic skills seem to be negatively affected by COMTRAIN. It is likely that the nature of the COMTRAIN task which heightens the user's awareness of outside resources as well as external requirements fits nicely into the world view of those who are externally orientated. On the other hand, the individual who is internally orientated may find that the COMTRAIN experience provides information which is difficult to assimilate since it focuses on many aspects of the organizational environment which must be beyond the company commander's sphere of influence. The time it takes to accommodate the realities of the environment with the commander's enduring perceptions of control may account for the initial deficits in performance.

Group	Activity-Specific Composite Scores				Monthly Composite Scores				
	Administration	Morale	Maintenance	Cdr	2nd	2nd-3rd	3rd	3rd-4th	4th
COMTRAIN									
Command proximal	7.25	6.33	7.87	7.88	5.83	1.11	6.94	.78	7.72
Not command proximal	12.21	11.21	13.00	13.00	7.33	2.69	10.01	2.69	12.70
Non-COMTRAIN									
Command proximal	12.57	12.33	12.70	13.53	7.42	2.62	10.04	2.80	12.84
Not command proximal	7.92	9.39	6.82	9.29	6.16	.80	6.96	1.68	8.64

Table 1. *Mean performance scores by COMTRAIN use and previous assignment*

Group	Activity-Specific Composite Scores				Monthly Composite Scores				
	Administration	Training	Morale	Cdr	1st	1st-2nd	2nd	3rd	4th
COMTRAIN									
Internals	7.83	10.40	6.50	8.55	5.10	.30	5.60	6.94	8.32
Externals	12.17	14.33	11.75	12.75	5.90	2.00	7.97	10.53	12.53
Non-COMTRAIN									
Internals	10.38	12.35	11.26	11.88	5.49	1.49	6.71	8.91	11.20
Externals	9.56	10.15	10.12	10.44	5.28	.87	7.03	7.73	9.79

Table 2. *Mean performance scores by COMTRAIN use and perceived control*

Similarly,commanders whose assignment immediately prior to command was not one proximal to the command experience seemed to profit from the use of COMTRAIN whereas commanders coming from a command-related job scored higher without COMTRAIN. While the benefits of COMTRAIN for inexperienced individuals is easy enough to understand, the negative impact on experienced individuals is more problematic. Using the reasoning developed in explaining the interaction of internal control and COMTRAIN it could be that those commanders with recent command-related experience find the information provided by the COMTRAIN experience difficult to assimilate into the perspective developed during the prior assignment.

EVALUATION BY GUIDE USERS

Company commanders who utilized the COMTRAIN guide were asked to evaluate the guide. Forty-three per cent of the commanders who utilized the COMTRAIN guide considered this kind of preparation very necessary. Thirty-six per cent of those commanders considered this kind of preparation moderately necessary. Twenty-one per cent considered it slightly necessary. None of the commanders who utilized the COMTRAIN guide considered this information unnecessary.

With regard to how helpful the COMTRAIN materials were, 29 per cent considered these materials very helpful, while 43 per cent considered them moderately helpful and 29 per cent considered them slightly helpful. No neutral or negative responses to this question were recorded.

Thirty-six per cent of the commanders using the COMTRAIN guide indicated that they would definitely recommend the guide to a friend taking over a company-level command. Fifty-seven per cent of the commanders answered that they would probably do so, and seven per cent answered 'perhaps'. No negative responses were received regarding this question.

Commanders were asked to indicate how they arranged to contact the individual specified in the guide. The available responses to this question were: (a) met at their request; (b) set up a meeting; (c) walked in and asked to talk; or (d) other. The purpose of this question was to determine the style and initiative shown by guide users. In no case did a guide user meet at the request of a staff member. This finding is important since it again underscores the lack of real socialization and orientation programmes being provided by battalion or company commanders. Thirty-eight per cent of our COMTRAIN users set up a meeting ahead of time in order to contact staff personnel. Fifty-four per cent walked in and asked to talk. Eight per cent used another method.

Another question asked was: 'In general, during the interviews, who raised most of the issues covered?' This question was designed to examine the adequacy of the socialization and orientation procedures that the battalion itself promoted for new commanders. Eighty-six per cent of our sample raised those issues that were discussed themselves. The remaining 14 per cent had experienced situations where some of the people that they contacted raised critical issues.

Two questions were asked regarding the adequacy of the guide itself. Eighty-six per cent of the guide users considered the guide 'okay as it is'. Fourteen per cent had specific recommendations for re-writing. Also, users were asked to list topics which should be added to the guide. Thirty per cent indicated one or two topics needed. No users generated more than two additional topics.

The final question in the evaluation by users was: 'Do you think that a different approach to command preparation for new commanders, of company-level units, is necessary?' Ninety-one per cent of the guide users answered 'no' to this question.

SUMMARY

COMTRAIN was found to improve performance ratings for commanders:
(a) without experience in the battalion prior to assumption of command; (b) with
an external orientation to perceived control; (c) with prior command experience,
but (d) without command exposure during their previous assignment. Transition
activities were found to impact most significantly immediately after transition with
less impact over time. Other variables found to affect early performance were
completion of the Officer's Advanced Course, tenure with the battalion and
previous assignment. Evaluations by COMTRAIN users were uniformly positive as
to its benefit.

REFERENCES

Buxton, W A (1977) *COMTRAIN: Training Materials for Company Commanders.* General
    Research Corporation, McLean, Virginia.
Champion, J (1971) Managerial succession in complex organizations. Unpublished manuscript,
    University of Washington.
Gibb, C A (1969) Leadership. In Lindzey, G and Aronson, E (eds) *The Handbook of Social
    Psychology* 4. Addison Wesley, Boston.
Pryor, M W, Flint, A W and Bass, B M (1962) Group effectiveness and consistency of
    leadership. *Sociometry,* 25, pp 391-397.
Rogers, M S, Ford, J D and Tassone, J A (1961) The effects of personnel replacement on an
    information processing crew. *Journal of Applied Psychology,* 45, pp 91-96.
Trow, D B (1960) Membership succession and team performance. *Human Relations,* 13,
    pp 259-269.

3.4 Training the Royal Air Force Training Designer

Squadron Leaders R K Littlejohn and B R Beaves
Royal Air Force School of Education and Training Support

Abstract: The RAF will have involved approximately 15,000 people and £250m in the achievement of its formal training commitment in 1982-83. Although the success of the Falkland campaign has highlighted the long-term benefits of effective training, such benefits are routinely difficult to quantify. Training investment has to be justified in a world of harsh realities. Moreover, rapid advances in technology not only demand frequent changes in trainable skills, but also result in competition between operational and training staffs for fixed procurement budgets. Consequently there is intense pressure for the timely and effective design of training. The corollary of this pressure is a demand for people skilled in advice and assistance to both the designers and the managers of RAF training.

In the early 1970s it was possible to meet this demand from spare capacity among education branch officers. However, natural wastage has eliminated most of the accrued experience in training design. Several major new equipment programmes coincided to overstretch the small pool of available expertise and persuade the RAF to divert resources to provide, urgently, training design advisers. The urgency and importance of the problem compelled a thorough analysis of the role of such advisers and the RAF Educational and Training Technology Development Unit was tasked accordingly. The design and implementation of the resultant course was undertaken by the Department of Training Design and Management of the RAF School of Education and Training Support.

The paper will describe the analysis and the resulting course designed to provide training in such 'soft' skills as cognitive awareness, problem analysis and social and organizational adroitness. It will show how experience quickly exposed weaknesses in the original design and how the design was enhanced for the second course which was completed in November 1982.

INTRODUCTION – THE PROBLEM

The Royal Air Force will have involved approximately 15,000 people and £250m in the achievement of its formal training commitment in 1982-83. The size and cost of this task reflect the fact that we conduct virtually all our training in-house, with little reliance on outside resources. The long-term benefits of our training are notoriously difficult to quantify. Nevertheless, we have to justify our investment in training in as harsh a financial climate as that prevailing in industry or the further education field. Rapid advances in technology not only demand a steady turnround in the skills for which we have to train, they also result in competition between operational and training staffs for those personnel who already possess the required skills.

For all these reasons there is intense pressure for timely and effective design of new training programmes. And following from this, there is a demand for people skilled in giving advice and assistance to both the designers and the managers of Royal Air Force training. In the early 1970s there was some spare capacity amongst education officers and we were able to train a number of them to meet the demand for training design advisers (TDAs). Since then, however, the experience which these officers gained has been lost to the Service by their diversification into wider responsibilities, by their promotion out of training design specialist work, and by natural wastage as they have left the Royal Air Force. Unfortunately too, we did not train replacements for them. The original training programme was a one-off response to a need which was met because the resources for doing so were available. After that we relied on a mixture of highly qualified officers who had been given university postgraduate courses to prepare them for more extensive training development work, and education officers with no special TDA training. At the beginning of the 1980s several major new equipment programmes coincided to over-stretch the small pool of expertise which remained. This persuaded the Royal Air Force to divert resources to provide, urgently, new TDAs. As a first step the Educational and Training Technology Development Unit (ETTDU) was tasked with carrying out a thorough analysis of the job which TDAs had performed on the projects to which they had been attached in the previous 10 years.

ANALYSIS STRATEGY

The first problem we faced was in identifying and tracing all those officers who, at some time or another, had served as TDAs. Surprisingly, there was no comprehensive list of those who were experienced, nor any readily available record of those who had been trained. However, the education specialization is comparatively small and has a well-developed informal information network. We were able to come up with 20 names from our own knowledge and these individuals in turn suggested others until, eventually, we consulted 43 current or past TDAs.

The long period of time we were covering also presented problems. The role of the TDA had apparently changed from the early 1970s when many had worked together in large teams. More recently they had been established as individuals working with small course design teams. Secondly, we had to ask some people to think back six to eight years when in the intervening time they had worked in completely different areas. In the event these problems appeared not to be serious. When we subsequently made a separate analysis of the responses from current TDAs, we found no significant differences from those of their earlier counterparts.

In conducting the job analysis we drew on all the resources available to us. The then OC ETTDU was himself an ex-TDA who had worked on two major course design projects. We therefore used his experience as a starting point and, conference style, drew up a provisional list of tasks which we believed were performed by a TDA. Within the School of Education there were other ex-TDAs and the list was refined by their comments. We then devised a document which we saw as lying between a questionnaire and an interview schedule.

Because there were comparatively few people to consult, and many of them were located together, we planned to visit them all. This also gave us a chance to see at first-hand some of the work that current TDAs were performing. This raised an interesting side issue. Data gathering by observation and interview appears to be more reliable than a questionnaire approach and, when the numbers to be surveyed make it practicable, the direct approach is preferred. There is the danger, however, that interviewees who have not been thoroughly prepared give 'top of their head' answers which may not be as full or as accurate as considered replies. To counter this, we used the interview to discuss the TDA's role generally and to talk through the document which we then left to be completed and sent on to us later. One result of this tactic was that we received only 33 responses from the 43 TDAs we consulted. It is debatable whether, on balance, we obtained a more complete pool of data than we would have by relying totally on interview. It might have been more effective for us to have sent the document in advance and collected it when we visited.

In the document, we presented the TDA with a list of 41 tasks (see Figure 1) and, for each, asked him to assess the frequency with which he performed it, its importance, and the difficulty it presented. There were different interpretations of

TASK PERFORMANCE INVENTORY

1. Obtain, analyse and review terms of reference.
2. Carry out job analysis.
3. Produce a performance inventory.
4. Design a project plan of action.
5. Assess time-scales for the project.
6. Identify sources of information.
7. Identify and ascertain resources for the team.
8. Advise tasking authority on plan, progress and results.
9. Design and use questionnaires.
10. Conduct interviews.
11. Liaise with other RAF departments.
12. Liaise with other Services departments.
13. Liaise with civilian manufacturers and specialists.
14. Monitor project progress.
15. Identify design problems.
16. Rectify design faults.
17. Define and write objectives.
18. Design tests.
19. Plan instructional strategies and methods.
20. Design validation (internal/external).
21. Produce an integrated training programme.
22. Identify relationships between ground, synthetic and flying training.
23. Prepare establishment bids.
24. Work with Command Headquarters Advisory Cells.
25. Give presentations.
26. Advise on and produce visual aids.
27. Obtain resources for task organization.
28. Organize documentation and printing.
29. Organize graphics and photography.
30. Carry out proofreading.
31. Write reports.
32. Work in aircrew or other specialist field.
33. Provide training advice to team.
34. Establish communications and reporting channels.
35. Relate training to environment.
36. Integrate extra-project activities.
37. Identify team and individual needs.
38. Advise on team accommodation.
39. Advise on training accommodation.
40. Analyse training programmes and statistics.
41. Brief visitors on project.

TRAINING DESIGN TASKS ADDED TO TDA LIST

1. Design training failure process.
2. Define attitude goals and write attitudinal objectives.
3. Liaise with instructional staff.
4. Monitor implementation of project.
5. Amend learning material after validation.
6. Apply project innovation strategies.
7. Review costs.
8. Obtain civilian recognition of training standard.
9. Edit training material.
10. Liaise with other TDAs.
11. Carry out network analysis.

Figure 1.

our categories to be ironed out. In addition, the frequency of some tasks was related to the stage of the project. Performing one frequently for a short period might be assessed as 'often' by one TDA and as 'sometimes' by another. This was never properly resolved and we subsequently treated assessments of frequency with some caution. The difficulty of a task decreased as the TDA gained expertise; in this case we asked for an assessment of the difficulty when the TDA first encountered the task.

TDAs were encouraged, if they wished, to add tasks and to expand on their responses. Altogether 55 additional tasks were listed but, after some discussion these were whittled down to 11 (listed in Figure 1); the others were repetitions or variations. Many of the comments made were peculiar to individual projects but others served to emphasize such things as the interrelationship of tasks or the importance of timing them.

RESULTS

Each task performed by a TDA involved a combination of problem analysis, social skills in establishing effective human interaction, and organizational skills in ensuring that the proposed solution and the client system were compatible. Performance of each task also depended on the TDA having the necessary supporting knowledge.

The ETTDU tasking did not require the design of TDA training. However, we believed that the job analysis could lead to a prescription of what was required. The TDAs' assessment of the frequency, importance and difficulty of each task allowed an initial consideration of where training might be relevant. Those which were unimportant and frequently performed did not justify training, nor did important but easy tasks frequently performed. For some other tasks, particularly where social skills were important, it appeared more appropriate to select a TDA who already had the necessary ability. The next stage was to determine which tasks were already covered by other Royal Air Force courses and which were best left to on-the-job training.

By then we felt that we were reaching the stage of an individual training specification. Potential TDAs should be aware of all the tasks identified, together with the assessments made by experienced advisers. Where training was judged to be appropriate, the TDAs could assess their own individual needs, and a suitable programme could be devised. At this point responsibility for the design and conduct of a TDA course passed to the Department of Training Design and Management (DTDM).

DESIGN FACTORS

There were several factors in the situation which were to persuade the DTDM, tasked with designing and conducting the training, to opt for an individual approach. In the first place higher management were referring to the training as a 'workshop' rather than a course, the implication being that it would not be a regular occurrence and that individual needs of the trainees would be paramount in the design strategy. Secondly, the eight projects for which the TDAs were to be trained differed significantly in many important aspects. Finally the analysis emphasized that the importance of the 'soft' skills of social and organizational adroitness in the TDA's role placed a high premium on the selection of the target population. In short, the training required was for selected people with well developed social and organizational skills inolved in widely differing projects — and it was training that was unlikely to be repeated on a regular basis.

The initial design planning suggested a common core of problem analysis skills consolidated by 'optional extras' selected by the trainees themselves from an inventory based on the analysis data. The framework was to be a four-week course which would include a field visit to a course design team and a seminar involving current and past practitioners in the dark arts of training design. To those who work within large organizations it will come as no surprise to learn that at the very moment when a coherent plan was developing, hidden factors emerged to cloud the issue.

The most important of these factors was the final selection of the eight trainees. The field of choice was restricted by background, experience, personal wishes and the problem of assembling eight people at one time from a group of people who tend to be posted every two-and-a-half years or so. Such a posting cycle with its inherent domino effect is a personnel manager's headache and this case was no exception. It was not surprising that the eight officers finally selected differed so widely in experience and background as to render the partially developed plan inoperable. Indeed, one of those selected had more relevant experience than two of the three DTDM directing staff.

At this stage, the original ambitious design was rapidly losing its attraction in the face of harsh reality. A further blow came in the form of an analysis of the training requirements submitted by training advisory staff at HQ Strike Command. As the majority of the TDAs to be trained were to work in Strike Command, there were compelling reasons for considering customer requirements. The emphasis of this analysis, which resulted from a technical conference of experienced trainers, was very much in favour of a standard package involving the theory and practice of course design and project management. Thus the customer and the designer held differing views, not so much on the basic product, but rather as to how it should be packaged. The inevitable compromise which was reached did not, as it transpired, produce the best solution.

FIRST COURSE

However, this is hindsight; at the time, ie during September 1981, the staff had a deadline to meet and an embarrassment of sometimes conflicting advice on how to proceed. Training objectives were set for the course and a four-week programme planned. The objectives covered three main areas. Firstly, the RAF's model for the design of training (Figure 2) formed the basis of the early part of the training. By a combination of instruction, discussion and syndicate exercises, the students would develop the necessary skills for analysis, statements of objectives, assessment, selection of training strategies and methods, course sequencing and validation. Secondly, by similar methods, the students would develop the necessary skills involved in the personnel and material resourcing of a training course with special emphasis on training aids, establishments and finance. Finally, and mainly through group discussion, the organizational and social skills associated with innovation and project management would provide students who had limited experience in this area with an opportunity to appreciate some of the appropriate methods of approach.

In order that the widely differing backgrounds of the eight students did not detract from the impact of the early part of the training, a reading list was sent for pre-course study. However, if such a device was to be successful, some encouragement was necessary to overcome human frailty. No such encouragement was given, the pre-course reading was not completed and the disparity of background remained a factor throughout.

The other significant item of preparation concerned the allocation of directing staff. The DTDM had prior commitments which would reduce the availability of directing staff during periods of the course. To overcome this problem and to provide the level of directing staff appropriate, staff were seconded from five other departments within the School of Education and Training Support and one outside

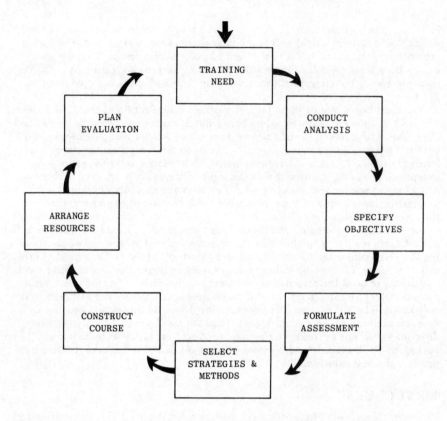

Figure 2. *Training design model*

agency. In addition, a financial limit was set for travel which allowed for two brief visits to course design teams operating in the field. Finally, five officers with recent experience of course design were gathered for a seminar aimed to acquaint the students with some of the practical problems associated with the task of a TDA.

Before assessing the course itself, it is of interest to mention briefly the projects to which the students were appointed. The projects included aircrew training for three new aircraft: the Tornado Air Defence Variant, the Nimrod Airborne Early Warning Aircraft and the VC10 Tanker. On the engineering side was the massive project for the re-equipment of the ground environment of the UK Air Defence System, and by way of contrast one student was to work on the design of training at the Joint Services ground defence centre. The mixture of flavours was compelling: aircrew training, engineering training and Joint Service ground defence training. It was compelling enough, as mentioned earlier, to suggest individual treatment, a suggestion which was the cause of disagreement before, during and after the course. If the staff were ambitious to attempt individual treatment, they were undoubtedly ill-advised to commit themselves to it publicly at the outset. When, inevitably perhaps, such individual attention proved beyond the capabilities of the directing staff, the frustration of expectations proved costly in terms of goodwill and valid feedback.

REVIEW OF COURSE

A comprehensive assessment of the success of the course is not possible, mainly because four of the students are still employed as TDAs on the projects to which they were appointed in November 1981. The success of the course can therefore only be measured in terms of how confidently the students took up their appointments and how their subsequent efforts, though not complete, benefited from the training.

Generally the students reported that they felt they had benefited from the course. During the end-of-course critique and through formal reports submitted by five of the students, there was a clear sense of satisfaction that they would be better able to meet their tasks as a result of the training. However, there were some significant comments made, particularly in the more considered written reports. The failure to meet the commitment to individual treatment was strongly criticized and much was made of the vastly different projects involved. Moreover, there were comments made about the number of staff involved in the course and about the absence of a coherent approach among the staff on some key points. Further criticism involved the slow pace of the course and the sequencing which tended to detract from its overall effectiveness. On the credit side, the staff noted with satisfaction the success of group interaction on the attitude of most of the students towards their new roles. In all but one case, the students developed a greater enthusiasm for their appointments as a result of the course.

Finally, and rather more disconcerting, was the opinion of one student that the model of training design which formed the basis of the course was flawed. It is not the aim of this article to justify the RAF's philosophy of training design; so it is enough to say that to the relief of most, but not to the surprise of the department, this minority view has proved to be just that — a minority view. Just as his experience has reinforced that individual's view, so observation of his working environment shows not only that it is an extraordinary one, but also that in fact the training design model is applicable to unusual as well as routine training design situations.

DESIGN MODIFICATIONS

To sum up the first course is to emphasize the thinking behind the re-design for the November 1982 course. The first course had achieved the objective of developing appropriate skills and attitudes in relation to the training design model, project management and the role of the TDA. However, it had not succeeded in developing individual students in matters directly related to their own projects, and the number of staff involved had occasionally led to dilution or even contradictory advice. Clearly the decision to attempt special-to-type training had been a mistake. Moreover, and at a higher level of management, a decision had to be taken about the future of the course itself. To mount a course at short notice had put pressure on the department, and the use of several non-specialist staff had been a necessary but unsuccessful response to that pressure.

It is fascinating to observe how, at this critical moment in the development of the course, the posting cycle already referred to turned inexorably to provide a change of key characters so complete as to amount almost to a 'clean slate'. The change of staff in the department made it more likely that a standard course approach would be favoured and that there would be no problem with the U-turn in policy. Changes in higher management delayed the decision on the future of the course until it could not prevent over-loading the department once more. Two months before the course actually started there was no clear decision to proceed because appointments of TDAs to several projects had not been confirmed. When the decision to go ahead was reached, the time-scale suggested that a repetition of the first course, 'warts and all', would be pragmatic. The projects concerned were equally diverse, although the previous training design experience of the students was uniformly small. However, the temptation to repeat the first course was firmly resisted by the department, although higher management were reluctant to allocate time for a complete re-design.

The November 1982 course was a comprehensive re-design, based on two major assumptions. Firstly it was assumed that there would be a regular requirement to train officers appointed as TDAs to major training design projects. Secondly, it seemed a natural corollary of this that a standard and general approach to the training would be necessary. One major constraint was to affect the re-design of the course: during the third of the four weeks allocated for the course, the department had a long-standing commitment to run a three-day course. It appeared to present a good opportunity for the TDA students to go out on a field visit — and so it proved.

Using this constraint as a positive rather than a negative design factor, the course profile (Figure 3) involved two weeks of thorough exposure to all the elements of the course design model and project management in preparation for a field visit in small groups to a number of selected training design projects. Each group would visit only one project and would deliver a detailed report to the rest of the course at the end of the third week. The final week would be concerned mainly with the provision of resources, especially finance, establishments and training aids.

COURSE PROFILE		
Weeks 1 & 2	Week 3	Week 4
Course design skills Project man't	Field visit	Resources

Figure 3. *Course profile*

The central theme of the course — the role of the TDA — would be developed by examination of the constituent skills of training design, observation of TDAs in the field, discussion of some of the strategies appropriate to various circumstances and would be consolidated during a seminar with selected TDAs from the field.

During the first course, the syndicate practical exercise had proved most effective in developing skills and attitudes. Consequently two types of exercise were developed, one involving practice of the elements of the training design model and the other requiring a response in the form of advice on design problems. The basis for this approach is a feeling that although chicken farmers do not need to be able to lay eggs themselves, they might be more effective if they had some experience of the pain involved. It is worth exemplifying the two types of exercise. To develop some level of skill in analysis, syndicates were shown a video film of a tradesman performing one of his standard tasks and were asked to produce a task analysis suitable for the derivation of training objectives. The film included an interview with the tradesman in which difficult areas were explained. The second type of exercise, requiring advice rather than hands-on skill, presented syndicates with a scenario involving the personnel and circumstances of a major training design project. Enough details were given to enable syndicates to present their solution in the form of advice on how to proceed with the analysis of the training requirement.

When the six officers who were to join the course were nominated it was clear that, as with the previous course, some background reading would be essential. Rather than issue a pre-course reading list, a device which had failed before, the first one-and-a-half days were allocated to a syndicate exercise which could only be completed by covering most of the material on the reading list, discussing it and arguing a case against the other syndicate under the critical control of the staff. The other major change was that directing staff would be exclusively from the one department except for a few sessions where common sense dictated the use of visiting speakers. Circumstances were more favourable in November 1982 than they had been in October 1981, and the benefits of this approach were felt by students and staff alike.

REVIEW OF MODIFIED COURSE

The course proceeded very much as planned, although minor adjustments were being made to sequencing and content throughout the four weeks. Again, it is difficult to measure the success of the re-design because the projects involving the students are far from completion. However, the initial responses have been very encouraging. As far as the students are concerned, they reported that they felt their own attitude changing as a result of the course. From being universally apprehensive about the nature of TDA work, and not a little sceptical about the chances of success, they developed a confidence and enthusiasm for the role. It is interesting to note the factors they cited as responsible for achieving this. The syndicate task which replaced the pre-reading list clearly achieved the vital aim of ensuring that all students had enough background to receive benefit from the first two weeks of fairly intensive training. The second factor was the profile which gave them two weeks to examine the skills involved in the job before visiting practising TDAs in the field. They not only found it effective to look at one project in depth, but benefited from the detailed reports of the other two groups. Moreover, they were emphatic that without the two weeks' preparation they would not have gained much from the visit — which also came at a psychologically apt stage of the course when a change of scene and pace was beneficial. Finally, they were convinced that the high correlation between the theory imparted in the classroom and the practice of training designers in the field was instrumental in confirming the credibility of the staff and enhancing the effect of the course overall. Thus the profile which had developed out of the pressure of prior commitments on the third of the four weeks proved to be a major factor in the success of the course.

CONCLUSION

The 18 months which cover this part of the story of training the RAF training designers have seen both new lessons learned and old ones reinforced. It is not unlike war itself which tends to be as unforgiving on those who ignore old lessons as it is on those who fail to embrace new developments. While our training designers are not exactly front-line combatant troops, they are directly affecting the performance of those who are, so there is every expectation that those selected for that role should be as professional as those who depend upon effective training for survival and success. We now have a training course which, in conjunction with special courses for the managers of training, contributes significantly to the effectiveness of training in the RAF.

3.5 Dimensions of Leadership

Jeanne Hebein

Human Resources Research Organization, Heidelberg, West Germany

Abstract: The purpose of the present study was to develop a comprehensive, descriptive model of generic skill requirements across four leadership positions within the non-commissioned officer corps of the US Army. In carrying out this project all of the non-technical tasks actually performed by job incumbents in the four leadership positions were identified, followed by a determination of the frequency, importance, difficulty, and criticality of each of the identified tasks.

These data then served as the basis for derivation of job dimensions (task categories) common to the leadership positions and a comparison of the importance, difficulty and frequency of performance of the dimensions for each duty position. These empirically derived job dimensions provided the structure and direction for in-depth performance interviews with job incumbents. Incidents of effective prototypical leadership performance within the limits of the identified job dimensions were discussed by the interviewees. Analysis of the interviews resulted in a list of the competencies and skills required for effective performance of an NCO in the specified duty position.

INTRODUCTION

In order to develop a means for describing similarities and differences in leader behaviours, roles and functions, fundamental common and unique dimensions need to be identified in a way that allows for their application to a wide range of leadership and supervisory situations. By determining the dimensions of leadership and by identifying the related tasks and skills required for leader performance, it is then possible to measure effective and ineffective leader performance for a given situation or organization.

A key step in identifying leadership dimensions and requirements is an analysis of the non-technical supervisory (leader) tasks performed by personnel in leadership positions. Based on this analysis, the skills and competencies required in carrying out these leader tasks can then be identified.

Various approaches have been utilized in an attempt to develop inventories of leader tasks and to determine what skills are required for task performance. The most common among these are:

1. The *ad hoc* or consensus approach (Clement and Ayres, 1976).
2. Job or task analysis of leadership situations (Powers *et al*, 1974).
3. Factor analysis of leadership tasks (Helme *et al*, 1974; Dowell and Wexley, 1978).
4. Identification of generic skills or competencies (Peterson and Rumsey, 1981; Klemp *et al*, 1977).

An assessment of the value and application of each of these approaches is contained in Hebein, 1982. The approach used in the present study included:

☐ An analysis of the tasks performed by NCOs in four duty positions.
☐ The classification of those tasks into job dimensions.
☐ The identification of the generic skills and competencies required for effective leader performance in the four duty positions.

METHOD

Two phases of data collection were carried out during the project. The objectives of the data collection efforts for Phase I were:

1. To identify the most important non-technical tasks performed by NCOs in the positions of first sergeant, platoon sergeant, section chief and squad leader.
2. To determine the frequency, importance and difficulty of performing each of these tasks.
3. To organize the tasks into job dimensions.
4. To compare the responses of NCOs in different duty positions and different MOS (military occupational speciality) types on the frequency, importance and difficulty of performing the tasks by job dimension.

For Phase II the objectives of the data collection were:

1. To identify the competencies and skills required in leader task performance.
2. To determine the differences and commonalities in competency/skill requirements among positions within a specified set of leader functions.

The specific methods used in conducting the study are described in Hebein (1983).

RESULTS AND DISCUSSION

The results and discussion of the data analyses for the NCO Leader Skills project are presented in the following sequence. First the results of the NCO leader task survey administered in Phase I of the project will be presented. These are based on mean ratings of importance, frequency and difficulty for the most important (upper quartile) non-MOS specific tasks within each job dimension for each duty position. Second, the results are presented of an analysis of variance to determine whether differences exist in the ratings by duty position of the importance, frequency of performance and difficulty of each job dimension. Reporting of the analysis of the competency and skill requirement interviews from Phase II completes the results section. The information presented includes a comparison across duty positions of the number of NCOs reporting these competencies and skills.

NCO LEADER TASK SURVEY

The complete set of leader tasks on which data was collected included 938 tasks. In order to reduce this number to a meaningful sub-set, two criteria were applied. Those tasks selected for analysis were (a) in the upper quartile of importance for all tasks and (b) performed by at least 50 per cent of the respondents within each duty position.

Altogether, 130 important tasks for all four duty positions were identified. Of these 130 tasks, 11 were common to all four positions. These 11 common tasks included:

Garrison tasks
1.   70 — Enforce standards of discipline, courtesy and dress.
2.   71 — Monitor soldiers health and welfare.
3.   73 — Brief new personnel on unit mission and policies.

Health and welfare tasks
4. 114 — Counsel personnel on disciplinary problems.
5. 118 — Counsel personnel on job performance.

Training tasks
6. 182 — Supervise individual training.
7. 184 — Plan individual training.

Maintenance tasks
8. 195 — Spot-check vehicles for preventive maintenance.
9. 199 — Review equipment readiness status.

Security tasks
10. 210 — Supervise key control

ARTEP tasks
11. 255 — Organize for combat operations.

In addition, 16 tasks were among the most important tasks for three of the positions. These tasks included:

General unit administration tasks
1.   16 — Prepare/maintain unit alert roster (first sergeant, platoon sergeant, section chief).

Supply tasks
2.   63 — Control equipment usage (platoon sergeant, section chief, squad leader).
3.   67 — Inspect basic loads (platoon sergeant, section chief, squad leader).

Tactical/combat tasks
4.   95 — Supervise area security (platoon sergeant, section chief, squad leader).
5.   96 — Implement tactical cover/deception (platoon sergeant, section chief, squad leader).
6. 106 — Supervise NBC protective measures (platoon sergeant, section chief, squad leader).

Garrison tasks
7. 111 — Supervise personal hygiene (platoon sergeant, section chief, squad leader).

Health and welfare tasks
8. 115 — Counsel personnel with personal problems (first sergeant, platoon sergeant, squad leader).
9. 147 — Apply motivational techniques (first sergeant, platoon sergeant, squad leader).

Group management task
10. 116 — Recommend personnel for promotion/reduction (first sergeant, section chief, squad leader).

Training tasks
11. 163 — Identify and enforce training safety (platoon sergeant, section chief, squad leader).
12. 170 — Organize/monitor unit SQT program (first sergeant, section chief, squad leader).

Maintenance tasks
13. 208 — Establish maintenance priorities (platoon sergeant, section chief, squad leader).

Security tasks
14. 209 — Report security violations (first sergeant, platoon sergeant, squad leader).

15. 214 — Conduct physical security inspection (platoon sergeant, section chief, squad leader).

ARTEP tasks
16. 259 — Develop perimeter defense (first sergeant, platoon sergeant, squad leader).

The level of importance and the commonality in rank for these 27 common tasks would indicate that they represent basic common functions of non-commissioned officers in performing leadership duties.

Another commonality among positions is the importance of the training job dimension. Training contained more important tasks for all four duty positions than any other dimension. First sergeants ranked 13 training tasks in the upper quartile on importance, platoon sergeants ranked 14 training tasks as important, section chiefs ranked 10 training tasks as important, and squad leaders ranked 11 training tasks in the upper quartile. This would support the concept that training is one of the most important functions of NCOs no matter what position they hold.

COMPARATIVE ANALYSIS OF JOB DIMENSIONS

The 130 tasks rated in the upper quartile on importance were divided into the 11 job dimensions presented in Table 1.

General unit administration
Administration of personnel
Supply
General military — garrison
General military — tactical/combat
Health and welfare
Group management
Training
Maintenance
Security
ARTEP

Table 1. *Job dimensions for leader tasks*

For each set of tasks within each job dimension for each duty position a grand mean was computed. This was done by summing the mean scores for each task and dividing by the number of tasks in the dimension.

These grand mean scores of importance, frequency and difficulty for each of the NCO leader task job dimensions were analysed using a 3 (military occupational speciality — MOS) x 4 (duty position) analysis of variance. Simple effects analysis examined the differences between duty positions using the Student Newman-Keuls test with the *alpha* set at $p < .05$.

The results of the comparative analysis of job dimensions identified those areas of greater importance, frequency of performance and difficulty for each duty position.

First Sergeants

The following job dimensions were of greater importance for first sergeants than for other NCOs:

☐ General unit administration.
☐ Administration of personnel.
☐ Garrison.

☐ Health and welfare.
☐ Group management.
☐ Training.
☐ Security.

First sergeants rated four of the important tasks as more frequently performed than did other NCOs. These were:

☐ General unit administration.
☐ Administration of personnel.
☐ Health and welfare.
☐ Training.

Also, ARTEP although not more important to first sergeants was more frequently performed by them than by other NCOs.

Nine of the 11 job dimensions were rated as more difficult for incumbent first sergeants than for other NCOs and eight task dimensions were rated as more difficult for new NCOs. Areas of difficulty for both included:

☐ General unit administration.
☐ Administration of personnel.
☐ Garrison.
☐ Health and welfare.
☐ Group management.
☐ Security.
☐ Training.
☐ ARTEP.

Tactical/combat tasks were rated as more difficult for incumbent first sergeants but not for new first sergeants as compared to other NCOs.

Platoon Sergeants

There were five job dimensions rated as significantly more important to platoon sergeants. These were:

☐ Supply.
☐ Tactical/combat.
☐ Training.
☐ Maintenance.
☐ ARTEP.

Platoon sergeants rated none of these areas as significantly more frequently performed than other NCOs. The one area that was more frequently performed was health and welfare.

Four of the five more important areas were considered to present greater difficulty for both incumbent and new platoon sergeants. These were:

☐ Supply.
☐ Training.
☐ Maintenance.
☐ ARTEP.

Section Chiefs

The only area which was rated as significantly more important to section chiefs as compared to other NCOs was supply. This area was also considered to be more difficult for incumbent section chiefs as compared to other NCOs. With regard to frequency of performance, only tactical/combat was more frequently performed by section chiefs as compared to other NCOs.

Squad Leaders

There were no job dimensions which were comparatively more important, difficult or frequently performed by squad leaders.

LEADER COMPETENCY/SKILLS INTERVIEWS

Table 2 contains a list of the leadership functions and related skills/competencies reported by NCOs during the interviews. When a skill was reported by an NCO during the discussion of specific incidents related to his/her leadership duties, that skill was scored as 'present' in that interview. If a skill was not reported during an interview, it was scored as 'absent' in the interview.

Supervising	**Organizing and Controlling Resources**
Directing	Inspecting
Assigning duties and tasks'	Monitoring
Delegating	Evaluating results
Informing subordinates	Organizing
Explaining/advising	Co-ordinating activities
Evaluating performance	Co-ordinating requirements/resources
Coercing	Implementing orders
Exhorting	Implementing procedures
Rewarding	Informing superiors
Punishing	Reporting and corresponding
Reprimanding	
Representing the group	**Individual Development**
	Instructing
Planning	Coaching
Establishing procedures	Setting individual performance standards
Scheduling	Giving feedback
Programming	Performance counselling
Allocating resources	Personal counselling
Setting unit goals	
Acquiring information	**Interpersonal Relations**
	Negotiating
Group Development	Use of informal networks
Team building	Establishing rapport with personnel
Resolving conflicts	Resolving conflicts
Setting group performance standards	
Critiquing performance	
Personal Ethics/Attitudes	
Achievement emphasis	
Concern for welfare of personnel	
Setting the example	
Professionalism	
Initiative	
Adaptability	

Table 2. *Leadership functions and related skills/competencies*

In order to determine whether there were differences in skill utilization as a result of duty position the data were analysed using analysis of variance substituting proportions for mean scores (see Kuechler, 1980). Thus the presence of a skill in the interview was scored as '1' while absence of the skill was scored as '0'. The sum of these '0's and '1's for each skill within a duty position or MOS type was the basis for a 4 (duty position) x 2 (MOS type) analysis of variance. Simple effects analysis examined the main effects means using the Scheffe test with the *alpha* set at $p < .05$.

Over all duty positions, the leadership functions reported by the greatest number of NCOs were supervising, organizing and controlling resources, individual development, and planning. Group development, interpersonal relations, and personal ethics/attitudes were reported by fewer NCOs.

The skills reported by a greater number of interviewees across duty positions included:

☐ *Supervising skills*
   Assigning duties and tasks
   Informing superiors
   Implementing procedures.

☐ *Planning*
   Acquiring information.

☐ *Group development*
   Setting group performance standards.

☐ *Individual development*
   Instructing.

Several skills were reported by only a small percentage of NCOs across duty positions. These included coercing, establishing procedures, resolving conflicts — superiors/peers. The remainder of the skills in the competency categories were in a mid-range on percentage of NCOs reporting that skill.

The results of the analysis of variance indicated that certain skills/competencies were more often utilized by NCOs in certain duty positions.

First Sergeants

Skills which were found to be of particular relevance to first sergeants were: directing, and establishing procedures.

Platoon Sergeants

There were no leadership skills found to be more frequently reported by platoon sergeants than other NCOs.

Section Chiefs

Skills which were more frequently utilized by section chiefs in comparison to other NCOs included critiquing performance (shared with squad leaders) and directing (shared with first sergeants).

Squad Leaders

Several skills were reported more frequently by squad leaders than by other NCOs. These included giving feedback, performance counselling and critiquing performance (shared with section chiefs).

CONCLUSIONS

The present study sought to determine the specific leader tasks performed by NCOs in four duty positions and to sort these tasks into functional job dimensions. The differences in the frequency, importance and difficulty of performing the tasks within each job dimension were identified. Finally, the competencies and skills required to perform a full range of NCO leadership functions were identified and the commonalities and differences among positions in the utilization of these skills were examined.

Of the 130 tasks ranked in the upper quartile for the four positions, only 11 were common to all, although many more were common to two or three positions. Thus there were variations between positions in the tasks which were ranked as most important for that duty position; in the frequency with which the important tasks were performed; and in the ratings of difficulty of a task by personnel in each duty position. Patterns emerged which indicated that:

1. Tasks rated as 'highly important' were also considered more difficult both for incumbents and new NCOs.
2. Tasks performed infrequently were considered more difficult.
3. Importance was not necessarily related to frequency of performance.

The results of the comparative analysis of job dimensions indicated that there were significant differences between positions on the importance, frequency of performance and difficulty of the dimensions. The more important dimensions for a position were representative of the major functions of that position, and indicated whether a position was more managerial, administrative or technical in nature. Fewer differences were found in the skill/competency requirements for the leadership functions. However, the differences that were found were related to the nature of the position, with specific skills indicating administrative and managerial functions.

REFERENCES

Clement, S D and Ayers, D B (1976) *A Matrix of Organizational Leadership Dimensions* (Leadership Monograph Series, Monograph 8). US Army Administration Center, Ft Monroe, VA.

Dowell, B E and Wexley, K N (1978) Development of a work behavior taxonomy for first-line supervisors. *Journal of Applied Psychology* 63, pp 563-572.

Hebein, J M (1982) *Leadership Skills: A Methodological Perspective* (HumRRO Interim Report). Human Resources Research Organization, Alexandria, VA.

Hebein, J M (1983) A methodology for identification of generic leadership skills. In Trott, A (ed) *Aspects of Educational Technology* XVI. Kogan Page, London.

Helme, W H, Willemin, L P and Grafton, F C (1974) *Prediction of Officer Behavior in a Simulated Combat Situation* (Research Report 1182). US Army Research Institute for the Behavioral and Social Sciences, Arlington, VA. (DTIC No. AD-779-445).

Klemp, G O, Munger, M T and Spencer, L M, Sr (1977) *Analysis of Leadership and Management Competencies of Commissioned and Noncommissioned Naval Officers in the Pacific and Atlantic Fleets* (TPD EG-33). McBer and Company, Boston, MA.

Kuechler, M (1978) How to use the SPSS regression procedure in multivariate analysis of dichotomous data. Paper presented at second annual ISSUE conference, Chicago, Illinois.

Peterson, G W and Rumsey, M G (1981) A methodology for measuring officer job competence. Paper presented at the annual meeting of the American Psychological Association, Division 19, Los Angeles.

Powers, T R, Caviness, J A, Jacobs, T O and Maxey, J (1974) *The US Coast Guard Academy Curricula: An Evaluation* (HumRRO Tech Rep 74-2). Human Resources Research Organization, Alexandria, VA.

ACKNOWLEDGEMENTS

The work reported here was performed at the Heidelberg Office of the Human Resources Research Organization (HumRRO), under contract with the US Army Research Institute for the Behavioral and Social Sciences (ARI). The research was conducted with the assistance of Dr Richard Miller, Dr Joseph Olmstead, Dr Batia Sharon and Mr Al Kaplan.

Section 4:
Career Updating for Educationalists

4.1 Retraining Teachers for the Microcomputer Age

Dr G Mills
University of Bradford

Abstract: The recent government initiatives in promoting the introduction of at least one microcomputer in most of the UK schools have led to an enormous increase in interest in any course which deals with computers in education. Local authorities and the Microelectronics in Education Programme (MEP) have found it very difficult to cope. In any case, the four-day courses which they provide only go part of the way towards satisfying demand. Some existing courses tend to be orientated towards the use of main-frame computers and may neglect the potential offered by the facilities of the new generation of relatively cheap microcomputers, particularly graphics and sound.

This paper describes a collaborative venture sponsored by Bradford and Leeds universities to provide an evening course in which the theoretical basis of educational technology is combined with the practice of microcomputing. Participants were expected to have either some preliminary facility with the computer language BASIC or prepared to attend for an additional three evenings during the first four weeks of the course. Half the time was taken in formal lecture/demonstrations while the remainder was spent obtaining hands-on experience in the Bradford University MicroComputer Applications Laboratory. The latter was used by the participants according to interest in either analysing/evaluating existing educational programs, writing/modifying programs or exploring the potential for teaching purposes of data-bases or languages such as LOGO and PILOT.

One interesting finding was that even amongst a group with sufficient motivation to enrol for an evening course, the proportion of teachers who were prepared to write BASIC coding for programs was relatively small. The main demand was for guidance in how to use a microcomputer effectively in class, particularly if the number of microcomputers available in school is very small. The techniques for dealing with teachers of a wide range of curriculum interest and involved with children of ages from five to 18 are described in detail.

HISTORICAL BACKGROUND

During the 1970s, a large number of secondary schools in the UK became linked to a main-frame computer. The number of terminals per school was usually small (often only one). Such terminals were mainly used for the teaching of computer science — rarely for other educational purposes. Some institutions, notably Leeds University Computer-based Learning Unit, did develop interactive learning packages on an experimental basis but they were not widely used. At the end of the 1970s, many schools began acquiring microcomputers to supplement such main-frames in the teaching of computing. The above initiatives were generally funded by the local education authorities.

Since 1981, direct UK government encouragement for the use of microcomputers in education has been sponsored by both the Department of Industry (DOI) and the Department of Education and Science (DES). The DOI has subsidized the purchase of microcomputer equipment up to 50 per cent of the cost for one system in every UK school, subject to the certain limitations. These include:

1. The microcomputer system must be on an approved list of UK manufacturers (the majority take-up to date has been for the BBC micro).

2. A minimum training in computer 'literacy' must be undertaken by at least two teachers in each school taking advantage of the half-price offer.

To complement the above hardware scheme, the DES set up in 1981 the Microelectronics in Education Programme (MEP). This was intended primarily as a software support and training programme. Indeed, it was stated categorically that it was not intended for the provision of microcomputer hardware in schools. One of the main results of the MEP has been the setting up of a network of Regional Information Centres. These centres have become heavily involved in the provision of four-day computer literacy courses to meet the requirements of the DOI scheme. Before these government initiatives were taken, a number of local authorities had set up organizations to encourage the use of microcomputers in education. Many of these originally standardized on a particular microcomputer system. These include Bradford (Commodore Pet), Hatfield (RML380Z), and Walsall (Tandy TRS80). At Bradford, the organization was originally based in the local authority computer division. At Hatfield and Walsall, they were based in teachers' centres. At Walsall, introductory courses for teachers were initiated in 1980.

TRAINING CONSTRAINTS

Due to mainly financial constraints which makes it currently very difficult for UK schools to appoint part-time temporary staff to cover for teachers undertaking part-time day-course training, three main course patterns have emerged. These are:

1. Short period — up to four days full-time.
2. From several to 20-plus weeks of one evening per week.
3. Full-time study for a whole academic session on a recognized course.

Regional Information Centres and local authorities have made herioc efforts in the past 12 months to meet the DOI requirements for short-period induction courses. Since the DOI scheme was extended to primary and junior schools (thereby more than trebling the number of potential schools!), their resources have been even more under strain. Most evening courses are sponsored by adult education institutions. These may be local authority based (colleges and polytechnics) or attached to a university. The normal pattern involves a set number of weeks, appointment of teaching staff specifically for that course and the payment of fees by the participants. Teachers on approved in-service evening courses may have their fees reimbursed in whole or part. Obtaining sufficient staff suitably experienced in microcomputer-based education to run such courses may be a problem in many areas. For teachers, their problem with evening courses is that out-of-school activities such as parents' evenings may restrict their attendance.

The 12-month full-time courses are available mainly because of governmental contributions of up to 75 per cent of the teacher's salary for the period of secondment which allows the local education authority to meet most of the expenses of a temporary appointment. In most cases, any microcomputer training will only form part of a diploma or master's programme. However, some teachers may be allowed to spend a substantial proportion of their time on computer-based educational project work (eg Manning, 1982).

Whichever type of course is adopted, one of the most important facilities which must be available is the provision of substantial hands-on experience on microcomputers. The ideal is one microcomputer to each participant. Where the ratio is more than two participants to each micro during the practical sessions, all my experienced colleagues find it unsatisfactory. In addition, many teachers are relectant to operate (except, perhaps, during an induction period) with a micro on a course which is different to the type which they have or expect to have access to at their school!

WHAT SHOULD BE TAUGHT?

Due to the unfamiliarity of most teachers with microcomputers, most courses start with the assumption of no prior knowledge either of micros or computer programming. In general, the following areas are covered:

1. Microcomputer hardware management — how to connect-up? How to use the operating system (eg load and save programs)? What to do if anything does not work? What support services are available?
2. An introduction to programming in BASIC plus demonstrations of advanced facilities such as high-resolution graphics and control facilities.
3. An examination of specific computer instructional and utility programs, including suggestions for using them in the actual classroom.

Additional topics which may be included are:

4. The social implications of microprocessor-based technology.
5. A comparative study of different computer languages for writing programs such as PASCAL, PILOT and LOGO.
6. Methods for authoring programs and practice in operating authoring languages.
7. Classification of programs including relating the type of teaching mode to the educational needs.
8. Methodical approaches to the evaluation of programs on presentation, technical correctness and educational content.

The four-day induction courses for teachers are based on areas 1, 2 and 3 above, with perhaps two to three hours out of 30 based on topic 4. At the other extreme, a course organized by the author on computers in education within a computing MSc/diploma programme concentrated almost entirely on topics 5, 6, 7 and 8. This proved feasible because all the postgraduate students so far have had experience in BASIC prior to attending their course in which the preferred computer language was PASCAL.

EVENING COURSE INITIATION AND ORGANIZATION

The University of Leeds Adult Education Centre had been involved in sponsoring courses in 'new technology' (ie microcomputers and their social impact) in Bradford from 1979, and wished to expand in this area. It became clear in early 1982 that there would be an enormous demand by teachers for courses on the use of microcomputers for educational purposes due to the DOI scheme. It was therefore agreed to initiate a new Bradford course starting in September 1982. This course would conform to their standard pattern of two hours each evening for two terms (12 weeks each) and would be run as a one-hour formal presentation plus one-hour practical. Bradford and Ilkley Community College had run a similar course in 1981-82 (which had been fully subscribed) under the direction of Frank Marrow and Joe Waters. It was known that they had encountered problems due to the wide range of interests from primary to A-level teaching. In fact, the College decided for 1982-83 to run two separate courses, restricting entry to those teaching in age ranges 4-11 and 11-plus respectively.

However, the philosophy of the Adult Education Centre was to mount courses for the general public. For the new course, they wished to maintain this tradition by allowing anyone to enrol who was genuinely interested in the subject of microcomputers in education. In addition, they were reluctant to refuse enrolments and would normally try to arrange an additional class if numbers were large. When the enrolments had exceeded 30 by seven days before the start, some last-minute organizational decisions were required.

One of the main factors affecting the organization was the availability of microcomputers. The practicals were based on the University of Bradford MicroComputer Applications Laboratory (MCAL) which then had some 15 various micros. Rather than split the course into two separate evenings, which would have posed problems in staffing, it was decided to operate with two one-hour practicals in the same evening separated by a formal one-hour class. The first activity on the first evening was to ask each participant to nominate either the early or late practical. Fortunately, they divided into roughly equal numbers! The final enrolment total was 43 (of whom eight were non-teachers), although the maximum number attending any one evening was 39. During the practical sessions, there were always a substantial proportion who were happy to 'share' a micro. Theoretically, there were enough micros to go round but, later in the course, a number of teachers were often not interested in working with an unfamiliar type of micro. At the start of the course, MCAL possessed only one BBC micro. This was later increased to three but all were in constant demand.

The other main organizational problem was how to cope with those teachers who enrolled for the course with no experience of a programming language. The enrolment leaflet stated that teachers with no experience would be required to attend additional sessions to achieve a certain minimum knowledge of BASIC — similar to what they would have been given on the four-day induction course. This was arranged by timetabling two-hour early evening periods on another night for weeks 2 to 4 inclusive. Over 50 per cent took advantage of this facility. It may be noted that at the start of the course, over half the teachers had no micro at school but nearly all had acquired one by the end of the course.

COURSE PHILOSOPHY — AIMS AND ACHIEVEMENT

The broad aim of the formal classes was to set the applications of microcomputers in education within a theoretical framework of educational technology. In early summer 1982, a provisional syllabus was prepared in which the course content was divided into 12 modules. Headings included the art of presentation, writing for different ability groups, analysis of educational objectives, structuring educational programs, utility modules, tutorial learning, simulation, games and case-studies, problem-solving modules, data-handling, etc. One deliberate omission was the use of microcomputers for control purposes (in the event, only two people expressed an interest in this area). Even so, by September, the author was already having second thoughts about whether all this could be sensibly covered, and he decided to issue a modified, less detailed syllabus to those enrolling.

During the course, it became clear that less than half the participants were intending to get involved with writing or modifying program coding. Therefore, those sections which had originally been scheduled for demonstrating coding, such as techniques for user-proofing, providing for varied responses, randomization in game activities, etc, were reduced considerably in scope and time-involvement. Unexpectedly, one area of wide interest was the use of data-bases. This was originally intended to be dealt with in one week but was extended to two weeks by popular demand. The more important themes of the course are summarized below:

1. A microcomputer differs from other teaching aids, in particular because of its interactive features. They particularly lend themselves to the incorporation of game situations to stimulate and provide more effective learning. The latter may eventually lead to significant changes in educational practice (Mills and Stonier, 1982).
2. The evaluation of educational computer programs must be on three levels:
   □ Mode and standard of presentation suitable for target population.

     ☐ Technical adequacy, eg user-proofed and fully debugged, and pedagogical
      soundness and significance.
3. There are four main types of computer program, and the choice of which
   type depends largely on the specific teaching requirement. The types are:
   ☐ Instructional — including drill and practice, programmed learning.
   ☐ Revelatory — simulations and case-studies.
   ☐ Exploratory — graphics and music aids, and programming (BASIC/LOGO).
   ☐ Utility — eg STATS packages, word-processing, data-base management.

ORGANIZATION OF PRACTICAL SESSIONS

For a course of this nature, the two prerequisites are hardware (micros), arranged in
such a way to encourage user interactions, and an adequate supply of educational
software. After a number of trials, the former was achieved by arranging the room
(10m x 10m in plan) so that the work stations formed an H shape. The software
was acquired from many sources. Some was 'public domain' (Commodore Pet),
some home-produced, some purchased, and some was obtained through US
connections. In addition, an adequate staffing level should be maintained. One
supervisor per 8-10 students is barely adequate (two staff per one-hour practical).

    The original aim for the practicals was to encourage teachers to work together in
groups in which at least one member would be technically capable of either writing
an original program or modifying an existing one, with the other members of the
group providing comments and assessment. In practice, the diversity of interest
coupled with the shortage of BBC micros inhibited this aim for the majority of the
class who tended to treat the sessions simply as an opportunity to view potentially
useful software. Conversely, in the second term several individuals became so
immersed in the computer project work that they frequently stayed in MCAL
instead of attending the formal one-hour sessions.

    To set the scene for project work, two practical evaluations were organized. The
first was to evaluate at least six (from a total of 14) allegedly educational programs
on eight presentation criteria. These were summarized as ease of understanding
instructions, relevance of the given information, conciseness of the introduction,
consistency of required user response, coping with mis-typing, aesthetic visuals, use
of non-essential material, and availability of information on the content/age range
of the target population. The second formal evaluation involved viewing a selection
from 10 different programs which made significant use of graphics with a view to
promoting discussion on questions such as: How necessary is graphics? Could it be
improved to enhance the teaching?

    During week 5, participants were asked to fill in a questionnaire on their
individual interests to assist in organizing the formation of groups for project work.
A summary of this information was fed back to the participants during week 7 to
help people to make contact and discuss a potential topic. During the less formal
practical weeks, a new selection of software was made available. For example, the
theme was instructional programs for week 7. From week 8 onwards, program
request forms were made available so that the organizers could hopefully obtain a
program on the requested topic for the following week. However, this facility was
little used. Among the projects which did reach a satisfactory conclusion were
the following:

1. A data-base program specifically of value in education, originally written for
   the Commodore Pet and designed so that it could readily be transferred to
   the BBC micro.
2. Collaboration between an undergraduate student and a teacher in introducing
   LOGO by borrowing a micro for one day per week.
3. Primary school teachers evaluating a counting and adding program written by

a final year undergraduate as part of her project, including classroom testing.

Apart from the above, significant collaborative work did not materialize although nearly 10 other participants are known to have written their own programs for use in their classrooms.

COURSE EVALUATION AND CONCLUSIONS

Apart from a general discussion amongst those attending the final week, no formal attempt was made to evaluate the course. The attendance followed a pattern similar to many adult education courses — over 75 per cent during the first term dropping to just over 50 per cent at the start of the second term and declining gradually thereafter. This was not so disappointing as it seems at first sight as several of those who continued on the course remarked of colleagues who did not that they 'had got what they wanted from the course'.

During the final week discussion, the following points were made:

1. Most teachers would emphasize the importance of facilities for identifying good software. Two specific suggestions for a future course were that teachers be allowed to borrow programs for a week and that the course organizers try to arrange a software fair.
2. There was some support for sectionalizing the materials. Three specific areas could be introductory (including acquiring simple programming skills), 'lower school' education, and 'upper school' education.
3. Teachers would generally prefer a definite published timetable of topics to be covered each week so that they could pick and choose if necessary. If necessary, specialist topics could be dealt with by using more guest speakers.
4. If possible, videotapes of some of the more important *Horizon* programmes on say, turtlegraphics, artificial intelligence, should be shown and their educational implications discussed.

REFERENCES

Manning, P (1982) A software teaching package (co-ordinates). MSc dissertation, University of Bradford.

Mills, G M and Stonier, T (1982) Trends and prospects for microcomputer-based education. *International Journal of Man-Machine Studies,* **17,** pp 143-148.

Tait, K (1982) Leeds University Computer-Based Learning Unit. *Computer Education,* **42,** (November).

4.2 The Use of the ARCS Model of Motivation in Teacher Training

John M Keller
Syracuse University, New York, USA

Abstract: The ARCS model of motivation is grounded in an expectancy-value theory of motivation. This is a type of social learning theory which assumes that behaviour is a function of interactions between the person and the environment. More specifically, in a motivational context, it assumes that effort is a consequence of motives or values, and of expectancy for success. Reinforcement serves to confirm or deny expectations. The ARCS model was developed from a synthesis of variables defined in various studies of human motivation. The model identifies four major influences on motivation: attention, relevance, confidence and satisfaction. Each of these categories includes specific concepts such as, respectively, curiosity, need for achievement, expectancy for success, and reinforcement. Included in the model are sample strategies and examples for the practical application of the model to instructional design and teaching. The model has had successful results in field studies with teachers who used it to improve the motivational appeal of their instructional materials, and of their teaching styles.

WHAT IS THE ARCS MODEL?

The ARCS model is a system for improving the motivational appeal of instructional materials, of instructor behaviour, and of the way in which lessons (or modules) and courses are designed. It provides strategies which a course designer or teacher can use to make instruction responsive to the interests and needs of learners.

WHY THE ARCS MODEL?

This model was created because of the lack of guidance that presently exists for improving the motivational quality of instruction. Much has been written about how to design instruction that will be effective if students *want* to learn, but there is relatively little that tells how to make the instruction more appealing.

WHERE DID THE ARCS MODEL COME FROM?

The ARCS model is the result of several years of research and application. A synthesis of the various approaches to studying human motivation (Keller, 1983) provided a basis for developing a useful set of categories and prescriptive strategies. All of the strategies in the model are derived from research findings and from practices that have resulted in motivated learners. This paper is an overview of the characteristics of the model, how it is used, and the results of two developmental tests.

CHARACTERISTICS OF THE ARCS MODEL

The ARCS model defines four major conditions (attention, relevance, confidence and satisfaction) that have to be met for people to become and remain motivated. Each of these subsumes several areas of psychological research (Keller, 1979), and several categories of motivational prescriptions (Keller, 1983).

Attention

The first condition, attention, is also a prerequisite for learning. At one level, it is fairly easy to accomplish. A dramatic statement, a sharp noise, a 'pregnant' pause, all of these and many other devices are used to get attention. However, getting attention is not enough.

The real challenge is to sustain it, to produce a satisfactory level of attention throughout the course. To do this, we have to respond to the sensation-seeking needs of students (Zuckerman, 1971), and arouse their basic curiosity (Berlyne, 1965). Ultimately, the best way to fight boredom and indifference is to stimulate their curiosity so the instructor can spend more time *directing* attention than in *getting* it.

Relevance

How many times have we heard students ask: 'Why do I have to study this?' When a convincing answer is not forthcoming, there is a relevance problem. To answer this question, many course designers and instructors try to make the instruction seem relevant to present and future career opportunities for the students. Others, in a more classical tradition, believe that learning should be an end in itself, something that students come to enjoy and treasure. However, there is a third way. It focuses on process rather than ends.

Relevance can come from the *way* something is taught; it does not have to come from the content itself. For example, people with a strong need for affiliation will tend to enjoy classes in which they can work co-operatively in groups. Similarly, people with a strong need for achievement enjoy the opportunity to set moderately challenging goals, and to take personal responsibility for achieving them. To the extent that a course of instruction offers opportunities for individuals to satisfy these and other needs, the person will have a feeling of perceived relevance, that this course is 'for me'.

Confidence

Losers and winners. We've all seen them both. However, we are not talking about the people who come in first or last in a competitive sport. We are talking about people who never quite make it, even when the odds are in their favour, versus the ones who always pull through no matter what the odds.

This characteristic is part of our third requirement for motivation. It has several popular names including 'will-power', 'guts' and 'the power of positive thinking'. More formally, it is called such things as 'expectancy for success' (Fibel and Hale, 1978), 'self-fulfilling prophecy' (Jones, 1977) and 'personal causation' (Bandura, 1977), to mention only a few. Essentially, it refers to a person's belief that if he tries to do something he will succeed, and its effects on performance can be dramatic.

Satisfaction

This category incorporates the things we know about ways to make people feel good about their accomplishments. According to reinforcement theory, people should be more motivated if we define the task and the reward, and we use an appropriate reinforcement schedule. Why, then, do people sometimes get resentful and even angry when we tell them what they have to do, and what we will give them as a reward? An important part of the answer seems to be 'control'.

When we require someone to do something to get a reward that we control, we may create resentment because we have taken over part of that person's ability to control his own life. This is especially likely to happen when the behaviour we control is one which the other person enjoys for intrinsically satisfying reasons. The establishment of external control over an intrinsically satisfying behaviour can decrease the person's enjoyment of the activity (Lepper and Greene, 1978). But, there are appropriate ways to use extrinsic rewards in learning situations. The challenge is to provide appropriate contingencies without over-controlling.

These four categories form the basis of the ARCS model. Within each are sub-categories that include prescriptive motivational strategies (see Keller and Dodge, 1982). However, given the purpose of this model for helping to identify specific ways to make instruction more appealing, there is still the question of procedure; how is the ARCS model used in an instructional development sequence? The following two sections provide a brief description of this process, and the results of using the model with two groups of teachers.

USING THE ARCS MODEL

The ARCS model is a systematic design model that interfaces with typical instructional design and development models. It can be conveniently separated into the steps of define, develop and evaluate.

Define

The define phase has two purposes. The first is to determine the general level of audience motivation. In some situations, a group of students will be highly motivated for a particular class due to their intrinsic interest in the topic, or because of external factors that make the class important to them. In other cases, the students' motivation will have to be stimulated after they arrive at the class. In the first case, the designer or instructor will have to maintain the motivation, but in the second case, strategies to establish motivation will be needed.

An important constraint of the ARCS model that became more explicit during the developmental testing is that it is designed to help make a course of instruction more motivating for an ordinary class of students. This means a class in which some people will be very co-operative and interested, others will be indifferent and bored, and some may even be slightly antagonistic. However, the group as a whole will be responsive if an effective set of motivational strategies is employed. The ARCS model is *not* intended to solve the problems of an individual person or group with severe personality difficulties.

The second purpose of the define phase is to determine the specific motivational problem categories (as defined in the ARCS model), and prepare motivational objectives. Included in the ARCS model materials is a checklist that helps identify the specific areas which are most likely to need special attention in the development of motivational strategies. Of course, it is always possible that a balanced focus will be needed in a given context; that is, a designer or teacher may not have an acute problem area, but might simply need to give balanced treatment to all four areas. The resulting motivational objectives will indicate the results of this defining stage.

Develop

The first step in development is to create a list of *potential* motivational strategies for each of the objectives. This list will almost always be longer than the final one. For any given motivational objective, there can be any number of specific strategies that will help accomplish the objective. Brainstorming is generally used at this phase. The goal is to move away from the analytical thinking that characterizes the define phase, and to begin thinking in an uncritical, more creative mode.

The next step is to produce an effective integration of the motivational strategies into the instruction. They should not take up too much time or detract from the learning objectives; they should fall within the time and money constraints of the development and implementations aspects of the instruction; they should be acceptable to the audience, and be compatible with the delivery system including the instructor's style. This involves a cyclical process of putting the motivational strategies into the instructional context, determining the quality of the 'fit', and then revising.

In this process, it is important to note that 'more is not always better'. For example, if a class comes to you already motivated, you do not want to inject an excessive number of motivational strategies. This would slow the class, and distract from their orientation to the task.

The strategies included in the model are proven, but their effectiveness, and the exact way in which they are implemented depends in part on the personality of the instructor, and the type of atmosphere that he or she wants (eg formal versus informal). Consequently, the final selection of strategies for a given instructional event is based, in large part, on the judgements of the designer and teacher rather than on objective criteria. In this sense, even though the ARCS model is a prescriptive model, it is more heuristic than algorithmic. It helps insure a solution to motivational problems, but it does not guarantee one as does a correctly applied algorithm. It requires experience and judgement, and perhaps even some trial-and-error from the designer.

Evaluation

It is important to base the evaluation of the materials on motivational as well as learning outcomes. Too often, decisions about the effectiveness of motivational strategies are based on gain scores or other achievement measures. This is not a good practice, because these dependent variables are affected by many factors, not just motivational ones (see Keller, 1979, for a more complete discussion of this point). To judge motivational consequences, we need to use direct measures of persistence, intensity of effort, emotion and attitude.

DEVELOPMENTAL TEST OF THE ARCS MODEL

The ARCS model has been used in two teacher training workshops. The first was in the spring of 1982 with 18 teachers of children between the ages of 12 and 14. All of the teachers were from the same school district, and most were from the same school. The workshop took place over a period of four months with afternoon meetings twice a month. It was conducted by a colleague of the author who was familiar with the motivational material surrounding the ARCS model, and included one session in which the author presented the specific strategies and procedures of the model.

During the four months of the project, the teachers went through the complete process of defining a motivational problem, formulating objectives, selecting strategies, preparing an implementation plan, enacting the plan, conducting evaluation, analysing results, and describing their conclusions. Most of the teachers worked on developing or revising modules of instruction to make them more interesting, but some worked on the motivational problems of specific students.

In general, the results of this experience were positive. Many teachers achieved the motivational goals that they had set. However, even those who did not tended to feel that they had benefited from the process, and they felt encouraged to try again.

An interesting consequence of using the ARCS model in this setting occurred.

Some of the teachers, in their conclusions, suggested that the key factor in the process was that they had simply paid more *attention* to the student, or class. At first, this seemed to be a disappointing outcome for the ARCS model. Why have a reasonably cumbersome, complex, time-consuming model if 'paying more attention' is all that is required?

Upon reflection, it became clear that the teachers were not giving themselves enough credit for what they had actually accomplished. After looking back at their action plans and logbooks, it was obvious that they had used specific strategies to bring about the change. For them, 'attention' was simply a convenient word to summarize a great many specific acts.

In the winter of 1982-83 a second test was conducted with another group consisting of 16 teachers ranging from kindergarten to senior high school within a single school district. This was a six-day workshop conducted by the author and two assistants for two days each in November, December and January. One day each month was spent in a working session with the teachers, and the other day each month was used for classroom visits and individual consultation.

At the end of the first session, the teachers had defined their problems. During the next four weeks, they were to work on collecting data to verify the problem, and to develop a preliminary strategy list. They were enthusiastic when we left, but when we returned, several had run into difficulties and become depressed.

We had encouraged the teachers to work on instructional improvement problems, rather than behaviour modification ones, but several had chosen the latter. Upon closer inspection of the details of the problems of some of these students, it became clear that it would be a challenge even for a professional psychotherapist to help them. The teachers who chose instructional improvement projects had, as a group, made better progress and felt more positive. We asked the concerned teachers to redefine their problems into something more manageable, and their progress improved quickly. However, in general there were slightly more difficulties with the second group than the first.

Why, we wondered, did the ARCS model work better with the first group of teachers, including the ones who chose behaviour modification problems? In the first group, the workshop leader had worked with the school district, and with the same group of teachers, on several other projects during the preceding three years. The earlier projects were concerned with helping the teachers learn to use systematic development and research procedures for creating and validating instructional improvement projects in the areas of curiosity and cognitive problem-solving skills.

In the second group, most of the teachers had not had an in-service training programme in several years, and some had never had one. Consequently, these teachers were starting from 'scratch' in terms of orientating themselves towards a productive experience in the workshop, and towards the specific processes of systematic development. They had to learn the generic design process as represented in the specific context of the ARCS model, and the content of the model itself. Despite the emphasis in the workshop on problem analysis, this group chose too many problems that were interesting and important to them, but fell outside the scope of the ARCS strategies or the time constraints of the workshop.

STATUS OF THE ARCS MODEL

The two developmental tests tended to confirm the basic assumptions of the ARCS model. The data collected by the teachers at the end of their projects indicated that many of them accomplished the motivational goal they had set, and they felt that the ARCS model was helpful to them. This provided support at both the objective and affective levels. Furthermore, the ARCS model works best with instructional improvement projects for which it was intended. It is not designed to help solve

motivational problems of individual students, although it can be helpful to a
teacher or counsellor who has exerience with behavioural change strategies, and the
development of individual learning packages. The ARCS model works best as a tool
to assist in improving the appeal of instructional materials and programmes.

REFERENCES

Bandura, A (1977) Self-efficacy: toward a unifying theory of behavioral change. *Psychological Review,* **84,** pp 191-215.

Berlyne, D E (1965) Motivational problems raised by exploratory and epistemic behavior. In Koch, S (ed) *Psychology: A Study of a Science* 5. McGraw-Hill, New York.

Fibel, B and Hale, W D (1978) The generalized expectancy for success scale — a new measure. *Journal of Consulting and Clinical Psychology,* **46,** pp 924-931.

Jones, R A (1977) *Self-Fulfilling Prophecies: Social, Psychological and Physiological Effects of Expectancies.* Halsted Press, New York.

Keller, J M (1979) Motivation and instructional design: a theoretical perspective. *Journal of Instructional Development,* **2,** 4, pp 26-34.

Keller, J M (1983) Motivational design of instruction. In Reigeluth, C M (ed) *Instructional Design Theories and Models: An Overview of Their Current Status.* Lawrence Erlbaum, Morristown, NJ.

Keller, J M and Dodge, B J (1982) *The ARCS Model of Motivational Strategies for Instruction.* Motech Learning Systems, Syracuse, New York.

Lepper, M R and Greene, D (1979) *The Hidden Costs of Reward.* Lawrence Erlbaum, Morristown, NJ.

Zuckerman, M (1971) Dimensions of sensation seeking. *Journal of Consulting and Clinical Psychology,* **36,** pp 45-52.

4.3 Assessment of Problem-Solving Judgement of School Psychologists: Implications for Staff Development

Dr G R Gredler
Syracuse University, New York, USA

Abstract: Increased attention is being focused on the diagnostic formulations of school psychologists in their examinations of school children for learning/behavioural problems. Little research has been conducted to determine the processes by which school psychologists formulate their diagnoses. The present study examines the decision-making process of advanced American school psychology students, practising school psychologists, and British educational psychologists (N=70).

A simulation module was designed to measure clinical problem-solving. Actual case material was developed incorporating several pieces of diagnostic information. Subjects were asked to select data cards they needed to come to a judgement concerning the referred child. Scores were obtained which reflected competence and effectiveness of their decision strategies. A panel of experts was used to establish the validity of the most effective procedures in the decision-making process.

Statistical analysis of data was carried out as well as ratings of interview data in post-diagnostic sessions. Data indicate a wide variability in quality of decision-making among both interns and experienced school psychologists.

This investigation indicates the usefulness of an objective analysis of the problem-solving process for school psychology students and practising school psychologists. Marked variability in diagnostic judgement was found not only in the school psychology student group but among practising school psychologists as well. Discussion will centre on use of this type of simulation module as part of the staff development programme with employed school psychologists. Such an approach should be helpful in pinpointing inappropriate diagnostic and intervention strategies used by school psychologists and should provide needed information to help in the improvement of their diagnostic judgement.

INTRODUCTION

A main responsibility of the school psychologist is to be able to render a diagnostic judgement about a child's learning and behaviour problems and make appropriate recommendations to parents and school personnel.

Clinical simulation modules were introduced in medicine by Rimoldi (1961). A typical patient management problem is composed of a description of the patient's complaint; the student then must choose from a list of options as to what the next step should be. The options to be chosen are categorized into units such as a general history section, physical examination data, laboratory examinations, etc. Possible actions to take are also included. These will range from those that definitely should be taken immediately to ones that are definitely contra-indicated. Scores are obtained which reflect the number of content units chosen and the sequence of helpful, harmful and irrelevant interventions chosen by the student. This type of approach would also appear to have merit for the school psychologist.

Problems in the classification of children's learning problems and use of diagnostic data by school psychologists has been intensively studied by McDermott (1980, 1981). In a study of school psychology students, interns and experienced school psychologists, he found some distinct differences among the groups in their analysis of diagnostic units of information obtained from three case studies.

Distinct time differences were found among the groups of school psychologists, with interns spending more time reviewing diagnostic data; also, newly graduated school psychologists devoted more time to reviewing projective test data. McDermott found that school psychologists, regardless of their training and experience levels, showed little diagnostic agreement; and indeed, that those with more training and experience tended to show even more disagreement.

Reasons for the inconsistency of diagnostic judgements of school psychologists may include over-use of state department guidelines, variable application of diagnostic standards from different classification systems, and inability to adequately conceptualize the dimensions of the presenting problem.

The approach in this study of diagnostic judgement was to take one case and investigate the diagnostic procedures of a group of school psychologists and advanced school psychology students as they reviewed actual case data.

Following the organization of a diagnostic management problem (DMP) as set up by Rimoldi (1961), Slater and Helfer (1971), and McGuire (1976) a DMP case for school psychologists was devised.

METHOD

Experience Groups

Subjects were school psychologists at various levels of training and experience.

Group I

Subjects in this group were school psychologists who had completed from one to 13 years as a full-time school psychologist and had completed prescribed psychology and assessment courses in school psychology. Some members of this group were also currently enrolled as students in a doctoral programme in school psychology but either had been or were employed currently in schools as a school psychologist.

Group II

Graduate students who had completed a series of assessment courses, had engaged in practicum experiences but had practised as school psychology interns no longer than eight weeks in schools.

Sample

The subjects were 22 advanced students in school psychology and 43 school psychologists.

Students represented the advanced graduate student pool from two large school psychology training programmes in the United States. Thirteen of the 43 school psychologists comprised the psychological services staff of two large English school districts. The remainder of this group consisted of the school psychologists employed in specific psychological service units in southeastern city and northeastern regional United States school systems and one psychological unit in a Canadian city.

The sample consisted of 52 per cent females and 48 per cent males. Age of the subjects ranged from 26 to 55.

Expert Group

Five school psychologists served as expert judges. These five experts included two

school psychologists of several years' experience who were currently in responsible
positions as directors of school psychological services in large school systems; two
school psychology trainers who also had extensive school experience; and one
school psychology trainer who had been a director of psychological services for
several years.

Materials

Case history data on a kindergarten child who had been referred by the classroom
teacher to the school psychologist was the main source of information for this
study. The case dealt with a five-year-old child. The case was of a young child
currently in kindergarten whose behaviour and learning was a problem to the
teacher. She had requested a psychological evaluation.

Case

The case material was built from actual case material obtained from the author's
clinical school practice. Forty-six pieces of data were available to the subjects.
These 46 pieces of information or 'diagnostic bits' represented 13 information
categories: (a) general history data, ie allergy history, pregnancy problems;
(b) referral problem information, ie statement from the teacher; parents' perception
of the problem; (c) readiness test data; (d) perceptual test information;
(e) intelligence test results; (f) motor co-ordination data; (g) projective tests;
(h) family history data; (i) behavioural observations; (j) token reinforcement
programme results; (k) behaviour ratings; (l) school achievement data; (m) and
miscellaneous data such as observations from the special help teacher; learning style
test results; data from a diagnostic teaching task; and demographic school data.

Procedure

The subjects were provided 46 pieces of data bits recorded on individual 3 x 5 cards
and placed in file jackets and a master index sheet on which were itemized the
types of information available on each of the numbered data cards. The school
psychologist was asked to choose whatever data that was felt to be needed to come
to a conclusion about the child's learning and behaviour problem and possible
interventions needed. With this kind of diagnostic management unit the subject
proceeds to work through the case data, selecting data cards in any order desired.
As many or as few information cards as desired can be selected by the subject. The
specific card chosen is checked off by the subject on a master index sheet as well as
the order in which the card was selected. Subjects were allotted up to one hour to
complete the activity. When confident of a decision the subject was then asked to
give conclusions and reasons as to the child's learning and behaviour problems and
plans for management of the problem.

Scoring of Protocol Data

The responses of the subjects were scored on a number of dimensions and were
divided into two major parts. In Part I protocols were examined as to the order of
choice of data cards made. This was an attempt to ascertain differences among
subject groups as to amount of information requested, and relative importance of
the categories to them. In Part II, protocols were scored as to the efficiency and
proficiency of the judgements made by the subjects. The following types of scores
were obtained:

1. *Efficiency score:* This consisted of the percentage of the subject's choices
   that are considered helpful in coming to a judgement about the child's

problems divided by the total number of the choices made by the subject.

2. *Proficiency score:* This score reflects the sum of all the positive and negative weighted items divided by the maximum number of points it would be possible to accrue if the subject selected every positive, helpful item.

3. *Overall competence score:* This is the weighted average of the proficiency and efficiency scores used in a formula where more weight is placed on proficiency than efficiency. The resultant scores of each subject were then compared to the judgements provided by the group of five experts.

The expert solution reflects the composite judgement of this group of psychologists. Data cards were classified into one of five separate categories as follows: primary choice cards (PC); secondary choice cards (SC); intervention choice cards (IC); non-helpful cards (NH); and nebulous cards (N). Criteria for each of these categories are given below:

1. *Primary choice:* Primary choice cards were those chosen consistently by four or five of the five experts. Such cards received a weight of 10 points.

2. *Secondary choice cards:* Secondary choice cards were those chosen by three of the five experts. They received a weight of five points.

3. *Intervention strategy cards:* Intervention cards were those chosen by four or five of the five experts. The total weight for this category was 50 points.

4. *Non-helpful cards:* These cards were chosen by either one expert or none. Each card so chosen was given a weight of minus five points.

5. *Nebulous cards:* These were data cards picked by only two experts. Such cards were not given either a positive or a negative weight. They figure, however, in the scoring process as they contribute to the efficiency and proficiency scores.

Research Questions

The following questions were asked:

Part I: 1. Do school psychologists at different levels of training and experience differ in their rank order emphasis of diagnostic information categories?

Part II: 2. Do school psychologists, whether advanced students or practising school psychologists, demonstrate acceptable overall competence in regard to their problem-solving judgement?

3. Do practising school psychologists show a higher level of competence in problem-solving when compared to school psychology students; and how do they compare with the judgement of experts? Do these subjects utilize diagnostic data similar to that chosen by school psychology experts. Or, instead, do they ignore certain pieces of information consistently, data which the experts find helpful?

RESULTS

Part I

To determine the composite order of category preference by the school psychologists and the experts, the number of times each category was requested was tabulated. Referral information from the teacher was the most frequently called-for data. Utilizing this approach to information usage, it is noted that the experts and the school psychology sample are in general agreement as to the composite order of category request. Wide variation occurred only in request of motor impairment data, perceptual test and achievement test data and accident information.

The 46 pieces of data were then grouped into 13 categories (see *Procedure* above). Ordering of category requests by school psychologists and experts gives some insight into the problem-solving process. The general pattern was for the school psychologist, school psychology student and expert first to seek orientating information about the child, ie reason for referral and parents' perception of the problem, then to look at certain aspects of the child's past history. This would include such information as developmental history data, information about siblings, mother's pregnancy data and child's medical history. This was followed by requesting IQ results. Finally, perceptual test data and achievement data and intervention information were requested. This same pattern of ordering information is seen in studies of psychiatrists (Gauron and Dickinson, 1966) and of school psychologists (Scherphorn, 1979).

However, such an approach is a crude method to utilize in order to gain insight into the process of problem-solving as used by the school psychologist. This approach to problem-solving analysis does not place sufficient emphasis on the way in which the school psychologist actually weighs and combines the data in order to come to a diagnostic judgement. And no in-depth information is provided as to how the school psychologist compares in his use of data with a group of experts who have reviewed the same case. For example, one piece of data — 'observations by special help teacher' — was given a rank order of 14.30 by the school psychologists and 17.0 by the experts. However, only 50 per cent of the sample of school psychologists chose this item; yet all five experts chose this data tool. The experts considered that the psychologist *must* have this intervention information before being able to arrive at an accurate judgement about the child.

Part II

Part II of the project investigated the proficiency and efficiency of the problem-solving process by school psychologists in order to provide insight into overall competence of their diagnostic judgement. Proficiency (P), efficiency (E), and overall competency (OC) scores were obtained for each school psychologist. Differences in degree of overall competence were defined as fair (.00−.39); good (.40−.59); and excellent (.60+). (Mean overall competence score of the expert group was .67.)

Chi square analysis indicated non-significant differences in competence in problem-solving ability between American advanced school psychology students versus American practising school psychologists (X^2 (2) = 1.92, NS). However, when the sample of the American school psychologists was compared with British educational psychologists as to overall competence in problem-solving, the resultant chi square was significant (X^2 (2) = 12.24, p < .01).

What is an acceptable level of performance on this type of problem-solving task also needs to be determined. Various methods of determining an acceptable level of performance are available which weight the subjects' level of experience and training at a point in time and determine whether or not to allot credit or penalty points. In this study, an acceptable level of performance was defined as demonstrating performance beyond that to be expected from random choice of data cards. Random choice of data bits resulted in an overall competence score of .17. Analysis of the various school psychology groups indicates that 23 per cent of the school psychology students and 25 per cent of the American school psychologists obtained overall competence scores as low as .17 or lower. None of the British educational psychologists received overall competence scores that low.

Reliability of Instrument

One attempt to establish the reliability of the method was undertaken when the school psychology protocols were analysed in terms of nine major themes. These themes reflected etiological, descriptive and prognostic statements concerning the child's learning/behavioural problems. Those subjects who were in the upper quarter in problem-solving ability (ie high overall competence scores) as outlined in Part II of the study were compared with the thematic content scores of the expert group as described in Part II. The resultant t-test was non-significant, indicating that both the 'good problem solvers' and experts demonstrated the same level of competence in describing the child's learning problems (+ (17) . 499, NS).

Such a comparison indicates consistency of response; that is, those who demonstrated high overall competence in problem-solving also demonstrated a high level of competence in the interpretation of the child's learning problems.

At the same time, these results provide some evidence of validity of this approach to measuring problem-solving judgement in school psychologists. This is because a group of school psychologists who demonstrated high competence in choosing important data bits of information were equally competent in being able to explain the etiological and descriptive factors important in the case problem. If this group had performed poorly on the task of thematic analysis, it would have been cause to question the validity of the measure as a suitable approach in understanding the decision process in school psychologists.

DISCUSSION

Results of this investigation of diagnostic judgement of school psychologists indicate a wide variability in diagnostic competence among practising school psychologists and school psychology students. These school psychologists demonstrated no greater competence than the school psychology students in making decisions about a child referred for a psychological examination. Many school psychologists consistently requested more data than did the experts and also ignored diagnostic data considered important by the experts. School psychologists frequently neglected to call for intervention data which the expert group thought important. When asked to discuss their diagnostic judgements, the school psychologists showed a similar wide variability in their ability to provide adequate etiological, descriptive and prognostic statements.

One group of school psychologists (the British sample) demonstrated a high level of competence in problem-solving and ability in identifying important diagnostic themes. Analysis of their responses to the DMP indicates they omitted fewer of the data cards thought necessary by the experts and chose fewer random or unnecessary data. Another group, the upper 25 per cent in competence in problem-solving, also showed a high level of ability to sense the problem, define it and offer proper management resolution.

Some subjects over-emphasized one aspect of the child's development, such as visual perceptual data, to the exclusion of other important information. Another factor which resulted in poor quality of diagnostic judgement was the fact that many subjects did not look at the intervention data available on the child. The results of this DMP unit indicate a number of school psychologists are uncomfortable and lack expertise in trying to explain the dynamics of a child's behaviour. Because the school psychologist is often sought out by the child's parents to discuss problem behaviour, inability to define the child's problem and provide appropriate management and intervention strategies can have serious results.

Results of this investigation indicate that additional emphasis on how diagnostic judgements are arrived at could properly be a part of the school psychology curriculum and in-service education.

It has been pointed out that transfer of problem-solving skills is less than has been assumed; therefore a reasonably large number of carefully selected problems should be provided to the student. Physicians were found to be more variable in their performance across tasks than had been expected (Elstein *et al*, 1978) and there is no reason to expect a different approach from school psychologists. Therefore, while important differences were found in this group of school psychologists , it must be pointed out that these school psychologists cannot be labelled as poor school psychologists on the basis of their performance on one DMP module. Use of simulation modules similar to the one used in the present study could help to provide opportunities to understand errors of judgement better, to clarify an individual's theoretical orientation, and to show how an individual makes decisions about learning and behaviour problems.

REFERENCES

Elstein, A S (1978) *Medical Problem Solving: An Analysis of Clinical Reasoning.* Harvard University Press, Cambridge, Massachusetts.

Gauron, E F and Dickinson, J K (1966) Diagnostic decision-making in psychiatry information usage. *Archives of General Psychiatry,* 14, pp 225-232.

McDermott, P A and Watkins, M W (1979) A computer program for assessing conjoint interrater agreement with a correct set of classifications. *Behavior Research Methods and Instrumentation,* 11, 6, p 607.

McDermott, P A (1980) Congruence and typology of diagnosis in school psychology: an empirical study. *Journal of School Psychology,* 17, pp 12-24.

McDermott, P A (1981) Sources of error in psychoeducational diagnosis of children. *Journal of School Psychology,* 19, 1, pp 31-44.

McGuire, C H, Solomon, L M and Boshook, P G (1976) *Construction and Use of Written Simulations.* The Psychological Corporation, New York.

Rimoldi, H J A (1961) The test of diagnostic skills. *Journal of Medical Education,* 36, pp 73-79.

Scherphorn, T G (1979) Information use by school psychologists for special educational placement decisions. Unpublished doctoral dissertation, Temple University, Philadelphia.

Slater, R E and Slater, C H (1971) Measuring the process of solving clinical diagnostic problems. *British Journal of Medical Education,* 5, pp 48-52.

4.4 Curriculum Development as Staff Training: A Departmental Case Study

John Bonington
Glenrothes and Buckhaven Technical College

Abstract: The further education (FE) system, and the Manpower Services Commission (MSC) are now jointly engaged in implementing government policy relating to youth unemployment. In contrast to the traditional 'received' course design, FE college departments are having to create innovatory curriculum designs. This paper gives background and description of a course design format adopted by a department in a local FE college, the use of which involves curricular responsibility at various levels of staff.

INTRODUCTION

Ten years ago it was true in the British FE system that:

> 'the emphasis on vocational training by experts from industry and commerce gave colleges their purposeful and practical, no-nonsense attitudes . . . and that the main influences have been external and little of the work has been internally created.' (Milner, 1973)

The establishment of validating bodies like TEC and BEC, acting as they do as curriculum catalysts (Makin, 1978), has changed the FE system internally (FEU, 1980), although not in quite the same way in Scotland as in England and Wales. It is no longer true that 'relatively little research into FE is being conducted and that curriculum development is non-existent' (Cantor and Roberts, 1979).

However, mainstream FE vocational course designs are still expected to be 'received' curricula (FEU, 1981a), arriving as 'a working syllabus, with order of topic development and which forms the basis of lesson plans' (Curzon, 1976). So it is that externally designed vocational courses offer what can be perceived as a tangible educational 'product' — a marketable product — allowing both tutor and student a perceived course 'identity', *and* providing a basis from which to structure responsibilities and rationalize resources. Given that the majority of FE staff have left other occupations which offered role identities, work-related norms (Booth, 1981) and defined products or services, then it is not surprising that they seem to relate easily to 'received' curricula and display anxiety when expected to generate curricula.

By marked contrast, because of youth unemployment, the FE system has also had to devise, since the mid-1970s, a very diverse range of vocationally non-specific pre-employment provisions. 'The so-called "local college" has borne the brunt of these changes and always showed itself able and willing to respond' (Kerr, 1982). This response has brought the FE system and the MSC into an extremely intimate relationship, the desirability of which some question. On a practical, working-relationship level it has forced FE colleges, as organizations, to communicate to others about their intentions, methods, processes and outcomes in ways that run completely counter to their established traditions (certainly pre-Haslegrave) and which many staff even now resent. Responding means that departments which wish to provide for or develop MSC-funded initiatives for young people, must be prepared to invest staff time and curriculum expertise in committing to paper what they are about. The MSC requires to know what it is buying, in effect, on behalf of the taxpayers and young people, for there can be no doubt that MSC has become local FE's biggest paying customer. As its role, influence, experience, and resources have steadily increased, the MSC has, like any responsible consumer, developed market knowledge of the strengths and weaknesses of providers, it has sharpened its negotiating and buying skills, and perhaps most importantly, by doing research and development of its own, it has refined and respecified the products it now wishes to purchase.

The MSC's role has meant an insistent and almost continuous need for internal documentation of provisions and, where course designs are departmentally generated, a need for clear and adequate curriculum design and development in order to *shape the perception* of staff task roles.

PROBLEMS OF CURRICULUM DESIGN AND DEVELOPMENT IN FE DEPARTMENTS

'Curriculum development in FE, has, like course design, always been rather piecemeal, and retrospective, in that FE tends to supply what its clients ask for' (Pratley, 1980). For mainstream vocational courses this means the needs of local or national industry, professional institutes, employers, established occupational groups (and even the MSC as promoter of provisions for 'strategic' shortages) evolving 'external' courses to be actioned by the system. This process of sifting and aggregating knowledge and skills into a valid 'product', often involving acknowledged experts, has shaped the character of mainstream FE into a style of presentation to students where 'content from a given syllabus and style form a tradition that gives content pride of place over process' (Tolley, 1983) and leads to inflexibility, although this is not true everywhere (Noble, 1980). The conflict between process and content has fundamental implications for design and successful implementation of provisions specifically aimed at non-academic young people (Mansell, 1982).

Staff role perceptions and expectations will continue to be modelled on approved practice and when, for example, 'no-nonsense' high pass rates on external courses are a work-related norm, then 'human modelling' shapes perceptions — it is 'true that people like best what they do well' (Gagné, 1977). It is this very reinforcement, leading to secure, conservative perception of role, allied with hierarchical management structures, that, departmentally, makes it all too true that 'the setting up of formalized channels crystallizes resistance and leads to greater rigidity' (Kaneti Barry, 1975) and also reduces the widespread availability and assimilation of innovative curriculum information.

College based 'curriculum development in FE rarely follows the boxes-and-arrows logic of the textbook' (Challis, 1981) not only because many in FE are openly hostile to the dissonantly perceived 'systems approach', exemplified by jargon 'about what to do with arrows' (Kaufman, 1972), but simply because they either don't have the time to do it or they lack the opportunity to develop the necessary analytical skills.

Worthwhile practice of any process-based curriculum (even if it is 'retrospectively' developed or more accurately redeveloped) must assume that all members of the course team are aware of the aims and goals which they seek to attain. Neglect to communicate, to implicitly assume such knowledge and understanding, is to make the most elementary error of effective management. But the explosive growth in staffing in many FE colleges has almost inevitably created a situation in which 'the apparent lack of clearly defined common goals and values generates a great deal of diffuse anxiety' (Cohen and Smith, 1976) the major practical outcome of which is a perceived 'discrepancy between management statements of values and styles and their actual managerial behaviour . . . There is

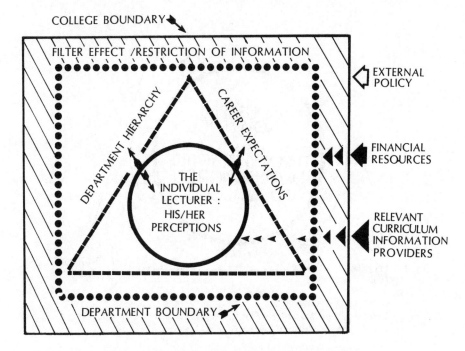

Figure 1. *The FE lecturer: departmental perspective*

a credibility gap which causes people to be cautious, conservative and self-protective' (Beckhard, 1969).

THE DEPARTMENT

The Department of Educational Services at Glenrothes and Buckhaven Technical College has responsibility for a range of college-wide media and learning resource services. By 1981 departments teaching included open learning courses, learning by appointment work, educational technology for 'in-service', provision for handicapped and other students with special learning needs, and a successfully established school/college 'link' programme based on the Industrial Institute, a pioneering, production-orientated industrial education facility founded in 1974 (Donald, 1977). Care had been taken from the beginning to provide in the institute a realistic work-experience, combining knowledge of the world of work and skills application to meet production demands, avoiding the temptation to simply provide 'watered-down craft level courses' (Pratley, 1980).

By 1981 the college had developed a wide range of provisions for the 15-18 year group, including a substantial commitment to the Youth Opportunities Programme (YOP) jointly funded by Fife Region and the MSC. The department's contribution was in offering short training courses, school/work 'bridging' courses for handicapped and low-achieving students, as well as the established 'link' programme. The department also began developing a work introduction course, a YOP special programmes provision (MSC, 1980) 'aimed primarily at the slow

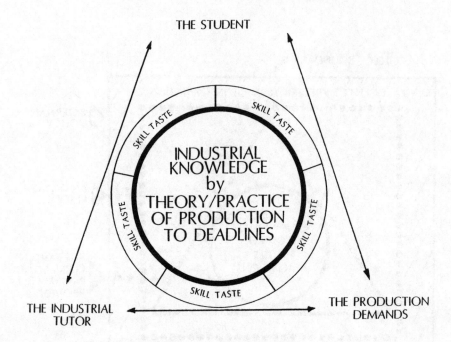

Figure 2. *The Institute of Industrial Practic and Orientation:*
the Industrial Institute work-experience link

learner who may have faced particular difficulty in dealing with the traditional
school environment' (McLeish and Mullin, 1981).

The department was not directly involved with any mainstream 'received'
course; it had a tradition of flexible, learner-centred activity, and it had for some
time been providing information on the services it could offer, to schools, to the
careers service, to the LEA, and to the technical services department.

Staff are drawn from the department's own establishment working with other
specialist lecturers, 'on loan' for extended periods from other departments, and are
a mix of professionally trained educational and other staff, including instructors.

The development of more systematic approaches to departmental curricula was
partly prompted by a realization that existing long-standing courses, particularly
the 'link' provisions, had changed and developed; it was also prompted by the
likelihood of expansion of pre-vocational work into new courses, such as the work
introduction courses. These courses were likely to generate a complementary
demand for higher quality planning and more systematic documentation in order
to obtain the MSC approval.

The college is allowed time each year for in-house staff development activities
and it was decided that the department would use this to promote, and hopefully
staff would effect, a more systematic curriculum planning and documentation. This
would in time become part and parcel of the department's working practice.

The immediate benefits expected were that:

1. By actually devoting time to retrospective curriculum design it would let us
   see where we had got to.
2. By developing a 'bank' of such information, preferably in aims and objectives
   form, it would aid design and redevelopment. This was felt to be particularly
   important in elucidating and clarifying knowledge and practice in two

'process' topics — industrial knowledge and work skills.

3. Carrying out such an exercise in teams would lead to a more effective understanding of how subject/topic content would be subservient to process, enabling new courses like the work introduction course or its successors, to be developed.

4. As the college department responsible for educational technology, we would be able to produce some evidence of its use and utility!

DEVELOPMENT AND IMPLEMENTATION OF THE COURSE PLANNING FORMAT

Staff development in FE aims to improve performance, help assimilation of changes, and enhance job satisfaction (ACFHE/APTI, 1973), satisfaction in this case being enhanced by heightened 'course identity' and 'process role'. By early 1981 the department's senior staff had digested the philosophy of keynote publications such as *Experience, Reflection, Learning* (FEU, 1978) and *Basis for Choice* (FEU, 1979) and it was agreed to initiate a planned programme of staff development, incorporating the learning strategy of experience, reflection, learning (FEU, 1981a).

As educational technologist charged with implementing the programme, I had the problem and had to recognize that, to achieve change, I was *dependent on the changes* (Gordon, 1979). Therefore the following characteristics were selected for the programme:

1. It must develop, in an almost organic way, out of an assured credibility born of recognition of the acceptance and exercise of curriculum development responsibility by senior staff (see Figure 3).

2. Clear and consistent communication of what is required must start at the top.

3. Development must be seen personally as a non-exposed, 'no-fail' activity (particularly the writing of objectives).

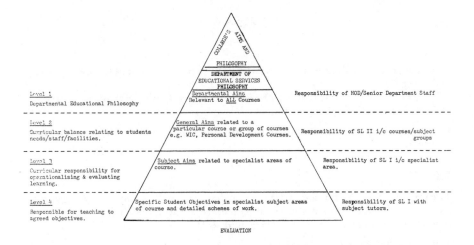

Figure 3.

4. All department staff do teach, so there had to be demonstrable egalitarianism in generating objectives.
5. Activity should be based on course groups not individual skill areas in isolation (see Figure 4).

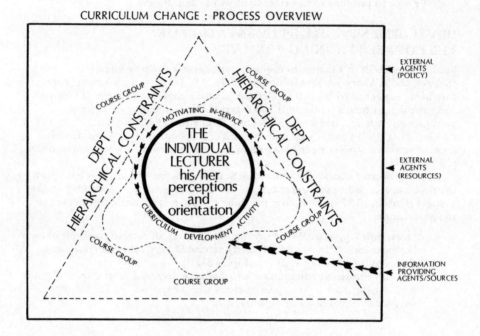

CURRICULUM CHANGE : PROCESS OVERVIEW

Figure 4.

6. As little educational technology 'jargon' as possible should be used (Booth, 1981).
7. Any in-service time ought to be devoted to productive activity not theory or lectures (like this paper?).

In practice the programme strategy was formulated and implemented as shown in Figure 5.

RESULTS

The programme, which is a continuing one, has achieved its aim — every course having now been examined and documented, using the agreed 'course planner' format. The format incorporates designated sections for:

Level 1   — departmental philosophy
          — departmental aims groups as:
              i) continuing education
             ii) industrial knowledge
            iii) personal development

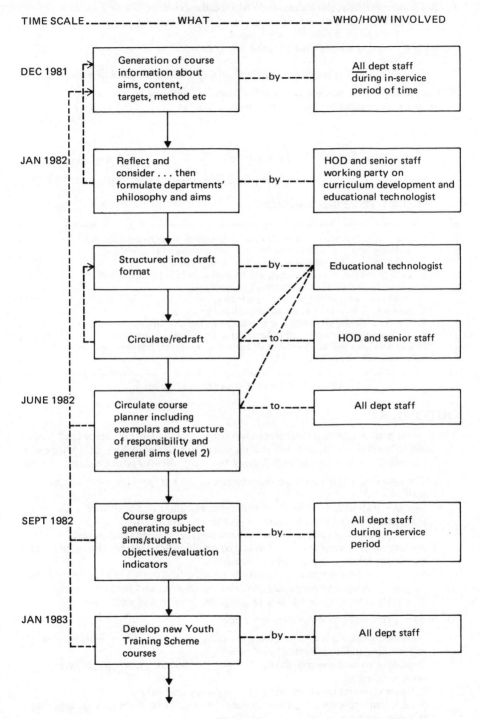

TIME SCALE _ _ _ _ _ _ _ _ _ WHAT _ _ _ _ _ _ _ _ _ _ WHO/HOW INVOLVED

DEC 1981

Generation of course information about aims, content, targets, method etc
_ _ _ by _ _ _ _
All dept staff during in-service period of time

JAN 1982

Reflect and consider . . . then formulate departments' philosophy and aims
_ _ _ by _ _ _ _
HOD and senior staff working party on curriculum development and educational technologist

Structured into draft format
_ _ _ by _ _ _ _
Educational technologist

Circulate/redraft
_ _ _ to _ _ _ _
HOD and senior staff

JUNE 1982

Circulate course planner including exemplars and structure of responsibility and general aims (level 2)
_ _ _ to _ _ _ _
All dept staff

SEPT 1982

Course groups generating subject aims/student objectives/evaluation indicators
_ _ _ by _ _ _ _
All dept staff during in-service period

JAN 1983

Develop new Youth Training Scheme courses
_ _ _ by _ _ _ _
All dept staff

Figure 5.

Level 2 — course title, duration, mode of attendance
          — general aims of course (or group of similar courses)
          — for whom the course is intended
Levels 3 — broad teaching aims for *each* subject area
   &   and
   4 — all subject areas, topics, their objectives, and indication of evaluation.

This approach is now the agreed basis for planning any new course in the department. An example of level three appears below.

Level 3:

Course Title: WIC Gardening and Landscaping

Teaching Aims of Course by Subject (use separate sheet for each subject area)

SUBJECT AREA: Basic Work Skills

The aims of this subject area are to develop in students a demonstrated ability to:
1. willingly accept and satisfactorily carry out orders and instructions.
2. satisfactorily carry out assigned tasks to completion.
3. understand the need for compliance to instructions or specifications.
4. assess the degree of achievement of assigned tasks.
5. co-operate with others in carrying out tasks.
6. proceed with tasks in a safe and disciplined manner.
7. display a satisfactory degree of self-discipline in individual or group tasks.
8. assume personal responsibility for completion of tasks or projects.
Note: these aims will be integral to all subject area activity, not dealt with in isolation, particularly PROJECTS.

Figure 6. *Course planner format: level 3*

OUTCOMES

The process produced many unforeseen questions, particularly at senior staff level. (Eg What is 'work'? Are basic work skills just a clutch of cognitive skills? Why can't the MSC define work skills better?) Among the most obvious *positive* outcomes are:

☐ The process of retrospection sharpened and altered 'process' perceptions and staff roles.
☐ Documentation redefined the profile of curriculum responsibility — the administrative tail less obviously wags the educational dog.
☐ The departmental staff structure has credibility in curriculum terms.
☐ An increased commitment to quality of teaching/learning is evident and infers a stronger relationship to 'course identity'.
☐ New course development, particularly relating to Youth Training Scheme, has been done more systematically, with better quality, and *faster*.
☐ New staff have a 'received' course design to refer to and assimilate.

There have been *negative* outcomes including:

☐ Increased workloads and pressures resulting from curriculum development extending outside in-service 'free' time!
☐ Demands, sometimes unrealistically high, for development time, better resources, etc.
☐ A closer questioning of existing system policy and values.
☐ A reluctance to embark on new courses because of the necessity of applying this systematic approach.

CONCLUSION

Curriculum development, on a systematic basis, is probably the most effective form of staff training because, if based on relevant research, it enables an individual to make an acknowledged contribution to a collaborative product and to exercise a degree of control over its subsequent development and revision. Our programme strategy was reasonably successful against a background of college innovation which in turn was approved of and supported by a progressive LEA, Fife Region.

Unlike Dr Wong of California, claimed to be 'the best in the business' because as a teacher he applies the ERIC research findings (The Times Educational Supplement, 1982), this paper only avers that this strategy does seem to work for reasons that are obvious in an FE context (Turner *et al*, 1982). Finally, and most importantly, did this help our students? On balance the answer is 'yes' because, like Dr Wong, we now know why we are doing what we are doing more systematically and with greater clarity than we were, and that benefits our students.

REFERENCES

Amnsell, J (1982) Curriculum-led college organisation. *NATFHE Journal*, 7, 8 December.

Association of Colleges of Further and Higher Education/Association of Teachers in Technical Institutions (1973) *Staff Development in FE.*

Beckhard, R (1969) *Organisation Development: Strategies and Models*. Addison-Wesley, Massachusetts.

Booth, R A (1981) 'Professionalism' and resistance to change in FE. Coombe Lodge Rep, 14, 8.

Cantor, L M and Roberts, I F (1979) *Further Education Today: A Critical Review*. Routledge & Kegan Paul, London.

Challis, B (1981) The Practice of Course Development. Coombe Lodge Rep, 14, 8.

Cohen, A M and Smith, R D (1976) *The Critical Incident in Growth Groups*. Univ Assoc Inc, La Jolla, California.

Curzon, L B (1976) *Teaching in Further Education*. Cassel, London.

Donald, B (1977) Glenrothes Industrial Institute and Berlin Freidrichshaven: a comparative study in the education of 16-19 year olds. Unpublished MEd thesis, University of Edinburgh.

Further Education Unit (1978) Experience, Reflection, Learning.

Further Education Unit (1979) A Basis for Choice.

Further Education Unit (1980) Loud and Clear?

Further Education Unit (1981a) ABC in Action: a report from an FEU/CGLI Working Party 1978-81.

Further Education Unit (1981b) Curriculum Control.

Gagné, R (1977) *The Conditions of Learning*. 3rd edn.

Gordon, T (1979) *Leader Effectiveness Training*. Futura, London.

Habeshaw, T (1980) Towards a system of continuing self-development for teachers. *British Journal of Educational Technology*, 11, 1.

Kaneti Barry (1975) Some constraints on change within departments of engineering in FE institutions. In Van der Eyken and Kaneti Barry (eds) *Learning & Earning: Aspects of Day Release in Further Education*. NFER.

Kaufman, R (1972) *Educational System Planning*. Prentice-Hall, Englewood Cliffs, NJ.

Kerr, S T (1982) Change in a local FE college. *Programmed Learning in Educational Technology*, 19, 3.

MacLeish, M and Mullins, R (1981) *A Programme for Opportunity: The YOP in Fife*. Fife Regional Council/MSC.

Makin, J P (1979) Staff development in FE colleges. Coombe Lodge Rep, 12, 10.

Milner, H S (1973) Is it FE? *Forum*, 15, 2.

MSC (1980) *Trainers Handbook: Work Introduction Courses*.

Noble, P (1980) *Resource-Based Learning in Post-Compulsory Education*. Kogan Page, London.

Pratley, B (1980) Signposts: a review of courses 16-19. FEU.

Pratley, B (1981) Starting from scratch: the 'What Have we got? model of curriculum development for vocational preparation. Coombe Lodge Rep, 14, 8.

Times Educational Supplement (21.1.83) How Dr Wong and ERIC aim to put the teaching profession right.

Tolley, G (1983) *The Open Tech: Why, What and How?* ACFHE.

Turner, C, Finlayson, J and Challis, B (1982) *Planning LEA Support for YOP: MSC Exemplary Projects.* Coombe Lodge.

ACKNOWLEDGEMENTS

For the graphic design skills Allan Salmond; for the typing skills Janice Kelly and Sarah McClelland.

4.5 The Use of Video in a National Training Programme for Teachers

Dr D G Gibson
St Andrew's College of Education

Abstract: The paper will examine the role of video material in a national staff training programme mounted by the Scottish Education Department in preparing teachers for the introduction of a 'foundation level' course in science education. The science course is aimed at a target population of secondary school pupils formerly regarded as 'non-certificate'. The course proposals suggest radical re-thinking about the kind of curriculum appropriate to such pupils and about the assessment techniques which should be employed.

A massive in-service training programme was thus required to provide the necessary staff development for first- and second-line pilot schools. Three regional curriculum development officers were appointed to co-ordinate the staff training programme. To assist them, a series of video programmes was commissioned from the educational technology department of St Andrew's College of Education. The video training package incorporates an interpretation of the syllabus and assessment 'guidelines' together with exemplar material from first-line pilot schools.

Thus, the paper encompasses the main theme of staff development and career updating (the pilot schools will themselves act as training centres for the wider school population) but also relates directly to the sub-themes of staff training and methodologies and resources associated with educational technology.

INTRODUCTION

In March 1980 the government announced their plans for the development of curriculum and assessment in the third and fourth years of secondary education in Scotland. The government's development programme set out a three-year programme of work designed to enable the secretary of state to decide in 1983 upon implementation of a new system. The government have now published a consultative paper (1982) which reports fully upon the development programme and sets out proposals for the phased implementation of a new system of curriculum and assessment. Broadly, the government have endorsed a curriculum structure with seven modes of study, comprising English, mathematics, science, religious and moral studies, physical activity and leisure, social studies and creative and aesthetic studies. Each syllabus is to be offered at up to three levels of attainment — foundation, general and credit — linked to a national system of certification for all.

In order to ensure that pupils would have a good opportunity to transfer between syllabus levels the development programme included an investigation of syllabus overlap. This issue has proved difficult to resolve. After close consideration by the Consultative Committee on the Curriculum, the Scottish Examinations Board and the department, there is general agreement that the solution may lie in defining broad bands of criteria for each level of attainment under the new system ('grade-related criteria'). The development programme involved several strands of activity. The main work lay in the pilot studies in foundation-level English, mathematics and science. These were based on a combination of internal and external syllabuses and assessment.

The principal conclusion of the pilot studies is that good courses can be produced and assessed for pupils for whom existing SCE courses are not suitable. The principal resource in the pilot studies has been the skills, experience and enthusiasm of the pilot school teachers and the devotion of substantial HM Inspectorate effort. Pilot studies have been supported by secondments of teachers to act as field development officers attached to the Scottish Examination Board. In-service training has been an important aspect of the development programme. The department has provided national courses aimed at producing a group of senior promoted teachers and principal teachers capable of assisting with further in-service training.

THE VIDEO PROGRAMMES

As part of this in-service training programme in science, the Scottish Education Department commissioned the production of a series of video programmes by the director of learning resources at St Andrew's College of Education in collaboration with two field development officers. Part of the early work involved filming in pilot schools across Scotland. Some of these videos were edited and shown extensively in the national in-service courses as examples of 'good practice'. Later, as they gained experience of in-service training requirements, the field development officers identified a clear need for an 'in-service training package' which could be used at local as well as regional level. The package would encapsulate the major issues of the development programme and provide teachers with support material related to the new techniques being advocated. This was seen as particularly necessary as the education authorities expanded the work into a 'second line' of about 200 schools. Introduction of foundation science into all schools is planned for 1984 with certification from 1986. After discussion, it was decided to produce a further series of four programmes concentrating on the central issues emerging from the considerable documentation originating from the SED.

GUIDELINES

The first programme deals with the national *guidelines* for foundation level science, produced on the basis of pilot studies in schools throughout Scotland. It is studio-based and solely concerned with a factual presentation. The two field development officers present the essential features of the guidelines including:

- [ ] *General objectives* of the course.
- [ ] The *structure* based on four broad but interrelated *fields of study*.
- [ ] The idea of *compulsory* and *optional* topics selected from the fields of study.
- [ ] The *specification* of each topic in terms of context, contents outline, specific objectives and pupil activities.
- [ ] *Moderation procedures*.

The programme lasts 12 minutes and is a studio-based factual presentation.

Most teachers sense that the most important aspect of the feasibility study in science is the development of an appropriate curriculum at foundation level. However, the development programme is also committed to examining the feasibility of national certification, and the difficulties inherent in assessment and certification at foundation level were perceived to be one of the major challenges of the whole exercise.

ASSESSMENT

The second programme thus considers the implications of both internal and external assessment in a national certification feasibility exercise. It tries to move away from a static factual presentation to incorporate classroom activities related to the material presented. It seeks to stress that assessment should be seen as an essential and integral part of the teaching-learning process. Assessment is geared to the five sets of general objectives:

A Knowledge and understanding.
B Handling information.
C Practical skills.
D Problem-solving.
E Attitudes.

It is proposed that internal assessment instruments should be used to assess pupil attainment of each of the sets of general objectives while external examinations will assess sets A, B, and D. It is hoped that the external examination will provide some validation of the schools' internal assessment.

One of the most interesting features of the development programme is that teachers are encouraged to select and use a range of assessment instruments for each set of the general objectives. It has to be pointed out, however, that most Scottish teachers have not had the opportunity of generating CSE-type syllabus and assessment proposals, and hence lack practical experience of using some of the assessment instruments being recommended. These are briefly mentioned in the second programme.

TEACHING METHODS

Programmes 3 and 4 are concerned with the potential pedagogic problems inherent in coping with two major areas which the development programme in science seeks to foster. Programme 3 focuses on *practical investigation*, which many teachers felt might be inappropriate for pupils at foundation level. The programme offers some guidance to teachers on this subject. Programme 4 concentrates on the issues concerned with *extended writing* — an area which science teachers had previously felt was the province of the English department but which the development programme had sought to promote, in keeping with a new spirit of fostering language across the curriculum.

PRACTICAL CONSIDERATIONS

A number of significant constraints existed during the period of production and use of the national training programme:

1. The decision to produce and use the video package was made at the time of expansion from the relatively small number of first-line pilot schools to the larger number of second-line schools, ie when there was already a greater demand for in-service material. Consequently, there was considerable pressure to film, edit and reproduce the material in the shortest possible time. With the imminent implementation of foundation science to all secondary schools in Scotland — a task which devolves entirely to the local authorities — the demand from local science advisers and even individual teachers for copies of the video for divisional and school-based in-service training has increased still further.
2. The work carried out at St Andrew's was additional to normal commitments and workload of the production team.
3. It was decided to use the two field development officers as presenters of the programme, although both were inexperienced in this area. Nevertheless, it was felt that teachers would more readily identify with them, and hence with the programmes, since it was their task to promote foundation science in the

second-line pilot schools. Feedback from the field development officers who have used the video programme in the course of their work has been most encouraging.

CONCLUSION

It is perhaps too early to judge how successful the video training package has been with the development programme as a whole. The response in terms of demand and feedback has been favourable. Whatever else may be claimed for the package, it has certainly been one means of putting the resources of a college of education directly at the disposal of a national educational development programme. This has brought a number of often disparate groups together — HMIs, local authority representatives, college of education personnel, and, most importantly, practising teachers.

REFERENCES

Scottish Education Department (1980) The Munn and Dunning Reports *The Government's Development Programme*. Edinburgh.
Scottish Education Department (1980) The Munn and Dunning Reports *Framework for Decision*. Edinburgh.

Section 5:
The Training of Craftsmen

5.1 Providing Extension Training for Offshore Personnel: An Educational Technology-Based Approach

H I Ellington and E Addinall
Robert Gordon's Institute of Technology, Aberdeen
and
J Blood
Omnitechnology Ltd, Aberdeen

Abstract: Omnitechnology Ltd is an Aberdeen-based organization that provides a variety of consultancy services to the offshore oil industry, including the development of custom-designed staff training schemes. This paper describes how the company recently developed an extension training course for the South Eastern Drilling Company (SEDCO), who wished to train their offshore barge engineers in the use of non-destructive testing techniques so that they could carry out emergency structural integrity inspections of drilling rigs after severe storms or accidents. It is shown how an educational technology-based approach was used to develop a suitable course built around three main components:

☐ A set of introductory tape-slide programmes.
☐ A set of comprehensive self-instructional manuals, incorporating self-assessment.
☐ Practical training sessions providing relevant 'hands-on' experience.

INTRODUCTION

Omnitechnology Ltd is a company that was recently set up in Aberdeen in order to provide a comprehensive range of technical and educational services to the offshore oil industry. Organizationally, it consists of three distinct layers, namely, a full-time managerial, secretarial and technical staff, a core team of consultants who are retained by the company on a permanent basis and are responsible for such things as the planning and operation of courses, and a much larger number of technical and educational specialists who make their services available to the company and are called upon as and when required. This highly flexible organizational structure enables Omnitechnology to tackle projects of a wide range of types: everything from the provision of teams of divers, to carry out underwater repair and maintenance work on offshore structures, to the planning, development and operation of custom-designed educational and training courses for offshore personnel. This paper describes a typical project of the latter type — the development of an extension training course for a major firm of offshore drilling contractors — the South Eastern Drilling Company (SEDCO).

THE PROBLEM WE WERE ASKED TO SOLVE

SEDCO is one of the world's largest firms of offshore drilling contractors, operating a fleet of semi-submersible drilling rigs (or barges) similar to the one shown in Figure 1. Such drilling rigs are chartered by oil companies to explore for oil in offshore concessions, and, if oil is found, to carry out further appraisal drilling in order to determine the physical extent, reserves and likely production rate of the field.

All the drilling rigs operated by SEDCO are subjected to stringent annual inspections, designed (among other things) to check their structural integrity. Rigs are also subjected to emergency inspections after severe storms or accidents involving collisions with other vessels such as supply boats. Both types of inspection

Figure 1. *One of the offshore drilling rigs operated by SEDCO*

involve testing key welded joints for possible cracks, and require the use of a battery of diagnostic techniques that come under the general heading of 'non-destructive testing' (NDT). These range from simple visual inspection and testing for superficial cracks, using magnetic ink or penetrating dyes, to carrying out sophisticated inspections of the internal structures of welds using ultrasonic waves or X-ray or gamma radiography. In practice, routine annual inspections involve the rig being taken off station, usually into a sheltered anchorage or dry dock so that access can be gained to parts of the structure that are normally deep under water. The NDT programmes that form an integral part of all such inspections are invariably carried out by firms of sub-contractors, who bring in teams of specialist staff in order to carry out the work.

In the case of emergency inspections, on the other hand, which are usually carried out while the rig is still on station, the requisite NDT work has to be carried out by SEDCO's own barge engineers. Thus, these engineers have to be trained in the use of the appropriate NDT techniques and in the interpretation of the results that they produce. What SEDCO wanted us to do was to develop an instructional system whereby barge engineers could be given such training *without* having to send them onshore for an extended course. In other words, they wanted us to produce some sort of individualized learning course that could be undertaken by the barge engineers on the rigs on which they worked.

HOW WE TACKLED THE PROBLEM

At the risk of stating the obvious, the key to producing a satisfactory course of the type SEDCO required — or, indeed, producing any sort of custom-designed educational or training package — is close collaboration between the consultants and the client at *all stages* of the development process. This serves a double function. First, it enables the consultants to learn exactly what it is the client wants, and to keep an on-going check that what is being proposed or produced is likely to prove satisfactory. Second, it enables the client to play a key part in the creative process by which the package is planned and developed, a factor whose importance should not be underestimated in work of this type. In the case of the SEDCO project, the men with whom we worked were Gene Hampton and Danny Sananikone, both senior members of SEDCO's engineering staff.

Work on the development of the course was carried out in three distinct stages, namely establishing the detailed course objectives, developing the overall plan for the course, and producing the actual instructional system components. Let us now look at each of these stages in turn.

Establishing the Course Objectives

As a result of detailed discussions with Gene Hampton and Danny Sananikone, we were able to identify the specific objectives that they wanted the course to achieve and to become fully aware of the constraints within which we would have to operate.

Basically, SEDCO wanted us to produce a course that would enable barge engineers with no previous knowledge or experience of non-destructive testing to be trained to such a level that they could carry out a full emergency rig inspection without supervision. This would involve giving such engineers:

1. A sound theoretical background to NDT, so that they could understand the principles on which the various types of tests are based and appreciate the range of applications and limitations of each technique; this would involve covering six different types of test, namely *liquid penetrant testing, magnetic particle inspection, eddy current testing, ultrasonic testing, X-ray radiography* and *gamma radiography*.
2. A thorough grounding in the practice of NDT, including a survey of the ways in which the various techniques are actually used by SEDCO and training in how to carry out the two techniques (magnetic particle inspection and liquid penetrant testing) that have to be carried out during emergency inspections.
3. Detailed knowledge of the nature of the materials and structures to be tested, of the procedures that are carried out during both routine and emergency rig inspections, and of the procedures for logging and reporting any defects detected.

SEDCO also wanted us to package the course in such a way that as much of the work as possible could be carried out while the barge engineers were working offshore, where they would have access to video playback equipment. They therefore wanted any audio-visual material that was incorporated into the course to be suitable for transfer onto video-tape.

Developing the Overall Plan for the Course

Once we have made ourselves thoroughly familiar with all the material that SEDCO wanted us to cover in the course, it became apparent that satisfactory coverage of the various objectives could best be achieved by building the course round three basic elements:

1. A set of self-instructional texts providing detailed coverage of the main cognitive content of the course, and incorporating a system whereby the students could monitor their progress (sets of self-assessment questions at the end of each section).
2. A set of audio-visual programmes, which would serve as an introduction to the self-instructional texts and also provide a link between the theory and practice of NDT by showing tests being carried out on the actual structures with which the barge engineers would be dealing in the course of the work for which they were being trained. It was agreed that these programmes should initially be produced in the form of tape-slide programmes, since this would not only minimize development costs, but would also allow for maximum flexibility of use. (The programmes could be used in their original form, either for individual study or for presentation to a group, could be transferred to video-tape for use offshore, and could be used as a source of individual slides and slide sequences for incorporation in lectures and other types of presentation.)
3. Facilities for the barge engineers to gain actual 'hands-on' experience of NDT through the provision of short practical courses or workshops. (It was, incidentally, always understood that these facilities would not be included in the actual course package, but would be provided on an *ad hoc* basis, with the courses or workshops being tailored to meet the needs of specific groups of barge engineers.)

With regard to the structure of the course, it was eventually decided that this should consist of two main parts, namely an introductory 'Stage 1' that would deal with the basic concepts and techniques of NDT, and a much more detailed 'Stage 2' that would cover the practical applications of NDT and its use in emergency rig inspections.

The Stage 1 resource materials would consist of a self-instructional manual backed up by a single introductory tape-slide programme. The self-instructional manual would contain the following main sections, each of which would be followed by a set of self-assessment questions in order to enable the students to check whether they had succeeded in mastering the material.

- ☐ NDT as a diagnostic tool.
- ☐ Liquid (dye) penetrant methods.
- ☐ Magnetic particle inspection.
- ☐ Eddy current testing.
- ☐ Ultrasonic testing.
- ☐ X-ray and gamma radiography.

We also decided to include an Appendix giving a general introduction to the physics of waves, since some of the barge engineers for whom the course was being designed would probably have no (or minimal) knowledge of this area. The Stage 1 introductory tape-slide programme would deal with the same basic subject material, with the exception of that covered in the Appendix.

Because of its greater length, we decided to split Stage 2 of the course into three parts, each of which would be introduced by a separate tape-slide programme. All three parts would, however, be contained in a single self-instructional manual, which would again include a set of self-assessment questions at the end of each section. A list of the three parts and their component sections is given below.

Part 1 The materials and structures to be tested
- ☐ the different types of steel and their basic properties
- ☐ structural steels used in offshore structures
- ☐ the welding of structural steels
- ☐ the integrity of welds; weld cracking

☐ the nature of the structures to be tested.

Part 2 How NDT is used and carried out
☐ how the various NDT techniques are used by SEDCO
☐ practical aspects of magnetic particle inspection
☐ practical aspects of the liquid penetrant method.

Part 3 Inspection procedures on SEDCO drilling rigs
☐ routine annual inspections
☐ emergency storm damage inspections.

The three Stage 2 tape-slide programmes would deal with the same basic subject material.

Producing the Instructional System Components

Work on the development of the instructional system components for the SEDCO course was itself carried out in two stages, starting with the production of the Stage 1 materials and only proceeding to the development of the Stage 2 materials once the former had been accepted by the client.

In producing the Stage 1 materials, we were greatly assisted by Norman Langton, Professor of Physics at Robert Gordon's Institute of Technology (and an authority on several aspects of NDT), who supplied much of the background information on which both the self-instructional manual and the introductory tape-slide programme were based. His contribution to the work is hereby gratefully acknowledged. In developing the Stage 1 tape-slide programme, we were also fortunate in having access to the facilities of Oilfield Inspection Services, an Aberdeen-based organization who carry out NDT contract work for the offshore oil industry. As it turned out, we were able to obtain virtually all the photographs that we needed for the Stage 1 programme during a single afternoon's work at OIS's headquarters, where practical demonstrations of all six of the NDT techniques covered in the programme were laid on for us. This invaluable contribution to the work is again gratefully acknowledged.

In all, the production of the Stage 1 materials took roughly two months, work being started in April 1982 and being completed early in June. Considering that the length of the self-instruction manual was 68 pages and that the tape-slide programme contained 75 slides, 49 of which involved the production of original artwork, we felt that we were entitled to be reasonably satisfied with this rate of progress.

Unfortunately, work on the development of Stage 2 of the course took considerably longer, largely due to circumstances that were completely outside our control. Unlike Stage 1, where all the photographs for the tape-slide programme could be taken in Aberdeen, Stage 2 required us to carry out a large amount of photographic work on an actual drilling rig. Furthermore, many of the photographs were of parts of the rig that were normally up to 70 feet under water, so that they could only be taken during an annual inspection or routine service, when the rig would be in light draught or in dry dock.

When we started work on Stage 2 (in July 1982), one of SEDCO's rigs was scheduled to undergo a major service (at Stavanger, in Norway) early in September, and provisional plans were made for us to carry out our photographic work during this service. Indeed, had everything gone according to plan, we would proabhy have been able to hand over the completed material by the end of the same month. However, due to a series of unforeseen delays, the rig did not dock at Stavanger until the middle of December, by which time the short days and deteriorating weather conditions made outdoor photography an extremely difficult exercise. Indeed, had our visit to Stavanger not happened to coincide with what we understand was virtually the only sunny, wind-free day during which the rig was in dock, we would probably *still* be waiting to take our photographs!

Since all the other work related to the production of the Stage 2 materials (writing of texts and scripts, preparation of artwork, etc) had long since been completed, we were able to finalize the package as soon as the Stavanger photographs were processed. The eventual length of the Stage 2 self-instruction manual was 86 pages, with the three introductory tape-slide programmes containing 60, 64 and 58 slides respectively. Thus, the completed course consisted of over 150 pages of text and over 250 slides — a fairly substantial package by any standards. Both stages of the course are now in regular use by SEDCO, and a supportive programme of practical workshops is already well underway.

CONCLUSION

At ETIC 82, two of the present authors made a case for increased collaboration between education and industry and showing how educational technologists are ideally placed to play an important role in such collaboration (Ellington and Addinall, 1983). The present paper provides a good example of how such collaboration can be carried out in practice, showing how two educational technologists working in the higher education sector have helped one industrial organization to produce an extension training course for another industrial organization. Since the paper also provides a case study on the application of educational technology methods to industrial training, we hope that it will prove of interest to colleagues on both sides of the education/industry 'divide'.

REFERENCE

Ellington, H I and Addinall, E (1983) Forming links between education and industry — how educational technologists can help. In Trott, A, Strongman, H and Giddins, L (eds) *Aspects of Educational Technology* XVI, pp 202-10. Kogan Page, London.

5.2 Educational and Training Technology at the German Singapore Institute

W K David Wong and Tom Wyant
Education and Training Technology Department, German Singapore Institute, Singapore

Abstract: This paper gives an outline of the educational and training courses at the German Singapore Institute. The main objective of running these courses is to train all existing and new instructors employed in the Economic Development Board centres and provide them with some form of acceptable basic pedagogical training.

BACKGROUND

In Singapore, manpower training is one of the government's main objectives. This is to maintain a continuing supply of skilled workers to meet the increasing demands of new and existing Singaporean industries. The Economic Development Board of Singapore (EDB) supports the government's objective by providing technical training for a new generation of apprentices, craftsmen, technicians, supervisory personnel and technical instructors. This is achieved by the operation of specialized industrial training institutes and centres, supported by co-operating countries.

GERMAN SINGAPORE INSTITUTE (GSI)

The German Singapore Institute of Production Technology was established in January 1981 as a joint project between the Federal Republic of Germany and the Republic of Singapore. Machinery and technical experts are contributed by the Federal Republic of Germany, whilst the Singaporean side provides buildings, services, counterparts and support staff. The German Singapore Institute training programme includes production engineering technicians specializing in machining processes, hydraulics and pneumatics, plastics technology, industrial computing, tool and die making, jig and tool design, production processes and instructor training. The workshops in the institute house an extensive range of sophisticated machinery, including numerically-controlled machines (NC), computerized numerically-controlled machines (CNC), hydraulic and pneumatic devices, plastic moulding machines, etc. After completion of the institute's two-year training courses, which are modelled on those carried out by the Meisterschules in West Germany, graduates receive a diploma in production engineering.

INSTRUCTOR TRAINING

One of the acute problems in the Singaporean technical training programme is the lack of qualified instructors. Existing instructors, whilst having competency, skills and knowledge in their own specialist areas, have received little or no training in the basic requirements of educational and training technology.

The prime objective of the GSI's Educational and Training Technology Department is that all existing and new instructors employed in the Economic Development Board centres shall receive some form of acceptable basic instructor training in the immediate future. To achieve this objective the following courses have been planned, organized and are currently running:

- ☐ Educational and training technology, Part I
- ☐ Educational and training technology, Part II

EDUCATIONAL AND TRAINING TECHNOLOGY, PART I

By the end of a four-week training course instructors will be able to:

1. Identify the main factors involved in a learning/teaching system.
2. State the purpose and importance of the identified factors.
3. Design and use detailed lesson plans, incorporating:
   - ☐ Aims and objectives
   - ☐ Selection of learning/teaching strategies
   - ☐ Design, production and use of supporting audio-visual aids and other available resources
   - ☐ Lesson evaluation schemes.
4. Design, produce, set and evaluate various methods of achievement testing.

EDUCATIONAL AND TRAINING TECHNOLOGY, PART II

This four- to six-month course is designed to be mainly self-instructional and self-directed. It is built around six modules as shown in Figure 1.

1. Investigation of a learning/teaching system
2. Design of a learning/teaching system
3. Implementation of a learning/teaching system
4. Management of a learning/teaching system
5. Evaluation of a learning/teaching system
6. Modification of a learning/teaching system

Figure 1. *Learning/teaching system modules*

A network analysis of the 73 topics contained in the six modules has been compiled and forms the master framework of the course design (see Figure 2). The network shows the logical, systematic development and relationship between the 73 topics. It also identifies for the trainee instructor the various learning strategies that are available.

At the beginning of each course every trainee instructor is interviewed and a personal profile is drawn of his or her particular training needs. This contains the topics chosen and the depth to which each topic needs to be studied (see Figure 3). The trainee instructor has a free choice of the topics that he or she may wish to start with. Once the choice is made, the trainee instructor utilizes the Radio Shack TRS-80 computer to type in the number of the selected topic. The computer then prints out the topics, objectives, details of reference or resource materials, standards to be achieved and information regarding forms of in-depth study, if the instructor wishes to pursue his or her studies further (see Figure 4).

A resource bank of materials is available and is based on the reference number allocated to each topic. Types of resource materials available are:

1. Cassette-tapes (recordings of lectures or factual information).
2. Video-taperecordings of selected micro-teaching sessions.
3. Articles, journals, handouts and newspaper cuttings.
4. Learner-controlled (user friendly) computer-assisted learning packages.
5. Tape-slide presentations.

When necessary, lectures, lessons, demonstrations, role-playing sessions and tutorials are available on request to the department staff.

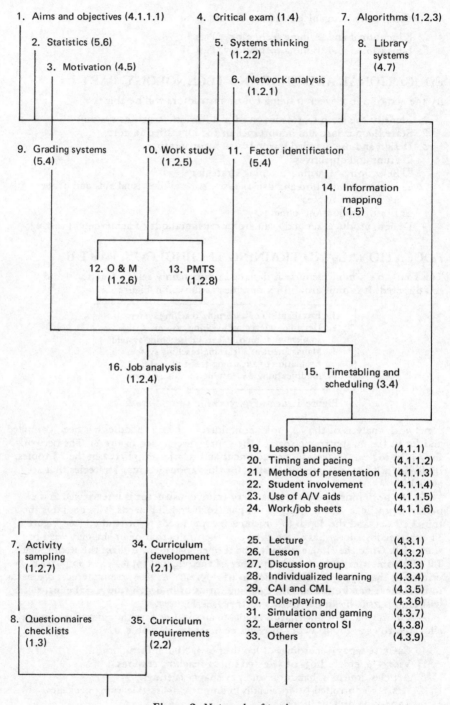

Figure 2. *Network of topics*

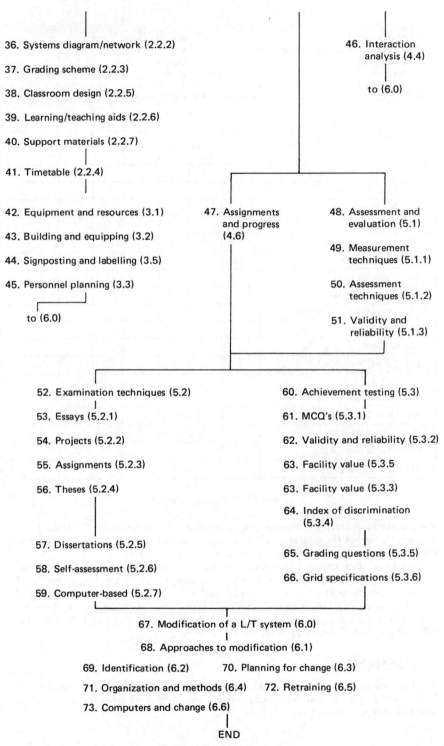

Figure 2. *Network of topics*

German Singapore Institute
Education and training counterpart/
student training
Progress checklist

Name: David Wong
Dept: Ed tech
Date: 17.2.83
Disk: *60-PROGCHEK/TOM:θ

NO	TOPIC	KNOW	COMP	APPL	ANAL	SYNT	EVAL	SIGNED
1.	Aims & objectives							
2.	Statistics							
3.	Motivation							
4.	Critical examination							
5.	Systems thinking							
6.	Network analysis							
7.	Algorithms							
8.	Library systems							
9.	Grading systems							
10.	Work study							
11.	Factor identification							
12.	Organization & methods							
13.	PMTS							
14.	Information mapping							
15.	Timetabling & scheduling							
16.	Job analysis							
17.	Activity sampling							
18.	Questionnaires/checklists							
19.	Lesson planning							
20.	Timing and pacing							
21.	Methods of presentation							

Figure 3. *Progress checklist*

Furthermore, materials, resources, teaching aids, etc, designed by the trainee instructors during the course, are retained and incorporated into the resource bank for the benefit of the instructors coming to the next course.

As part of their course requirement, trainee instructors will be called upon to give lessons or demonstrations to an audience comprising trainees from the Part I courses which may be running in parallel to the Part II course. It is also envisaged that the graduates of the Part II course, will be capable of running a Part I course in their own training centres, initially under the supervision of the staff from the Educational and Training Technology Department.

ASSESSMENT

For both courses instructors are assessed on their micro-teaching sessions, practice lessons, development and use of audio-visual aids, design of assessment/evaluation schemes and project work.

Education instructor training course Module No. 1: Investigation of a L/T system	6. Network analysis (1.2.1) GSI – TGW – Sept – 1981 Disk No. 40 COMAPSI/TOM:0

Introduction	Network analysis is a management technique for the planning, organizing and controlling of projects.

Objectives	After completing this module section the student will:
	1. Draw a network analysis of a subject of his choice, showing:
	  1.1 A logical development of the subject matter
	  1.2 Correct numbering off of the nodes
	  1.3 Clear identification of the subjects and topics.
	  From the network the student should develop ideas to assist him in the planning, organization and development of his lessons, teaching methods, subject development, etc.

Practical work	1. Completion of the exercises given in the course handout 2. Drawing of a network of a syllabus or curriculum
References	☐ *Learning to Change* (UNESCO) pages 32, 68-70 ☐ Various management books (Resources Centre) ☐ Course handout ☐ Articles and publications
Aids	☐ Transparencies ☐ Handouts
In-depth work	☐ Design of a new syllabus by network analysis ☐ Investigatory work on the use of the computer and an educational syllabus or curriculum ☐ Self-instructional techniques based on personalized syllabi

Name: David Wong   Date: 17.2.83   Grade: Signed:

Figure 4. *Content map*

GENERAL COMMENTS

The integration of modules, network and topics gives a fair degree of flexibility to the department's tasks. The staff spend most of their time in designing and developing learning materials for the courses.

The department has also made it possible for any training centre to receive any module it requires for use in its own premises. For example, a short course can be extracted and tailor-made from 'Module 5: Evaluation of a learning/teaching system' where a need has arisen to encourage staff to write and evaluate multiple-choice test items.

CONCLUSION

Finally, the authors would like to bring home the point that equal opportunities are provided for all instructors to strive to fulfil themselves in terms of acquiring knowledge and skills. It is estimated that at the end of a five-year period all instructors from the Singapore Economic Development Board training centres will have received updating of educational and training technology and there will be co-operation among the training institutes and centres, in the production of learning and teaching resources, as well as in the research and development of educational technology.

5.3 The Changing Requirements for Craftsmen in the Process Industries

Dr Michael Cross
Senior Research Fellow, The Technical Change Centre

Abstract: 1. What problems occur in the repair and maintenance of plant which may be due to deficiencies in the skill, knowledge, attitudes or utilization of craftsmen? 2. What changes in training content, training method, and manpower utilization would help to overcome the problem? 3. How can the decision-making processes about recruitment, training and utilization be improved to ensure a self-correcting system which continues to meet the needs of the plant? 4. What trends (especially technological, organizational, attitudinal) are occurring or foreseen? 5. What further changes in training content, training method and manpower utilization will be necessary to meet the needs of the future?

OBJECTIVE OF THE RESEARCH

The terms of reference adopted are: (a) to establish the process industries' need for craft skills and knowledge for the 1980s onward, and (b) to determine the most appropriate and effective scheme of training to provide the skilled manpower in craft trades which the process industries require.

METHODOLOGY

Empirical data were collected from 36 companies in which 114 formal interviews were conducted. A further 107 formal interviews were also conducted with trade unions, government departments, consultants, machinery suppliers, etc to examine the research findings in a wider context, to validate them and to explore their implications. The case study firms were chosen as ones being known to be 'technical leaders' in their sectors. In all, 14 sectors have been considered and these are: brick (2, 2);[1] cement (1, 2); man-made fibres (2, 2); pharmaceuticals (3, 4); cigarette (1, 2); plastic (4, 7); food (5, 8); brewing (2, 3); chemicals (5, 7); glass (3, 4); asbestos (3, 4); packaging and paper (3, 3); rubber (1, 2); and metal manufacture and casting (1, 6). Data were collected on a range of topics relating to personnel and employee relation policies, maintenance strategy, production scheduling, etc, and they relate to the sites visited (36 in all). The data, however, also relate to a further 54 sites as policy and practice were determined from the main site visited. At the main sites over 6,800 craftsmen were employed and the study has examined how their jobs are changing, the factors influencing those changes, and processes by which current and future craft skill requirements can be satisfied.

SUMMARY OF MAJOR FINDINGS

Distinct common/general craft skill requirements are now emerging, and there is as yet little means of translating this demand into an effective training supply scheme.

[1] *Number of cases considered, final number of cases to be considered*

In broad terms these new craft skills can be broken down into four 'levels':

- ☐ Traditional craftsmen.
- ☐ General craftsmen (cross- and dual-skilled).
- ☐ Machine specialist craftsmen.
- ☐ System specialist craftsmen.

At the moment companies are providing the above range of skills by increasing the use of contractors (especially upon process control equipment), by creating 'false' technician grades, by wholesale training reviews to improve the technical abilities of existing craftsmen, and by selective training programmes.

The major barriers to progress in supplying the necessary skills is the low level of existing skills, poor existing training provisions, common craft rate pay structures, lack of appropriate training material and courses, the lack of a clear and agreed definition of the skills required, the speed of the existing system to react to changing demand (improvements are being made), and the failure when installing new plant to define new skills and training requirements.

SUMMARY OF MAJOR CONCLUSION

1. In order to ensure a supply of the necessary calibre of craft labour there is a need to establish a career structure and a suitably flexible payments structure to allow for skill acquisition. At the moment single craft rates are causing dissatisfaction amongst craftsmen and will result in them leaving their employers to join either maintenance contractor/service support firms or to join other better paying employers. This is causing and will continue to cause skill shortages.
2. There is a need to explore the possibility of developing both an occupational and a regional training system rather than the current sector and national systems.
3. The *effective* diffusion and utilization of the more complex microprocessor-based control system will be impeded, especially in terms of incremental additions to existing plant, without the provision of a competent and motivated craft workforce.
4. Much greater efforts are needed to monitor the emergence and development of new craft skill requirements and their translation into appropriate training courses. Such schemes as Open Tech and NTI will help, but by themselves will probably prove insufficient.
5. Methods of training delivery and assessment need to be examined and explored.
6. Enough training material exists at the present for a start to be made, but a means for its collation, validation and dissemination needs to be found. (An initiative has been taken by the Technical Change Centre with respect to this need; funds are being raised from both industry and the Manpower Services Commission.)

FUTURE PROGRAMME OF WORK

1. Continuation of existing programme of work, building up a monitoring of skills exercise with 56 companies.
2. Running of three industrial workshops with companies already involved, leading to a series of agreed recommendations in relation to training for maintenance in the process industries.
3. Running of four employment workshops with colleagues at the Technical Change Centre.

4. Detailed examination of the supply of specialist, high-level skills by maintenance contractors/equipment suppliers, with specific reference to process control equipment.
5. Extension of existing programme of work into the food processing industries to involve 250 firms. (Funds are being sought from the Department of Employment/Manpower Services Commission.)

Section 6:
Career Updating for
Professionals and Managers

6.1 Date to Update

Cynthia Stoane
Glenrothes and Buckhaven Technical College, Fife

Abstract: Professional updating is important not only from the point of view of knowledge; it also makes practitioners reconsider their practice and question their own competence. This paper presents a case study of a method used to provide practitioners with opportunity to make decisions about their practice, to offer individualized feedback about their decisions and to allow them to assess their own competence. The materials used were relevant to practice, the practitioners using them were made aware of their relevance and importance and were able to use them at the time, place and pace which suited them. The method described is applicable for the in-service training and updating of teachers, psychologists, social workers, business executives and trainers.

INTRODUCTION

The professional updating of teachers, psychologists, social workers and technologists, to name but a few practitioners, is recognized as vitally important. Methodologies and technologies are changing so rapidly that the practitioner could quickly become outdated in his practice unless he continues his education in some way. There is no shortage of books and journals designed for the continuing education of those in practice, but receipt of literature does not guarantee reading nor indeed learning (Byrne, 1969). In-service courses and conferences may be offered, but lack of time and money, and distance from colleges and conference centres frequently deters busy practitioners from attending. A further deterrent is a lack of communication between those in practice and 'experts' in an idealized situation. Courses for the continuing education of professionals are organized, in many cases, by the experts. Lecturers in colleges can have very different experience and perceptions from practitioners in the field and perhaps little idea of what it is like to work there. As a result courses offered often have little relevance to the real situation and frequently do not take into consideration the problems which practitioners actually face.

RATIONALE

If professional workers are to update their knowledge effectively and frequently, they must be provided with courses and materials which are relevant to practice and they must be made aware of their relevance and importance. In order that such aims be met, practitioners must have the opportunity to question their competence to practise, become aware of deficiencies in their knowledge and thus see the need to update. The remainder of this paper describes a method used to provide general practitioners in the medical profession with an opportunity to make decisions about their own practice, to offer individualized feedback about their decisions and to allow them to assess their own competence in a non-threatening way. Such a method has applicability to the in-service training of most professionals.

METHOD

Distance Learning

This method was first designed at the Centre for Medical Education at the University of Dundee and used a distance learning approach to overcome problems of time, distance and, in many cases, shortage of money. Distance study has been found to be an effective answer to the problems of continuing education for the following reasons:

1. Materials can be used at learner's own time, at his own pace, and at a convenient place. In addition, learning can be carried out in the privacy of the home, if preferred.
2. Relevant material, designed specifically for one centre, can be widely disseminated.
3. Active involvement and feedback can and should be built into the learning process.

Self-Assessment

A self-assessment exercise was designed in diary form, and mailed from the university to 4,000 general practitioners throughout the United Kingdom. Each diary describes the day-to-day management of a patient by general practitioner Dr Mackay. The decisions he had to make, the drugs he prescribed, the way he handled the patient, the social and psychological decisions he made, and where he looked for information to help him in his decision-making, are all discussed.

A doctor reading the diary might strongly agree or disagree with some of the choices. What Dr Mackay did is not necessarily correct. The participator is asked to make decisions about the way he would have managed the patient, either recording his answers on a reply-paid card which he returns to Dundee, or telephoning his answers on a 24-hour answering machine. This also provides opportunity to record comment or question. He then receives a personalized letter comparing his answers with the author's and, along with the letter, the next diary.

There are four diaries in the series. All cover areas of importance to general practitioners, provide opportunity to make decisions about practice, offer individualized feedback about decisions, and allow doctors to assess their own competence.

Case Study

As an example, the second diary studies the problems with a mongol child. A young couple have a new baby — a mongol. Hospital staff are uncommunicative with both the father and the general practitioner. Mother and baby are discharged from hospital, mother rejecting the baby. Dr Mackay faces the problem of management with little help. In his words: 'Haven't seen a new case of mongolism for a time; must check the books'; and he goes on to detail what he learns when he does so. 'Nothing like a case in the practice to improve your knowledge', he ponders. This is subtle teaching. The reader doctor is made to feel that his problems are understood. This is a non-threatening approach.

In a further extract Dr Mackay writes: 'Found a good book by Janet Carr', and he discusses its content. The reference list is thus presented in a non-threatening form. He also finds a need for and demonstrates an awareness of the roles of other disciplines, such as the social work department or the education department in the management of the parents and child. Help organizations (eg Downs Baby Association) are mentioned.

As the story begins to have a happy ending, with the diagnosis of mongolism as slight, mother's acceptance of the child and father's marital problems solved, the doctor is made to feel that this is as a result of the hard work of the good general practitioner, who is prepared to question his decisions and his knowledge, continue his education and update himself. How easy it would have been to turn them away to cope by themselves.

DISCUSSION

Feedback

A frequent complaint about courses offered for in-service training is that insufficient feedback is provided. Many courses are too didactic, offering little opportunity for learner participation and therefore little opportunity to measure competence or achievement. Provision must be made for two-way communication (Lewis, 1975). As there cannot be regular face-to-face contact in a distance learning approach of the nature described, the opportunity should be built into the course for the learner to obtain immediate feedback and to contact a tutor for more detailed feedback or assistance if and when necessary (Durno, 1974). It was therefore an aim of this course to provide doctors with the opportunity to become actively involved in decision-making about their competence: to compare their own decisions with those of experts and, hopefully, to speculate about the differences of opinion and become aware of possible deficiencies in their knowledge. This problem-solving approach can provide the active involvement which has been recognized as essential for effective learning (McGuire, 1967).

The print method used to provide individualized feedback to the learner is the cheapest but also one of the slowest methods. Adaptability to other media, such as the computer, will be apparent (Stoane, 1980).

Relevance to Practice

It is important that the writers of such materials should bear in mind the overall aims of the approach:

☐ To provide materials which are relevant to the practitioners for whom they are written.
☐ To make the practitioners aware of the relevance and importance of the materials.

The first aim can be met by involving in the writing team not only subject experts but also recognized experts from the field. In the medical example described this meant that a consultant worked hand in hand with a practitioner to combine theory with everyday practice. In the case of in-service training of teachers, a college lecturer or an educational psychologist might work with a practising teacher.

The second aim calls for expertise from educational developers and researchers who will design into the materials activity and assessment which will indicate its relevance. In this way potential users will not only be encouraged to take up the course initially but will also be motivated to continue (Premi, 1974).

Research has shown, however, that many people can be aware of the relevance and importance of educational material yet, for various reasons, not make use of it (Byrne, 1969; Stoane, 1982). It has been reported that incentive provides the motivation to take up a course of study and this can take the form of a reward, such as a certificate, or even something more tangible. Compulsory enrolment too cannot be ruled out as an incentive and a driving factor. The 'friendly reminder' to continue study (Harden, 1980) is a motivating factor.

Convenience and Flexibility

It has already been said that a distance learning approach can provide the learner with the opportunity to study in the place, at the time and at the pace most convenient to him (Holmberg, 1975; 1982). Some flexibility must also be provided in follow-up activities so that they meet individual needs and preferences for study.

Administration

Administrative arrangements for the individualized feedback should be carefully planned so that there is immediate turn-round and the mechanism is as smooth as possible. Delay can cause frustration to the learner, resulting in lack of motivation to continue. The use of a telephone consultancy or a telephone answering system for very personalized feedback is well worth considering.

CONCLUSIONS AND RECOMMENDATIONS

The method described used a diary approach as an interesting and motivational way of presenting information for professional updating. The combination of materials which were relevant to practice and which used non-threatening self-assessment techniques led the potential learner to realize the importance of and need for updating. The use of a distance learning approach proved attractive to busy professionals in service.

But how, we may ask, is an effective piece of in-service training to be recognized? In a recent working paper (Neville, 1982), it is stated that this will be by the observable and desirable changes in achievement of a trained teacher's class (or a doctor's patients). Unfortunately this is difficult for most trainers to observe and to correlate with the training. As a result, most training is judged, at best, on the teacher's (ie the student's) reactions as expressed to the trainer; at worst, it is judged by the extent of the continuing demand for the course or materials. Doctors who received the diaries found the approach to be effective. They liked the method and claimed to have learned from it. The method described has applicability to the in-service training of other professionals, including teachers in schools and colleges, psychologists, social workers, technologists and business executives.

REFERENCES

Byrne, P (1969) Postgraduate education for general practitioners. *British Journal of Medical Education,* **3**, p 50.

Durno, D and Gill, G M (1974) *Journal of the Royal College of Practitioners,* **24**, p 648.

Harden, R M, Stoane, C and Dunn, W R (1980) Learning at a distance: evaluation at a distance. In Winterburn, R and Evans, L (eds) *Aspects of Educational Technology* **XIV**. Kogan Page, London.

Holmberg, B (1981) *Status and Trends of Distance Education.* Kogan Page, London.

Holmberg, B (1976) *Distance Education.* Kogan Page, London.

Lewis, R (1975) The place of face to face tuition in the Open University system.

McGuire, C (1967) Simulation technique in the teaching and testing of problem solving skills. Michigan Annual Meeting of *National Association for Research in Science Teaching.*

Neville, C *et al* (1982) Development and use of materials for in-service training of teachers. *Council for Educational Technology* Working Paper 21, p 30.

Premi, J N (1974) *Canadian Medical Association Journal,* **3**, p 1232.

Stoane, C and Stoane, J (1980) Answers at a distance. In Percival, F and Ellington, H (eds). *Aspects of Educational Technology* **XV**. Kogan Page, London.

Stoane, C, Harden, R M and Dunn, W R (1982) Doctors who did not participate in a continuing education programme. *Medical Education,* **16**, pp 296-299.

ACKNOWLEDGEMENTS

The author acknowledges *Pharmacia Limited* for financial support of 'A Doctors Diary' and the Centre for Medical Education, University of Dundee for permission to describe the method.

6.2 The OUTPUT Method: A New Approach to Management Training

Keith Elliott
Senior Lecturer, Social Studies Dept, Liverpool Polytechnic
and
Don Wright
Senior Executive, Trustee Savings Bank, North West

Abstract: This article explains the five-stage OUTPUT study method and its relevance to learning situations. It then goes on to show that the thought process inherent in the OUTPUT method is in itself a systematic approach which can be applied to most management role situations which have their core in analysis and information usage. It can be applied continuously by managers, thereby avoiding the idea of a specific solution to a specific activity which is used on only infrequent occasions.

The study skills literature (Main, 1980) is full of sensible advice, but it has been said that its fault is that students find it impossibly hard to follow (Howe, 1982). We felt that the separate pieces of advice needed integration into a single, simple study method that students could remember and use.

Research and 'chalkface' experience suggest that learning is likely to be more effective when, during study periods, there is:

1. A clear defined target or objective.
2. Study with clearly framed questions in mind.
3. Activity rather than the passivity of, say, merely re-reading old notes.
4. The creation of notes and their conversion from one form to another.
5. A final testing of recall of the material to determine if the target has been achieved.

These well-established features of purpose, activity and recall have been integrated into a single new method which we call the OUTPUT method. It is so called because it enables the inputs of time and effort to be converted into outputs of more effective learning. The method consists of five parts — MAP OUT, SEARCH OUT, LOOK OUT, PRINT OUT and CHECK OUT — and is shown in Figure 1.

MAP OUT

It has been said of Christopher Columbus that when he set out he did not know where he was going, when he got there he did not know where he was and when he returned he did not know where he had been. This first stage is designed to prevent students from falling into the 'Columbus syndrome'.

When you map out a journey you should know your constraints, that is, for instance, you should know how much time you have for it so that you can decide whether you can complete it in one attempt or divide it into shorter stages. Similarly, when starting to study, students need to MAP OUT what they are to study by looking at the overall picture of the study topic. Sources of information must be identified and collected and then there should be a fairly quick survey of the material to provide a general idea of its complexity, familiarity, content and format. In the light of this initial MAP OUT a target can be set that is clear and attainable within the time slot available, and adjusted by the learner to his own perception of his progress and ability.

MAP OUT *enables a target to be set geared to the time available.*

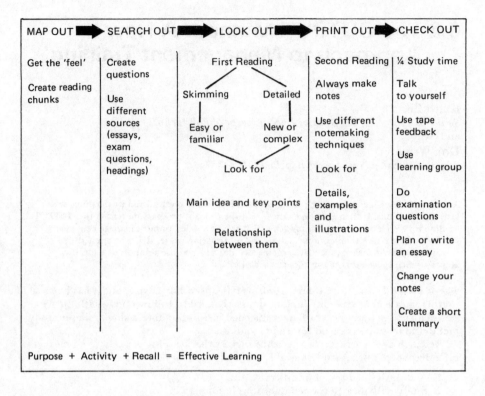

Figure 1. *The OUTPUT study method*

SEARCH OUT

It is vital to be purposive when studying. The creation of questions is a crucial preparatory stage because it provides a focus and aids concentration. OUTPUT's second stage therefore is to search out the subject area to create a series of questions. These questions can cover a number of categories and be initiated by different sources.

Categories	Sources
Content itself	Exam questions
International comparisons	Essay titles
Recent developments	Tutorial topics
Methodology used	Heading and subheadings from
Sources employed	the text
Criticism and evaluation	
Links to other subject areas	

In skills classes students are able to create many questions on any topic in just 60 seconds and very quickly it is realized that they provide a sense of direction.
SEARCH OUT *concentrates study activity and makes it active and purposive.*

MAP OUT and SEARCH OUT are the vital preparatory stages. We have found that students can be trained in their usage very quickly and that they readily see the benefits of not diving straight into the information-using stage, ie LOOK OUT.

LOOK OUT

Here students are on the LOOK OUT for the information that will enable them to answer their questions and to achieve their target. It is the stage when information is gathered in by reading or listening. At this stage it is vital to realize that there are probably three levels of learning as shown below. Level one, the lowest level, is concerned with details and facts. It is the level so often considered to be the only one by students at O Level where they are faced with rote-learning facts. Level two is a more interesting stage when relationships between the facts are considered. At level three overall theories or structures that make sense of the relationships and facts are considered or created. Students need to be made aware of these two higher levels of learning if they are to 'deepen' their learning (Marton, 1975).

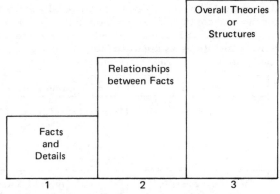

Figure 2. *Three levels of learning*

To encourage this we suggest that notes are *not* made during the LOOK OUT (or LISTEN OUT) stage. This is for three reasons. First, if notes are made on first reading, before the student knows what is to come and what the thread of the argument is, then they will inevitably be too long, and will almost certainly involve copying down chunks of the text word for word. This form of 'written photocopying' can cause major problems later when these notes are used for essays and the student is accused of plagiarism! Second, knowing that the text is to be read twice, with notes made on second reading, discourages the slow reader's habit of regression or backtracking and so can encourage faster reading speeds. Third, and most important, knowing that you can read the text again enables the first reading to concentrate on the higher levels of learning. The facts and details themselves can be noted on second reading.

The nature of the first reading, whether or not it can be skimmed, will depend on the assessment of the material made at MAP OUT. For simple and familiar material a skimmed first reading would be possible but for more complex and unfamiliar material a normal detailed first reading would be required.

LOOK OUT *provides the information that answers questions.*

PRINT OUT

This stage is concerned with building up a structure of relevant notes. As memory fades over time it is important to PRINT OUT information of the relationships and structures identified at LOOK OUT. The separation of LOOK OUT from PRINT OUT emphasizes the importance of identifying the key points and the general thread of the argument or analysis *before* engaging in note-making activity.

The print-out of notes can take place now that the key idea(s) are firmly in mind following the first skimmed or detailed reading. Reading through for the second time the focus can be more on the supporting details, examples, and illustrations. The selected main ideas and supporting details and examples can then be put into note form.

The normal and traditional note form is the vertical note in which linear notes are made using the lines in sequence. The emphasis here tends to be on the words rather than space, or on the relationship between words. An alternative form which we find students enjoy using once they are trained in its use is 'horizontal space' note-taking. Here the 'tyranny' of vertical lines is overcome by the simple device of turning the page sideways — ie by using 'horizontal space'. This enables patterns and relationships to be shown and, crucially, it encourages brevity.

Apart from the patterned note (Buzan, 1974) there are other horizontal space notes. Particularly useful is the horizontal frame shown in Figure 3. It enables comparisons and contrasts to be seen by looking horizontally and is vital when preparing for 'compare and contrast' essay and examination questions. The horizontal frame is also particularly valuable to managers when they are producing alternative solutions to 'situations' as discussed later in the paper.

PRINT OUT *builds up a storehouse of information.*

	Vertical Notes	**Horizontal Space Notes**
Type of note	Traditional linear	Patterned note (Buzan, 1974) Horizontal frame Flow diagrams Hierarchy Trees or pyramids
Format	The notes use lines in sequence	Page usually turned sideways. Notes use space to create shapes and patterns.
Emphasis	Is on words only	Is on space, and relationships not just words.
Advantages	1. Useful specially when listening and there is only one hearing. 2. Can provide the base for later conversion into horizontal space notes.	1. With the page placed sideways notes are likely to be concise. 2. The focus on relationships and patterns eases recall.

Figure 3. *A horizontal frame about notes*

CHECK OUT

At this final stage of the OUTPUT study method students should CHECK OUT that they have hit their target by ensuring that they can recall the material and that they have answered their questions. By doing this students secure a basis of understanding and make revision a continuous all-year-round activity. The techniques that can be used all emphasize activity; they include writing examination answers, talking to yourself (possibly with a tape), and the creation of fresh notes by converting those made at PRINT OUT into a different form. The knowledge that the study period will conclude with a CHECK OUT session will in itself create a sense of purpose and increase concentration. This stage is therefore so crucial it should take up about a quarter of study time.

CHECK OUT *cements understanding and eases learning and recall.*

OUTPUT IN MANAGEMENT TRAINING

The response to our training courses and to our book, *Studying the Professional Way* (Elliott and Wright, 1982),[1] which sets out the OUTPUT method in full, has confirmed that the method is memorable, popular and embraces all the key elements necessary for successful study. We have always felt that one of the strengths of the method is its flexibility and its applicability as a thought process to learning situations; consequently we have started to apply OUTPUT to the area of management skills. Today's manager is faced with a variety of information sources, both verbal and written, all of which require assimilating, summarizing, storing and subsequently using; very similar skills to those used by the effective student.

The OUTPUT method has an obvious use for the manager in his role as an 'information filter', and an improvement in the application of 'learning skills' benefits all managerial staff (Figure 4). The practising manager also carries out many functions which include an analytical or mechanistic component, such as problem-solving, decision-making, managing change — areas in which separate training programmes are available to ensure managerial competence.

The proliferation of training courses and their individual systems and methods can create some problems for managers when they attempt to apply their new skills in the workplace. Each course will have its own specific 3, 5, 8 or 10 step approach (Kepner and Tregoe, 1965), and provided the manager can remember how many steps there are and which system applies to which process, he can proceed with his particular management activity. The practical result of the numerous systematic methods (Leigh, 1983) is that they fall into misuse during a normal hectic management day — the usual management training dilemma.

The OUTPUT study method is in itself a systematic approach, but it has the benefit of being applicable to most routine management role situations which have an analytical and information usage core. Consequently it can be applied continuously by managers, thereby avoiding the idea of a specific solution to a specific activity which is used on only infrequent occasions. The application of the OUTPUT stages to these areas of management is shown in Figure 5.

From Figure 5 it can be seen that the approach is very similar to that adopted by successful students although in practical terms the completion of the cycle will take much longer than in a learning situation. For example, data usage at LOOK OUT and implementation and feedback at CHECK OUT can often take weeks or months to complete. The significance of the method is that it ensures managers reach rational, objective solutions and strategies which will in the long run save time and money.

Managers are usually extremely busy, and when faced with 'a situation' there is a tendency for them to opt for an obvious remedy or course of action. By applying the first two stages of OUTPUT managers can avoid the dangers inherent in such an approach. MAP OUT ensures that they define the 'situation' carefully and consider where data can be acquired, whilst SEARCH OUT helps to detail those important areas which require specific attention. The process of generating SEARCH OUT questions opens the manager's vision to the alternatives available and thereby helps to avoid stereotyped answers (de Bono, 1982).

The importance of these stages cannot be over-emphasized. They do not take long, particularly when SEARCH OUT questions can often be categorized, for example, in terms of human, technical and financial criteria. Managers are always conscious of time, but by taking steps to concentrate their subsequent activity

---

[1] *Copies of 'Studying the Professional Way' (£3.95 inc p & P) and further information regarding courses in learning skills and management training may be obtained from: Skills of the Eighties, FREEPOST, Birkenhead, Merseyside L42 2AB.*

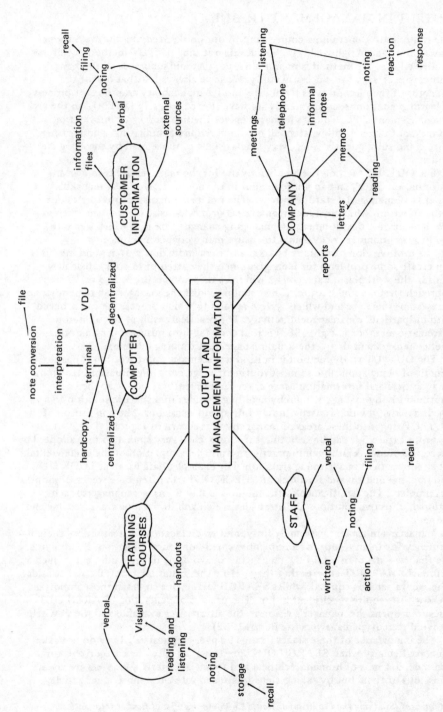

Figure 4. *OUTPUT, learning skills and management information*

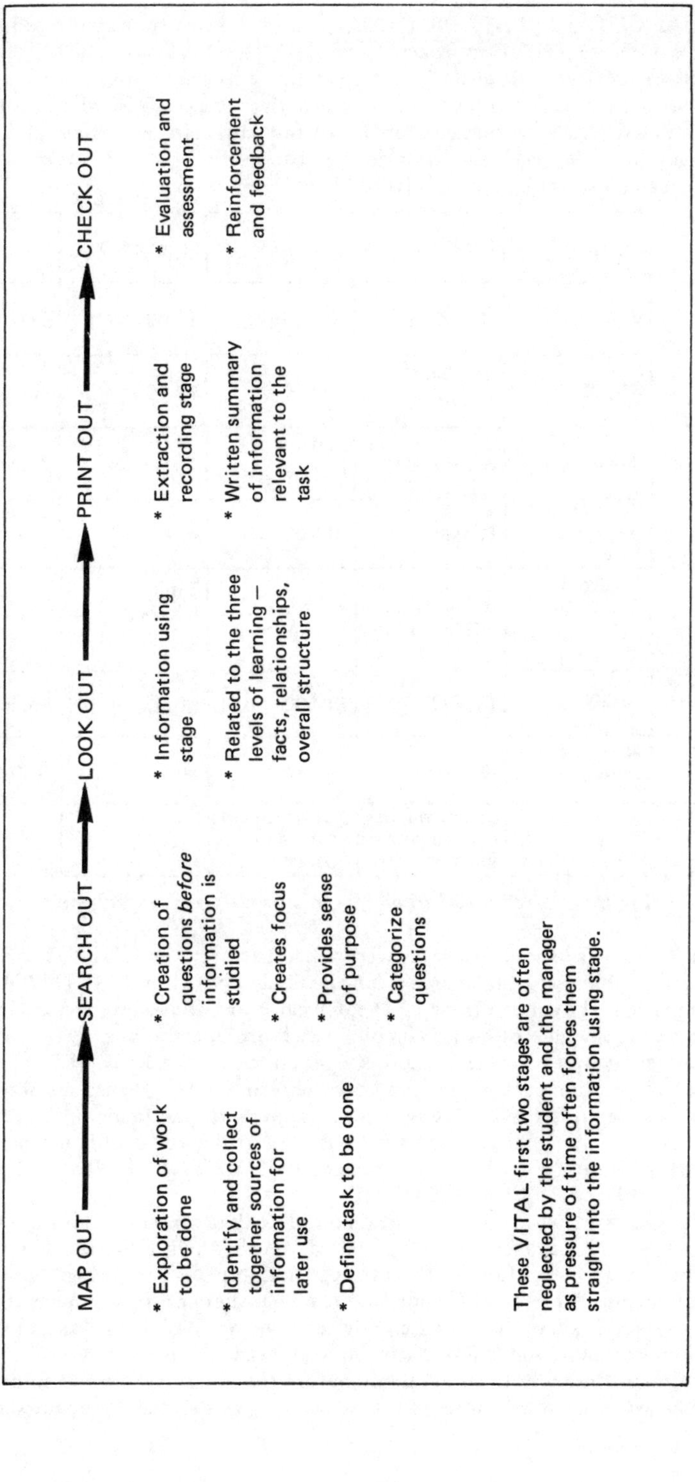

MAP OUT → SEARCH OUT → LOOK OUT → PRINT OUT → CHECK OUT

MAP OUT

* Exploration of work to be done

* Identify and collect together sources of information for later use

* Define task to be done

SEARCH OUT

* Creation of questions *before* information is studied

* Creates focus

* Provides sense of purpose

* Categorize questions

LOOK OUT

* Information using stage

* Related to the three levels of learning — facts, relationships, overall structure

PRINT OUT

* Extraction and recording stage

* Written summary of information relevant to the task

CHECK OUT

* Evaluation and assessment

* Reinforcement and feedback

These VITAL first two stages are often neglected by the student and the manager as pressure of time often forces them straight into the information using stage.

Figure 5. *The OUTPUT method applied to management*

through MAP OUT and SEARCH OUT they can save much time in the following three stages of the OUTPUT approach.

The PRINT OUT stage is also of vital importance to the manager, for here the relevant data are extracted and recorded, alternatives are established and action plans formulated. The systematic recording of the data using a horizontal frame note can ease the analysis of the 'situation' by showing all the relevant data and options on a single sheet of paper (Figure 6).

	Location A	Location B	Location C	Location D	Require
Space	9,000 sq ft	12,000 sq ft	6,000 sq ft	12,000 sq ft	>11,000 sq ft
Rental	£10,000	£10,000(3) 10,500(2)	£8,000	£9,500	min
Lease	5 yrs	3 and 2 yrs	Variable to 10 yrs	3 yrs max	3-5 yrs
Services charged first year	Painting and renovation — no cost	£2,000	£1,200	£3,000	—
Location	Adjacent to present	— opposite side of town — 10 mins drive — 8 miles	5 mins	5 mins (airport)	<15 mins
Cost of move charged first year	£1,500	£2,000	£1,500	£1,500	minimum
Time	Available 30 days	90 days	60 days	Now	<60 days
Extras		Owner will pay rent on current location	Owner pay cost of move for 5 yr lease		

Figure 6. *Horizontal frame for location of office decision*

During the ETIC workshop, delegates were asked to apply the OUTPUT approach to a standard problem-solving exercise. The general application of OUTPUT to problem-solving is shown in Figure 7. The delegates involved were particularly concerned about the lack of data available, which became obvious as soon as they tried to answer the questions that had been generated in SEARCH OUT. (Examples of the kind of questions developed and how they can be categorized are shown in Figure 8.) This demonstrates a strength of the approach: practising managers often start from the position: 'What data have I got? Let's solve the problem'; more useful is the position: 'What have I got to achieve?' (MAP OUT) 'What information do I need to achieve it?' (SEARCH OUT).

Whilst we accept that in the real world complete data are not always available, this should not lead managers to take a limited view of their activities. They need to improve their creative thinking and to produce action plans that bring about long-term solutions. The OUTPUT method can help them do this by providing a framework which ensures that as much relevant data as possible are collected to allow the generation of viable alternative solutions; the data should be recorded in a horizontal frame to facilitate comparison, before the most appropriate solution can be implemented to answer a 'situation' that was clearly defined at the outset.

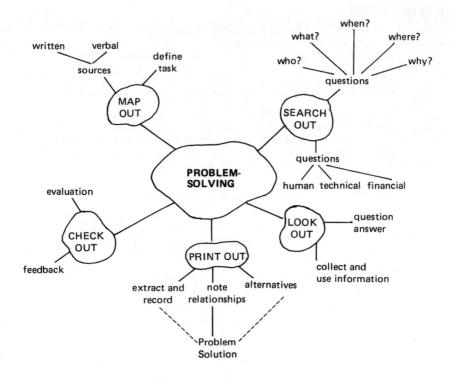

Figure 7. *OUTPUT and problem-solving*

What is different from standard?
    ☐ What standards expected?
    ☐ How great is deviation?
    ☐ Rising or falling?
Who is involved?
    ☐ One section/group?
    ☐ Confined to particular age/sex/education?
What equipment/system is involved?
    ☐ Is it specific to unit/tool/machine?
    ☐ Has specification been changed?
    ☐ Is equipment new?
When does it happen?
    ☐ At one time of day/month/year?
    ☐ Coincides with people/system change?
Where does it occur?
    ☐ Confined to one part of organization?
    ☐ Spread geographically?
Are there any relationships/causal connections?
    ☐ Do factors relate?
    ☐ Are any factors irrelevant?
What are possible causes of problems?
What is urgency of solution implementation?
What is possible solution?

Figure 8. *SEARCH OUT*

REFERENCES

de Bono, E (1982) *de Bono's Thinking Course*. BBC Publications.

Buzan, T (1974) *Use your Head*. BBC Publications.

Elliott, K and Wright, D (1982) *Studying the Professional Way*. Northwick Publishers, Worcester.

Howe, A (1982) Study skills as a province of educational technology. In Osborne, C W (ed) *International Yearbook of Educational and Instructional Technology 1982-83*. Kogan Page, London.

Kepner, C H and Tregoe, B B (1965) *The Rational Manager*. McGraw Hill.

Leigh, A (1983) *Decisions, Decisions*. Institute of Personnel Management.

Main, A (1980) *Encouraging Effective Learning*. Scottish Academic Press, Edinburgh.

Marton, F (1975) What does it take to learn? In Entwistle, N and Hounsell, D *How Students Learn*. Readings in Higher Education, **1**, University of Lancaster.

Section 7:
Theory and Applications of Educational Technology

7.1 The Mutual Influence of Large-Scale Integrated and Very Large-Scale Integrated Components in the Development of Equipment and Education Technologies

M Kovács

LSI Application, Information and Learning Centre, Budapest

Abstract: The following problems are dealt with: structural modification in the electronics industry; technical development from the point of view of increasing circuit complexity; development trends in digital techniques; modifications in the field of education, vocational and professional training; teachware and preparation for the application of the microelectronic devices in Hungary.

INTRODUCTION

Currently amongst the most important problems are how fast creative work can be developed and how fast new techniques can be adapted. The electronics industry has been in critical circumstances for a long time. In the field of digital technique qualitative changes as a consequence of sudden development are taking place every five or six years. These qualitative changes have caused radical alterations not only in the whole industry, but also in our way of life. Consider first the mutual influence of the electronic components and equipment industry in the field of digital techniques. The capabilities of the electronics industry are determined by the properties of components. It was necessary to find new solutions to produce large digital equipment. This fact has strongly influenced research work and resulted in great improvements in the electronic components — as regards reliability, power, dimension and price — by two to nine orders of magnitude within the last 30 years (see Figure 1). This improvement has particularly been the consequence of technological research which has resulted in greatly increased circuit complexity. Ready-made circuits instead of discrete components have introduced a large structural modification in the electronics industry (see Figure 2).

As a result of the LSI/VLSI technology, the production of the electronics of digital equipment will consist mostly of processing solid material instead of mounting different components. This means that electronic equipment production is continuously rising to the level of the integrated circuit technology. Figure 2 shows changes in circuit complexity, the decrease in prices of active elements, and structural modification between component industry and equipment industry as regards design and mounting of electronic equipment affected by semiconductor technologies.

The appearance of small-scale integrated circuits set the designer free from problems of designing traditional circuits with discrete components. A number of ready-made logical functions have been provided by medium-scale integrated circuits so that design has become quicker and easier. More complicated problems can be solved more flexibly. The appearance of LSIs has brought about a revolution in electronics. The introduction of microprocessors and microprogramming (stored in the Read Only Memories — ROM) has promoted a structural change in digital system techniques. Figure 3 presents system design transformation as a function of system complexity. Today it is obvious the LSIs cannot be considered as just one component among others. Microprocessors and microcomputers are the most

CIRCUIT UNIT	GATE PER UNIT	PRICE OF AN ACTIVE ELEMENT	DESIGNING AND MOUNTING OF THE DIGITAL EQUIPMENT /%/	
			COMPONENT FABRICATION	EQUIPMENT FABRICATION
TRADITIONAL /1948-1968/	1	/$/ .10		
MM/MICRO-MODUL/ /1952-1966/	1	.10		
IC SSI MSI /1963-..../	1-10 10-10²	.01 .01-.001		
IC LSI /1969-..../	10²-10⁴	.002-.0001		
IC VLSI /1975-..../	MORE THAN 10⁴	UNDER .0001		

Figure 1. *Trends of the typical active component characteristics in the field of digital technique*

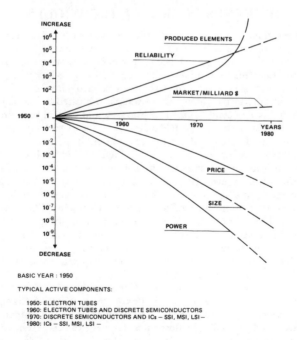

Figure 2. *Structure modification in the electronic industry*

BASIC YEAR : 1950

TYPICAL ACTIVE COMPONENTS:

1950: ELECTRON TUBES
1960: ELECTRON TUBES AND DISCRETE SEMICONDUCTORS
1970: DISCRETE SEMICONDUCTORS AND ICs — SSI, MSI, LSI —
1980: ICs — SSI, MSI, LSI —

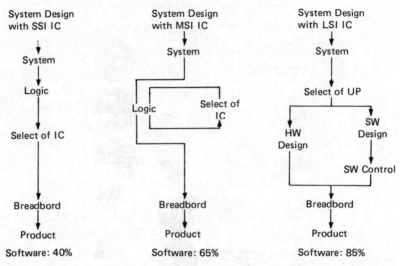

Figure 3. *System design transformation in function of system complexity*

exciting technical features of our times; it is predicted that these devices will not only revolutionize the digital electronics field, but will influence the way of life of present and future generations.

DEVELOPMENT TRENDS IN DIGITAL TECHNIQUES

Economic changes must be investigated to pick out developmental trends. Continuous and discontinuous forms of economic movements may be distinguished within global economic change. The basic factor in constructing the envelope curve is complexity, because this determines price, reliability, speed, power, system design, and how changing cost rates of software and hardware work. This leads to the conclusion that qualitative changes have been established by increasing circuit complexity, which involve evolutions in technology and system technique. We have analysed the life curves of the digital ICs from the point of view of complexity.

Figure 4 shows the life curves of the integrated circuits. The envelope curve has been constructed from the development curve (Figure 5) which is derived by graphic integration from the life curves. The envelope curve (Figure 6) shows the trend of scientific-technical evolution, which is the envelope of each stage of the qualitative changes. Each stage is roughly on a two-orders-higher level of circuit complexity in accord with the state of technical development. The next stages will probably be defined by complexity as well, because the application of electron beam and X-ray lithography would result in much higher circuit density; but at the same time use of X-ray means the steepness of the envelope diagram is constantly increasing, and hence that the production and the competitiveness of representative IC-types are effective for an ever shorter time. Predicting the course of development is our objective, so we have to take into consideration the consequences of the expected qualitative changes. By recognizing expected qualitative changes in advance we can reduce our backwardness. The span of life of equipment has been considerably shortened by rapid obsolescence. To meet the requirements of dynamic growth we have to construct our equipment with the most up-to-date devices. In Figure 7 the life curves of some microprocessors are depicted.

The method of envelope extrapolation can help us to recognize the expected duration of the next qualitative changes and our position in the development.

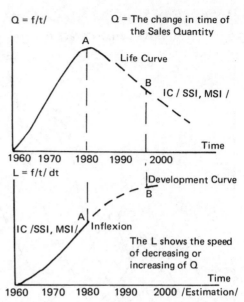

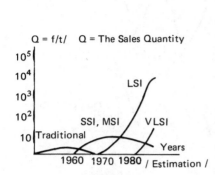

Figure 4. *The life curves of the digital ICs from the point of view of complexity*

Figure 5. *Life curve and development curve of the digital SSI, MSI ICs*

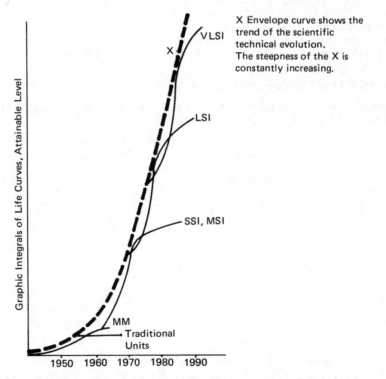

Figure 6. *The envelope of the evolution diagrams of the digital circuits*

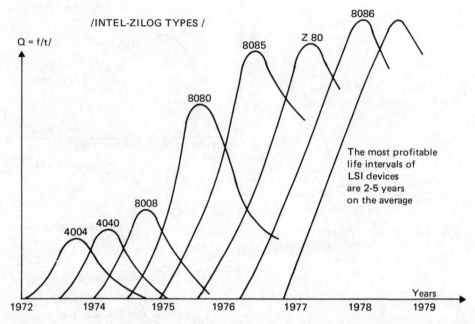

Figure 7. *Life curves of some microprocessors*

New techniques often cause fear and anxiety because processes in silicon crystal of the semiconductor are (even for the majority of electrical engineers who got their degrees long ago) mysterious and, for most people, quite unimaginable.

REARRANGEMENT OF THE SPECIAL FIELD

According to the forecasts (Figure 8) the need for experts in electronics will be as follows (USA data):

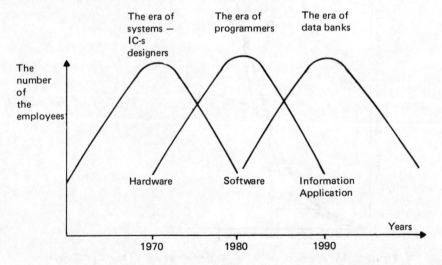

Figure 8. *Structural modification in the professions*

1. The seventies were the period of *hardware* circuit designers, that is, most experts dealt with the design of integrated circuits and systems as well as with the production of equipment.
2. The eighties are the period of experts producing *software* programs, since in this period hardware devices (elements, apparatus, etc) accepted at an international level according to quality from both a technical and an economic point of view were already available. Thus, the application of such devices is highlighted, which mainly means software programming tasks.
3. In the nineties, however, the need will be greatest for experts working in the field of *informatics*, who know where hardware elements — indispensable for applications — can be economically purchased and put quickly into operation.

EDUCATION, VOCATIONAL AND PROFESSIONAL POSTGRADUATE TRAINING

By the appearance of the LSI circuits, the classical concepts of 'component' and 'system', applied up to now in design, have changed. The circuit designer does not use components in construction work any more but applies systems as components instead. This fact itself involves several problems.

One of these problems is that the knowledge of the system, which now appears as a component, and the evaluation of its facilities, presents tasks different from those so far encountered. Learning the new design methods should be ensured as widely as possible. At the beginning of the design phase, when selecting the components, the risk is much higher than in the case of conventional elements, because the components chosen — since each is itself a system — predetermine the possibilities of the application.

As a result of the increase in the application of microelectronics and of the degree of integration obtained with former technical and economic results, marked and rapid changes will arise in the structure of expert employment. Evidence of this fact already exists. In any field of industry, agriculture, medicine, electronics, education, scientific research, office work, household, etc, it would be difficult to find an area where the application of LSI and VLSI circuits has not yet been started.

It is absolutely essential to maintain the competitiveness of products, to adapt them to new technical discoveries and to be more efficient; indeed these processes must be accelerated. According to different estimates, microprocessors will bring changes in more than half of all workplaces in the next 10 to 15 years. Thus, engineering education and the elaboration of the ideas concerning the advantages of electronics and their appropriate use must be provided within a short time.

TEACHWARE — ORGANIZED PREPARATION FOR THE APPLICATION OF MICROELECTRONIC DEVICES IN HUNGARY

In order to solve the problems noted above, networks of LSI teaching, service and consultant engineering offices have been founded throughout the world to promote the efficiency of technical work and the implementation of results. These organizations help to exploit the benefits of structural improvements both in engineering and in business. Following examples from abroad 14 national institutes were created as a basis for consultation, teaching and information to promote the practical application of LSI in Hungary. The LSI Application, Information and Learning Centre (LSI ATSz) was founded in 1980.

The LSI ATSz follows the example of the similar institutions abroad. Its tasks and activities are the following:

1. To develop an up-to-date information base that reflects improvements in this area and is able to support a system that helps the research and development of microcomputers and their application through providing information, advice and education.
2. To develop a data-base for such things as LSI ICs, parameters of microcomputers, present and future developments in international and Hungarian program systems applied in Hungary.
3. To develop a catalogue of microcomputer programs and to organize a program library service.
4. To develop an information base to promote the compatibility of different software packages and to keep the choice of elements reasonably restricted.
5. To elaborate suggestions for reducing the duplication of effort both in software and hardware.
6. To integrate long-term conceptions of research and development activity in the area of the application of LSI and to elaborate suggestions for the introduction of results.
7. To provide hardware and software services for our member institutes.
8. To initiate national and international co-operation concerning the application of LSI and to participate in such co-operative activity.
9. To educate by organizing courses, visits and the development of educational materials.
10. To give information concerning the state of the art and the results of the national and international research.
11. To explore the possibilities of microcomputer applications in Hungary and to support their implementation.

REFERENCES

Romhányi, J (1982) *Information Sources*. Budapest.
Szántó, P (1979) Számitógépes információs hálózatok az USA-ban= TMT 26.7-8, pp 305-24.

Keyword Index